AF854635

Robert Macklin was born in Queensland and educated at Brisbane Grammar School, the University of Queensland and the Australian National University. He began his journalistic career at the *Courier-Mail* and subsequently wrote for *The Age* and *The Bulletin*, and was associate editor of the *Canberra Times* until 2003.

His critically acclaimed *Dark Paradise* swept aside the curtain of euphemism to expose the horror of colonial sadism in the penal colony of Norfolk Island. His comprehensive and compelling history of Australia's Special Forces, *Warrior Elite*, is required reading in the fields of military security and intelligence. His bestselling biography of Rob Maylor, *SAS Sniper*, revealed in graphic detail the battles against Islamist fanatics.

Robert has won numerous literary prizes including, with Peter Thompson, the 2009 Blake Dawson Prize for Business Literature for their classic, *The Big Fella: The Rise and Rise of BHP Billiton.*

Robert is the author of 27 books including the biography of Kevin Rudd, four novels and major works of history. He is a graduate of the Australian Film and Television School and has written and directed documentary films in 33 countries in Asia and the South Pacific. Robert now lives in Canberra and Tuross Head and divides his time between his books and screenplays.

ALSO BY ROBERT MACKLIN

Novels

The Queenslander
The Paper Castle
Juryman
Fire in the Blood

Non-fiction

Seven Cities of Australia
The Jesus Delusion
Jacka VC
Kevin Rudd: The Biography
Backs to the Wall
War Babies
My Favourite Teacher
The Great Australian Pie
SAS Sniper
Redback One
SAS Insider
One False Move
Dark Paradise
Warrior Elite

With Peter Thompson

The Battle of Brisbane
Morrison of China
Keep off the Skyline
Operation Rimau
The Big Fella: The Rise and Rise of BHP Billiton

Books of the Film

Newsfront
The Journalist
Glass Babies

HAMILTON HUME

THE LIFE & TIMES OF OUR GREATEST EXPLORER

ROBERT MACKLIN

hachette AUSTRALIA

Aboriginal and Torres Strait Islander people are advised that this publication contains names and images of people who have passed away.

hachette
AUSTRALIA

First published in Australia and New Zealand in 2016
by Hachette Australia
(an imprint of Hachette Australia Pty Limited)
Level 17, 207 Kent Street, Sydney NSW 2000
www.hachette.com.au

This edition published in 2017

10 9 8 7 6 5 4 3 2 1

Copyright © Robert Macklin 2016

This book is copyright. Apart from any fair dealing for the purposes of private study, research, criticism or review permitted under the *Copyright Act 1968*, no part may be stored or reproduced by any process without prior written permission. Enquiries should be made to the publisher.

National Library of Australia
Cataloguing-in-Publication data:

Macklin, Robert, author.
Hamilton Hume: our greatest explorer/Robert Macklin.

ISBN: 978 0 7336 3879 4 (paperback)

Hume, Hamilton, 1797–1873.
Explorers – Australia – Biography.
Australia – Discovery and exploration.

994.02092

Cover design by bookdesignbysaso.com.au
Cover images courtesy of Mitchell Library, State Library of New South Wales (*Australian Alps as first seen by Messrs. Hovell and Hume* by George Peacock Edwards) and Cooma Cottage/National Trust (drawing of Hume)
Map by Kinart
Text design by Bookhouse, Sydney
Typeset in 12.25/17.25 Bembo Pro by Bookhouse, Sydney
Printed and bound in Australia by McPherson's Printing Group

FSC www.fsc.org MIX Paper from responsible sources FSC® C001695

The paper this book is printed on is certified against the Forest Stewardship Council® Standards. McPherson's Printing Group holds FSC® chain of custody certification SA-COC-005379. FSC® promotes environmentally responsible, socially beneficial and economically viable management of the world's forests.

This is for Robert John and Sophia Macklin

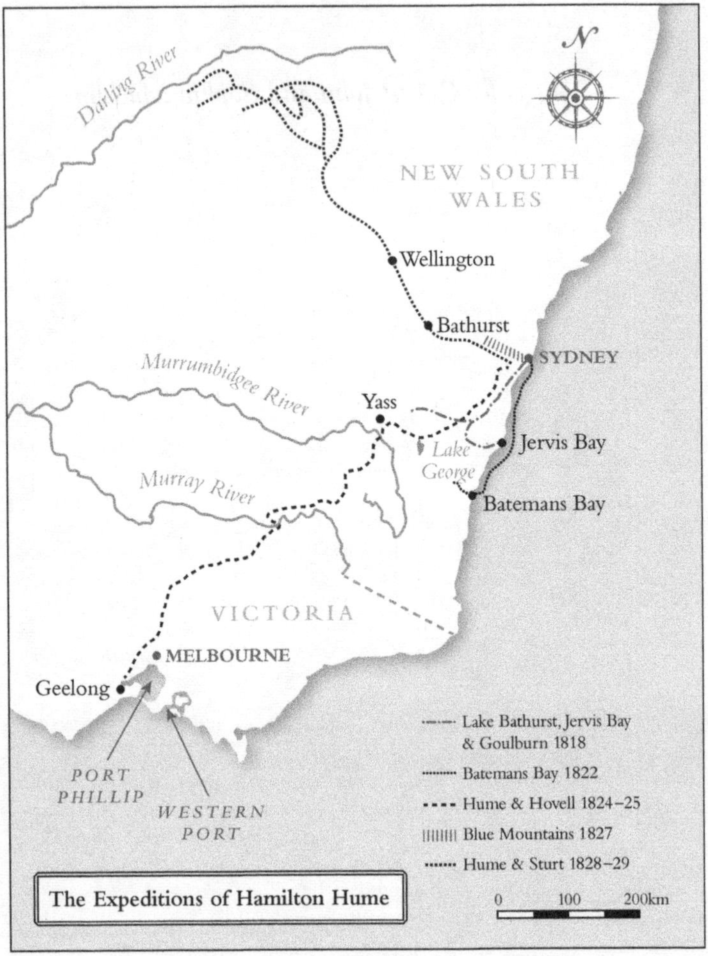

The Expeditions of Hamilton Hume

Contents

'Presuming myself (altho' an Australian) capable from experience of undertaking such an expedition, I represented my willingness to do so to His Excellency, who promised his sanction and protection; and under this impression I, in company with Captain Hovell, prepared and purchased at our private expense such conveniences and necessaries as were suitable for an undertaking of this kind . . .'

Hamilton Hume to Governor Sir Thomas Brisbane, 20 April 1825

Prologue

They emerged from the bush like skeletal ghosts, the convicts first, staggering in short steps, all in rags but one – he was barefoot and naked, wild eyes staring from a face of black bristling whiskers. It would be days before he returned to his senses. They were followed by the mounted naval man, his clothing torn and hanging loose; no sign left of the haughtiness, the pomposity that had marked the start of the journey.

Then, finally, came the tall, angular bushman who had guided and shepherded them all the way, there and back – across the swollen creeks and rivers, through the valleys and up the sharp, rocky ridges, down again to the boggy swamplands, the wide plains, the thick bush that had become almost impassable, where the horses collapsed from exhaustion and the dogs died on their feet; the open country where they slaughtered one of the remaining bullocks for the meat to sustain them and the hides to cover their bleeding soles.

He got them through. They didn't understand how. Willpower was part of it, but only part. There were the Aboriginal people.

He talked to them in their lingo and they told him where to go, what to avoid, how to find the springs and waterholes. But there was something else, something much more important: it was his knowledge of the landscape and his feel for the bush, almost mystical in their strength and certainty. No one else understood it, and certainly not the naval man with his useless instruments and his skittish fears. Perhaps even he, the bushman, didn't fully comprehend it. No matter; he got them through.

And on the way they saw what no white man had ever seen: a countryside that stretched in glory from one end of the horizon to the other; fertile land, virgin plains big enough to run a million sheep and cattle, broad enough to support 10,000 farms, rich enough to found a nation.

The country was Australia. The bushman, Hamilton Hume.

Introduction

Hamilton Hume's long life spans the first 80 years of the British conquest and settlement of Australia. It was a tumultuous time as the alien, northern culture crashed and foamed upon the country's endless coastline and then remorselessly spread itself across the continent in the final act of European colonisation of the planet.

There were those among the newcomers who would commit unspeakable crimes against the people who had been the land's custodians for millennia. And they did so with barely a slap on the wrist from their British colonial masters. Some tolerated the Aboriginal people's presence; others engaged with them; and yet others still – Hume among them – embraced them.

Among the whites, those first eight decades began with a desperate struggle for survival. There were times when it all seemed to have been in vain. And even when their occupation took root, all the fierce conflicts of an isolated community in a remote and unfamiliar world threatened to overwhelm them. It had begun as a place of exile and punishment, where the British notions of social division sparked a bushfire blaze of conflict within the community and found expression in hatred, mutiny, plunder and rebellion.

Were it not for the explorers extending the boundaries of settlement, that community would have imploded in mutual loathing and rage. The explorers gifted it with a safety valve; the land itself – the immensity of its presence, the promise of its bounty – eventually conjured for them a vision: that this Great Southern Land provided the last great opportunity to create a nation, blessed by its attributes and unique in its opportunities, a raw young country that could take its proud place in the wider world.

Hamilton Hume above all others was the quintessential explorer, the pathfinder for the newcomers. He led them through the hostile terrain and past its fretful custodians to the best grazing lands, the finest streams and watercourses. And they rewarded him with celebrity. When Hume set out on a journey to the unknown, it was news. When he returned, people gathered to hear what wonders he had discovered – and what new pastures they could appropriate.

Australian-born, he occupied a particular place in the society of the day. He was certainly not 'one of us'. Indeed, he and his compatriots were termed 'currency', as opposed to the British-born 'sterling'; or alternatively 'white natives', to differentiate them from the 'black natives' that surrounded and threatened their settlements. Mrs Felton Mathews, the British-born wife of a surveyor, recorded her views in her 1833 journal when she and her husband passed through the Hume property near Campbelltown. 'Mr Hume,' she wrote, 'is a native, but decidedly the best informed and most agreeable of any I have seen. They are usually ignorant, awkward and vulgar, or else shallow, conceited and coxcombical.'[1]

However far he rose through the colonial ranks, he was never able to overcome his nativity. It was said – correctly – that where other explorers and intruders on Aboriginal tribal land were attacked, Hamilton Hume was able to mix freely with the people and to gain their trust. And while this might be accounted a great virtue among his fellow bushmen, it merely confirmed colonial society's judgement of his place in the pecking order.

It mattered little that his father was a free settler and his mother the matron of the colony's most important girls' orphanage. Moreover, his charming wife was herself a daughter of the manse, though she too was Australian-born. The location of his birth would haunt him through his long life, until in its closing chapters he would at last strike back, confronting a representative of the 'class' from which he was forever excluded. His target was the man with whom his name is inextricably linked in what began as 'the worst equipped, poorest planned major expedition in Australia's history':[2] Captain William Hilton Hovell. In taking his stand against Hovell, Hamilton Hume became the unwitting embodiment of a vital element in Australians' perception of their own history and identity, a figurehead in the so-called culture wars that still bedevil his compatriots today.

The great journey Hume and Hovell took in 1824 from the tentative southern reaches of Sydney's settlement to the coastline at Port Phillip, site of the Victorian capital, would transform perceptions of Australia. For the first time their discoveries held out the clearest promise that that this ragged penal colony could become a nation in its own right. And despite the seemingly impassable mountains, the wild rivers, the threat of starvation and the timidity and incompetence of his 'sterling' companion, the Australian got them through.

But Hume's achievements have not always been recognised. The English-born (Sir) Ernest Scott, who came to Australia in 1892 as a newspaper reporter, set the tone of Hume's Anglophile detractors for a succession of academic historians. Becoming a Hansard writer in the Victorian parliament, Scott's unwavering pro-British views attracted the colony's establishment and, despite his lacking any academic qualifications, he was invited to apply for the chair of history at Melbourne University. His treatment of the Hume and Hovell expedition – in which Hovell was portrayed as the figure of consequence and Hume the upstart bushman – provided a template for the distinguished cohort who passed through his hands at the university. They included the future history professors (Sir) Keith Hancock, Fred Alexander, (Sir) Stephen Roberts, Manning Clark and N. D. Harper. Their influence is impossible to overstate.

They and their successors have ensured that the manner in which our history is framed in our schools and universities is still firmly Anglophile. Indeed, it is not so much Australian history as the British history of Australia – a very different beast. For, in their telling, the 168,000 men, women and children transported largely for trivial offences, or rebellion against British appropriation of their Irish homeland, still bear the opprobrium of the 'Australian convict' label. Their degradation and forced labour in a British slave economy for the first 70 years of settlement is excused or even applauded.

Indeed, it goes some way to explaining that while biographies of British-born figures, from Arthur Phillip to Matthew Flinders to William Bligh, have filled Australia's bookshelves, this is the first full-scale biography of the native-born Hume to find a commercial publisher. The only other book devoted to the explorer – *Currency Lad: The Story of Hamilton Hume and the Explorers* by R. H. 'Bob' Webster – was privately printed by his family in 1982.

Hume's life and times transfigured the country of his birth; and in all the significant events of that period – from the destruction of Aboriginal society to the spread of the squatters and pioneers, the advent and excesses of the gold rush, the barely recognised or understood bushranger rebellion, the political movement for self-government and the beginnings of the White Australia Policy – Hamilton Hume played a role, sometimes at the forefront, sometimes at the margins, and occasionally as an unwilling participant. As his story weaves its way through those eight tumultuous decades, it may well give succour and strength to those who believe that the time has arrived for Australia to understand and appreciate its colonial beginnings, while insisting that we should no longer be defined by them.

Perhaps we no longer need to hide the atrocities perpetrated against the Aboriginal people; we no longer need to seek our sense of nationhood in the shedding of blood at Anzac Cove in pursuit of British colonial ambitions; we no longer need persist with the logical absurdity of a foreign monarch as our head of state. On the contrary, Hume's story and the lessons he derived from his native land and its people provide the clearest signal that the time has come to embrace our Aboriginal heritage, our cosmopolitan migrant population, our distinctively egalitarian native traditions and our geographical good fortune to become pathfinders ourselves in the brave new world of the 21st century.

Today there are the beginnings of a new urgency in the issue. But the debate is as old as our history. In 1855, a prominent Australian wrote, 'Circumstances have greatly altered of late, and from a comparatively obscure and insignificant position, Australia has risen to occupy a prominent place and interest with the civilised world; in the train of which, occurrences which 30 years ago were of little interest, now assume a new importance.'

The writer was Hamilton Hume.

CHAPTER ONE

Beginnings

Hamilton Hume's father Andrew sets off for Australia on the Guardian, *reaches Port Jackson, and is sent to Norfolk Island.*

The journey that brought the first of the Hume family to Australia is one of the great seagoing adventures of the eighteenth century. When Hamilton's father, Andrew Hamilton Hume, boarded a converted warship, the 44-gun HMS *Guardian,* in September 1789 for the long voyage to Port Jackson he could not have guessed at the cataclysm awaiting.

He was 27 and had already gained a reputation as a young tearaway. In fact, like D'Arcy Wentworth, who he would join at the unexpected end of the journey, he had severely blotted his social copybook, and a sojourn in the colonies was the only reasonable career move left to him. While Wentworth had been twice accused of highway robbery and a third court case was in train, Andrew Hume had been cashiered from his regiment.

The eldest son of a Presbyterian minister in the farmland of Ireland's County Down, Andrew had joined the Moira

Volunteers, risen to the rank of captain and become engaged to the daughter of the Earl of Moira. But when his colonel made a slighting remark while on parade, an outraged Andrew seized him by the leg and unhorsed him. A duel followed and Hume had the temerity to ignore gentlemanly convention – to aim high – and shot him. Fortunately, the colonel recovered, but Hume was disgraced and the aristocratic engagement permanently severed.

Family connections secured him a position with Duncan Campbell, the wealthy shipowner whose fleet serviced the West Indian slave plantations and whose broken-down hulks housed the overflow of convicts from British prisons. Campbell played a significant supporting role in Australia's colonisation. He was an uncle by marriage to William Bligh and gave him his first command as captain of one of his sugar traders; and it was through the Campbell connection that Fletcher Christian became a Bligh favourite on the trader and later the *Bounty*. For Andrew Hume, the experience as overseer of convicts on Campbell's hulks was a natural springboard to his appointment as one of eight 'superintendents' on the *Guardian*, each of whom had additional farming, surveying or engineering skills, only five of whom eventually arrived in Australia.

The captain of the *Guardian*, Edward Riou, was one of the rising stars of the Royal Navy. Like so many of his fellow officers, he had joined as a 12-year-old, and he had served as midshipman on the *Resolution* during the third and fatal voyage of Captain Cook. (Coincidentally, Bligh was himself a senior warrant officer on that expedition.) Riou had fought with distinction in the French Revolutionary Wars and was only 27 when given the command of the *Guardian*.

When Andrew Hume joined the passenger list, Riou's mission was to take desperately needed supplies to the infant colony at Sydney Cove. By then the population of about 700 convicts and their 300 jailers was facing starvation and under sporadic attack from the Eora people, whose tribal land they had appropriated. The *Guardian* was loaded with two years provisions for the settlement, clothing for the marines and material for convict dress, medicines, sails, hospital blankets and bedding, tools, farming implements and 15 casks of wine. It contained a portable garden created by Sir Joseph Banks, which included no fewer than 150 fruit trees, some already in blossom. There were also several free settlers and their families, 25 convicts with trades such as carpentry and butchery, and an assistant chaplain for the colony, the Rev. John Crowther.

Riou made good progress to the Cape of Good Hope, where he loaded seven horses, 16 cows, two bulls, small flocks of sheep and goats, and a pair of deer. He then set forth on 11 December for the easterly run before the roaring forties to what was still called New Holland. However, he chose to steer a little further south than usual, in the hope of encountering an iceberg to replenish the fresh water for his large cargo of thirsty livestock. On 23 December, according to his bosun, John Williams:

> We fell in with a large island of ice, about twice as high as our mastheads. We sent our boats to pick up loose ice that was about, by which means we had like to have lost our boats and men for the weather came on thick and began to blow very hard, so 'twas with a great deal of trouble that they got to the ship.

> We cleared them of the ice they had picked up then we hoisted the boats in and stood off from the island of ice for two hours. Then [we] tacked and stood to the eastward [but] the ice was so lofty that it drifted faster than we expected by the wind having so much hold of it. The [fog] being so thick that we could scarce see the length of the ship, the wind blowing so fresh that we ran foul of it. [The iceberg] knocked away our rudder, broke the tiller in three pieces, broke one of the after-beams in two, knocked the sternpost from the keel and damaged the ship in a shocking manner.[1]

As the massive ice island floated away, the sea poured in through great gashes in the *Guardian*'s side. By now the wind was roaring, the fog had been replaced by sleet and the waves rose above the decking. Riou ordered cargo to be thrown over the side to lighten the load, and all available hands – including Andrew Hume, the other superintendents and the convicts – set to the pumps where they worked without a break for the next 24 hours. Next to be jettisoned were the animals, all but a few sheep cast unwillingly into the icy ocean. The pumpers still seemed to be fighting a losing battle, so with the gale screaming through the rigging the captain ordered the launch, the two cutters and the jolly boat to be hoisted out into the great tumbling seas.

The biggest of the boats, the launch, was forced to drop first and on the windward quarter to make room for the cutters, but when it reached the water it was thrown back towards the ship. Its crew battled to keep it free of the ship while at the same time the gunner, Mr Somerville, holding one end of a coil of rope, climbed into the jolly boat, which hung over the stern. But when the jolly boat reached the water it was drawn under the ship and overturned. Somehow, Somerville clambered back aboard the craft and was able to right it. Then, according to Williams, the captain ordered the launch returned for supplies and the cutters came close aboard to receive them for transfer. In the chaos of the raging sea, some officers and men threw themselves into the boats, though the one convict who attempted it was physically restrained.

With the captain's permission, Thomas Clements, the sailing master, as well as the purser, the doctor, Parson Crowther – indeed, all the officers but for one midshipman and Williams himself – abandoned the vessel to her fate. Reports of the numbers vary, but according to Williams, some 56 men left the ship more than 2,000 kilometres from land.

While a no doubt anxious Andrew Hume remained on board, both cutters, the jolly boat and the launch – all with minimal provisions – disappeared into the sleeting rain. The jolly boat sank with all hands; the cutters were never heard from again. Only the launch with 15 people aboard would survive. They would be picked up days later by a French merchant vessel and taken to Mauritius. The Rev. Crowther would take the next ship home and resign his commission. Word of the tragic loss of the *Guardian* quickly spread.

Meanwhile, in the wild Southern Ocean more than 150 men, women and children remained on board the stricken ship. But Riou was not about to surrender to the sea without a fight. According to bosun Williams, 'The commander had a strong resolution for he said he would sooner go down with the ship than he would quit her. We had two chances – either to pump or sink.'[2]

They could still make it into the sail room and managed to retrieve a triangular four-course sail, line it with oakum and rags and manoeuvre it beneath the leaking keel. As the remaining casks floated up to the main deck, they also provided a measure of buoyancy. The two events made only a marginal difference, but to sailors alone in the vastness of the Southern Ocean they represented the priceless commodity of hope.

The *Guardian* by now was little more than a great rudderless raft. Williams said, 'Sometimes our upper-deck scuppers was under water outside, and the ship lying like a log in the water and the sea breaking over her like she was a rock in the sea.' But hope combined with fear – and the captain's indomitable will – were sufficient to keep the men at the pumps.

However, there was dissension from some of the remaining passengers. One of Andrew Hume's fellow superintendents, Philip Schaefer, claimed that Riou 'called me a fervent rascal and ill-treated me'.[3] According to one later report, '[Some of] the people at one time had carried their disobedience so far as to threaten [Riou's] life and had made a raft of the booms on which they were determined to take their chance, rather than remain any longer on board the ship.' But Riou's remonstrances 'prevailed on them to give up a plan which must inevitably have plunged them into certain destruction'.[4]

By manoeuvring the remaining sails, Riou was able to make some headway towards the African coast. As the days turned to weeks – and the weather remained favourable – that sense of hope among the seamen grew until it became an article of faith. In the eighth week of their ordeal, they spotted a sail. And when it answered their frantic signal it revealed itself as a Dutch trader. It could not approach too close for fear of upending the remains of the *Guardian*, but at least it could attach a tow rope, keep them company and guide them to shelter. Finally, they sighted the Cape of Good Hope, nine weeks after the collision. Two whale boats came out to meet them, roped themselves to the bow and slowly pulled the *Guardian* to berth.

Riou gave the captain of the Dutch ship a letter for the Admiralty and eight weeks later the captain delivered it to a fishing vessel lying off the English coast. When the letter reached London, it went immediately from the Admiralty to King George and as word spread Riou was hailed as a national hero.

At the Cape, Riou signalled his intention to take the ship, with a skeleton crew, to Saldanha Bay on the west coast. In fact, he was unable to reach his destination and was forced into False Bay, where the *Guardian* was beached and later destroyed in a gale.

The survivors counted their blessings. Among them were the 20 remaining convicts, most of whom had distinguished themselves throughout the ordeal. They would continue to New South Wales and Riou's report of their conduct saw 14 of them pardoned. Some of the passengers were hospitalised, and others had second thoughts about their journey and, like Parson Crowther, returned to England.

Coincidentally, while at the Cape Riou was able to refresh his acquaintance with his old shipmate from the *Resolution,* William Bligh, who was returning to England after his own remarkable feat of maritime doggedness. In the wake of the mutiny on the *Bounty,* he and 19 of his loyalists had sailed his open boat for 47 days from the South Pacific to Kupang in the Dutch East Indies. He too would be feted on his return to

England, though not without protest from the well-connected families of Fletcher Christian and other officers of the *Bounty*.

Riou's fame was unequivocal and celebrated in the phrase 'as gallant as Riou'. He was marked for speedy advancement in his naval career, but would not live long enough to enjoy the ultimate fruits of his success, being killed in the 1801 Battle of Copenhagen.

Andrew Hume, who seems to have laboured ceaselessly at the pumps with convict, sailor and free man alike, suffered an enduring legacy: he lost all his hair and would wear a wig for some years later. Otherwise, he recovered physically, and when the *Lady Juliana* arrived en route to Port Jackson he was among those who joined her for the final leg of the journey.

He was particularly fortunate in his choice of vessel. The *Lady Juliana* was officially one of the Second Fleet, which has gone down in history as the Death Fleet and one of Britain's more reprehensible colonial misdeeds. However, not all its ships should be tarred with that brush. (The *Guardian* itself was numbered in the flotilla, yet it could hardly boast a more honourable and compassionate master.) The *Juliana* carried no fewer than 223 female convicts, and by the time they reached the Cape almost all were in excellent spirits.

According to John Nicol, a steward who had joined the vessel in the extended period before she sailed from Portsmouth, 'There were not a great many very bad characters [among them]. The greater number were for petty crimes and a great proportion for only being disorderly, that is, street walkers.'[5] By the time the *Juliana* left England it had gained the reputation of a floating brothel.

'When we were fairly out to sea, every man on board took a wife from among the convicts,' wrote Nicol. 'The girl with whom I lived – for I was as bad in this point as the others – was as kind and true a creature as ever lived. I courted her for a week and would have married her on the spot if there had been a clergyman on board.'

However, though the woman bore him a child before the *Juliana* reached Port Jackson, the shipboard romance did not survive once they reached the colony. Other liaisons were even more tenuous. Indeed, when the ship spent seven weeks in Rio de Janeiro, they not only replenished their provisions but the women filled their purses as they entertained the Brazilian and expatriate gentry.

The governor, Arthur Phillip, was less than pleased to see the *Juliana* arrive. While the store ship *Justinian* – another of the fleet – had reached Sydney on 2 June, unloaded her relatively meagre cargo and departed immediately for the satellite colony of Norfolk Island en route to China, his penal colony was facing imminent starvation. His biggest vessel, the *Sirius*, had been lost in February while attempting to berth at Norfolk Island and now he had an additional 250 dependants, only a small fraction of whom would be productive members of his ragged settlement.

He immediately assigned as many as possible to a further nine-day journey to Norfolk Island, where his young protégé, Lieutenant Philip Gidley King, had established a satellite colony to exploit the tall pines trees and the flax plants Cook had recorded during his 1774 visit. He and his naturalists, Johann Forster and William Wales, believed they would provide much needed masts, spars and sailcloth for British ships. And Norfolk's arable land could help feed the Port Jackson settlement. Unfortunately, the pines would prove too brittle for masts and the early farming attempts were sabotaged by native rats and caterpillars.

The flax also caused problems. It was very different from the familiar European variety, and Governor Phillip was unable to find anyone with expertise in its conversion from plant to cloth. So when he learned that Andrew Hume had some experience farming it in County Down, he assigned him, soon after his arrival, to the tiny island colony.

By now the true hell ships of the Second Fleet were arriving at Sydney Cove. The *Suprize, Neptune* and *Scarborough* had been contracted from the firm Camden, Calvert & King, which undertook to transport, clothe and feed their 1,006 convicts for a set price per head, whether they landed alive or dead. It was not an uncommon practice. The company (and others like it) had been transporting black slaves from Africa to the West Indies under the same conditions for at least two centuries.

They made only one stop on the way – at the Cape of Good Hope – where they took on board the 20 surviving convicts from the *Guardian.* Those on the *Neptune* were deliberately starved, kept in heavy irons in fetid conditions below decks and rarely allowed out for fresh air and exercise. Scurvy ran rampant. Before they reached Sydney, 162 convicts would perish at the hands of their tormentors.

On the *Scarborough*, the convicts attempted to rebel but were betrayed by one of their number, the forger Samuel Burt. The ringleaders were then, Burt wrote, 'flogged with the greatest severity, and others chained to the deck, and it is supposed will be tried and executed immediately on their arrival at New South Wales.'[6] The *Suprize* also arrived with a cargo of ill-treated and ailing survivors.

The colony's chaplain, Rev. Richard Johnson, who had waited in vain for his successor, Parson Crowther, was shocked to the core as he stepped aboard the *Neptune.* 'I beheld a sight truly shocking to the feelings of humanity . . . they were wretched, naked, filthy, dirty, lousy and many of them unable to stand, to creep, or even to stir hand or foot.'[7] No fewer than 124 of them would subsequently die in the makeshift tents that operated as the penal settlement's hospitals.

By contrast, the free men aboard the *Neptune* were well looked after. They included Lieutenant John Macarthur, whose wife and son travelled separately on the *Scarborough*, and D'Arcy Wentworth, who took a convict mistress, Catherine Crowley, while on board. Wentworth would also be immediately assigned to Norfolk Island as an assistant-surgeon. And once the *Suprize* was thoroughly cleaned, he and his pregnant mistress joined Andrew Hume on it for the journey to Lieutenant King's tiny domain. Their son, William Charles Wentworth, was born on board as the *Suprize* stood off the island.

Back at the Sydney settlement, the captain of the *Neptune,* Donald Traill, and the other ships' masters, sold the rations they had denied the convicts for a tidy profit. Governor Phillip's protest was mild at best and at worst a dereliction of duty. 'The scene of misery . . . was occasioned by the contractors having crowded too many on board these ships,' he noted, 'and from their being too much confined during the passage.'

There was, however, a brief public outrage when news of the horror reached London. An inquiry was held and private action taken in the courts against the contractors. The government then took over the case, and in time it simply faded away. Camden, Calvert & King were actually contracted to supply the Third Fleet. Traill and his chief mate, William Ellerington, were also privately prosecuted for murder in the Admiralty Court, but acquitted on all charges even before the judge summed up the evidence.

CHAPTER TWO

Further Fortunes of the Humes

Andrew Hume meets and marries Eliza Kennedy, Hamilton Hume is born, and disease begins to devastate the Aboriginal population.

Andrew Hume's sojourn on Norfolk Island was not a happy one.

The situation on the island had improved under King's managerial hand after the first disastrous crops, but ill-health then forced King to take a leave in England and on his return violence and thievery were rife. He quickly reasserted control, but the arrival of yet another load of convicts – many of them women from the *Juliana*[1] – brought the total population to 700 and put a severe strain on resources.

The convict barracks were concentrated on the southerly shore of Sydney Bay, with small outlying settlements in the north and west. Andrew Hume lived in the northern Cascade Bay area, where some of the convicts in his charge collected the flax plants for processing. King was already impatient with the lack of progress in the endeavour when Hume arrived. The initial attempts by a seaman-weaver, Roger Morely, the previous year had at least begun it through 'retting', where the inner stalk of the plant is rotted away, leaving the outer fibres intact. However, that was the limit of Morely's knowledge, and he could go no further.

Andrew had received no formal training in the field, but he managed to produce a small piece of cloth during King's absence, which he sent to Governor Phillip with a request for more convict labourers and equipment. King was unimpressed with this effort, and it may well be that Hume's irascible personality also contributed to the subsequent falling out between the two men, since King was accustomed to unquestioning naval obedience.

Moreover, during his English visit King had persuaded Captain George Vancouver, who was about to leave for the Pacific, to call by New Zealand and persuade two Maori experts to come to his aid. Vancouver kidnapped them and delivered 'Toogee' and 'Hoodoo' to Norfolk. However, it soon became clear that the Maoris knew little and cared less about flax-dressing; it was 'women's work' and they would have no part of it. By this time, King had sent Hume back to Port Jackson.

In July 1790, the smallest of the First Fleet vessels, the armed tender *Supply,* was sent to Batavia on an urgent mission to buy provisions. She returned in September, having chartered a Dutch ship to follow with more stores. But still there were doubts that the Antipodean experiment would survive. The convicts lived under slave conditions, with free use of the lash by their jailers. Their guards detested them almost as much as they hated their own exile among the 'savages'. The few free settlers attracted by promises of land grants and free labour were quickly disillusioned by the unfamiliar landscape, the resentful Aborigines and the dwindling food stocks. Discontent was rife.

Marine Major Robert Ross, the lieutenant-governor who was fiercely at odds with Captain Phillip, reported:

> I brought six sheep from the Cape at a great expense, and every one of them is either dead through the badness of the country or killed by some villains among the convicts who, in spite of every punishment that can be inflicted, still persist in their former villainous practices. Four of them have been executed since our arrival here, and three more are very likely to suffer the same fate very shortly . . . I believe this country to be the outcast of God's works.

A female convict complained in a letter that:

> Notwithstanding all our presents, the savages still continue to do us all the injury they can, which makes the soldiers' duty very hard, and much dissatisfaction among the officers. I know not how many of our people have been killed. As for the distresses of the women, they are past description.

And a letter from an unnamed free settler printed in the Edinburgh weekly, *The Bee*, reported:

> The state we were in when the dispatches went from this place in the *Supply* sternly threatens us again, there being no more than seven months in store at the present allowance. We have little to look to from our granaries; and the livestock, which consists of goats, pigs and poultry, are so degenerate and few in number from want of food that the whole would not afford the colony two days subsistence.[2]

In 1792, Hume secured a position in charge of government livestock at Toongabbie, 30 kilometres west of Sydney Cove. There some 500 convicts were clearing the land for a 640 acre (259 hectare) farm and he undertook his duties with a will. But, according to family records, he had developed an intense hatred of the convict system at a time when flogging was the order of the day. Andrew was disgusted by its brutality and refused to employ it.

Some of the officers and settlers given male convicts to work their land grants or females to serve their household needs treated them no better than their contemporaries in the American south used their black equivalents. Virtually every convict woman was forced to barter her sex for the necessities of life. And rarely did the men – particularly the Irish – escape the lash. Indeed, the Rev. Richard Johnson's assistant and eventual successor, Samuel Marsden, who finally arrived in 1793, would be cheerfully dubbed 'the flogging parson' by his fellow landholders. Accordingly, Andrew stood out among the English slave-drivers as 'unreliable'.

That year he applied for a land grant of his own. Governor Phillip responded with 30 acres (12.5 hectares) of rough Toongabbie bushland. Andrew continued to run the government store in the settlement part-time, being described in the government *Gazette* as one 'who attends to the delivery of provisions'. In the government pecking order, he ranked in the first 23 public employees.

While Andrew was a big, handsome man with a fine singing voice, and could be a charming gentleman in the rough and rambunctious community of the day, he was also, according to family history, 'impetuous, fearless [with] a most violent temper'.[3] It was a colourful combination and it attracted one of the more personable and charming women of the colony in Elizabeth 'Eliza' More Kennedy.

The youngest daughter of the Rev. John Kennedy, Vicar of Teston and Nestlehead in rural Kent, she had arrived in Australia in 1794 on the *Suprize* as companion and nursemaid to the children of her widowed brother James, a free settler. Her father's church had a strong evangelical tradition, supported the anti-slavery movement and had opened one of the first Sunday schools in England. Eliza had been well educated, trained as a teacher and taught at the school. Soon after her arrival – once James was able to engage convict servants to care for the children – she found employment as senior mistress at the newly established Orphan School for Homeless and Unwanted Girls at Parramatta. Her salary was £40 a year, a substantial sum at the time.

She quickly created a favourable impression and would gain a well-deserved reputation as a friend of the Aboriginal people. She attended church services in the district and this might well have been where she and Andrew met. They were married by Rev. Johnson in September 1796 at St John's Anglican Church, Parramatta, at the time little more than a hut. He was 34, and she was two years older.

Eliza's nephew John Kennedy would also migrate to the colony in 1796 on the *Royal Sovereign* as a settler and would take up a land grant of 160 acres at Prospect Hill, an evening's walk from Parramatta. Since Prospect Hill was also the site where the first emancipists were given their grants, it may well be that the Kennedys, like the Humes, were regarded by the colonial elite as somewhat irregular – perhaps even dangerously free-thinking – in their social orientation.

Eliza and Andrew lived at his Toongabbie store while she maintained her position at the nearby Parramatta orphanage, and she continued there before and after the birth of their first son, Hamilton, on 19 June 1797. He would be followed by a daughter, Isabella, the following year and two other sons to survive early childhood – John in 1800 and Francis Rawdon in 1803.

Andrew Hume's testy nature, belligerent when drinking, made life difficult. And in the remarkably litigious community of the time he figured frequently in the civil and criminal courts. Though he was invariably acquitted of crimes as varied as rape (of a certain Ann Smith) and cattle theft, his unhappy relationship with King, which had begun on Norfolk Island, came to a head when the naval man succeeded Hunter as the governor of New South Wales in 1800. In September of that year, King wrote to the colonial secretary in London that 'On arriving here I found the stock in very bad state and the superintendent in charge of them [Hume] being a worthless character who had been tried for robbing the stores and rape.'

Andrew was dismissed from his post and the Hume family moved to a small land grant on the Hawkesbury, where they planted wheat and vegetable crops and ran a small herd of cattle. But like their fellow smallholders they endured the twin disasters of flood and fire. Indeed, their property would be destroyed three times in three years. Neither could they escape the fierce tensions of the penal settlement.

On 5 March 1804, a group of up to 300 Irish 'politicals' – transported rebels against the British occupation of their homeland – rose up at the government farm at Castle Hill. Led by Phillip Cunningham, they armed themselves with muskets and pikes from surrounding farms, took control of Toongabbie and attacked Parramatta. Their plan was to advance on Sydney Town and declare New South Wales the Republic of New Ireland two weeks later on St Patrick's Day. Governor King declared martial law and Major George Johnson led 29 troops of his New South Wales Corps into battle, assisted by 50 volunteer militiamen. However, when the rebels were lured by a priest to a meeting under the white flag of truce, Johnson arrested Cunningham and his second-in-command, Samuel Humes. Johnson's troops, now reinforced by 150 marines and crewmen from the HMS *Calcutta,* renewed their attack and in the advance shot 15 rebels without loss of any of their own.

Troops and volunteers pursued the disorganised rebels into the countryside and muster records from before and after the uprising show a sudden absence of more than 150 names. Firing could be heard for several days. Over the next three months a group of Quakers buried the dead where they had fallen, the only reminder of their fate a circular cairn of stones around the shallow graves.

Nine of the 300 renegades captured or surrendered were hanged and the bodies of Cunningham and Samuel Humes were publicly displayed on the gibbet at Parramatta for several days. Four received 500 lashes and exile to the Coal River (Newcastle) chain gang. Others received 200 lashes, and many were sent to Norfolk Island. There they came under a standing order for Irish prisoners that if foreign ships were seen on the horizon they were to be mustered into the wooden stockade; and if the ships landed the stockade was to be set alight.[4]

Four years later, rebellion came from the other end of the political spectrum, and this time it would affect Andrew Hume directly. Governance of the penal settlement was becoming little short of anarchic as the New South Wales Corps (nicknamed the Rum Corps) fought a seemingly endless battle against the authority of the naval governors. By now John Macarthur had resigned his commission in the Corps and established himself as one of the leading landowners in the infant colony. But his influence as a gimlet-eyed éminence grise for the privileged could hardly be overstated.

On taking over from King in 1807, Governor William Bligh – more sensitive than most to any challenge to his authority – attempted to stop the corps trading in rum, which had become the unofficial currency in the colony. A sharp deterioration of relations between the governor and the military culminated in Bligh ordering Major Johnson to arrest John Macarthur.

Instead, at Macarthur's instigation, Johnson issued an order charging Bligh as being 'unfit to exercise the supreme authority another moment in this colony'. On 26 January, exactly 20 years since Arthur Phillip had asserted British sovereignty over half the continent, Johnson advanced on Government House to arrest his successor. For a second time in his turbulent career Bligh fell victim to mutiny and was held under house arrest until his replacement could be installed. In the interim, Johnson appointed Macarthur colonial secretary, the de facto head of the settlement.

Andrew Hume was swept into the swirling currents of contention and in the wake of the Rum Rebellion was reinstated as government stock-keeper at Toongabbie. Five months later, in yet another power shift, he was dismissed by the acting lieutenant-governor Joseph Foveaux, who had transferred from Norfolk Island where he had gained a reputation as one of the more sadistic commandants. He had ruled by the lash and developed a system of 'selling' female convicts to his officers and men.

There was a sharp irony in Foveaux's attack on Hume, whom he charged with 'speculation and malfeasance', since Foveaux had used his own position to enrich himself with land grants and a growing herd of beef cattle on the island and the mainland. Again Andrew was acquitted, though by then Eliza had been forced to return to her position at the orphanage to feed the family. In 1809, the lieutenant-governor of Van Diemen's Land, William Paterson, arrived in Sydney as acting governor. At the behest of his wife, Elizabeth, the patron of the orphanage, Eliza became the first woman in the colony to receive a grant of land and cattle – some 60 acres at Prospect Hill.

These early travails and Eliza's guiding hand would turn the Humes into a close-knit family. Very little has survived of their correspondence with friends and relatives but it is clear that from childhood Hamilton came to know and love the country of his birth. The effect of the family's difficulties on the young man's character may be found not only in his own sharp temper when crossed, but also in the obvious pleasure he discovered in the solitude of the bush. He was usually joined by his younger brother John and often a near neighbour, John Batman, who, like Hamilton's brother, was three years his junior. Batman would remain a friend throughout Hume's life and would later be one of the beneficiaries of Hume's expedition to Port Phillip, when he became the acknowledged founder of Melbourne.

It was during these early hikes through the countryside that Hamilton first encountered the bushranging phenomenon that would play such a significant role in the colony's social and political affairs during his lifetime. It would highlight the stark divisions within the community and would culminate, for Hume, in the death of his beloved brother.

It had begun before he was born. In 1796, Governor Hunter mentioned in dispatches 'a gang or two of banditti who have armed themselves and infest the country all around, committing robberies upon defenceless people'.[5] More commonly, 'bolters' from the chain gangs either joined briefly with an Aboriginal group or kept themselves alive through raids on the settlement before either surrendering or perishing in the bush.

One of the rare exceptions was John Wilson, a Lancashire man who had been transported in the First Fleet for having stolen 'nine yards of cotton cloth called velveret of the value of tenpence'. In 1792, he absconded into the bush and joined an Aboriginal clan who gave him the name Bunboee. Over the next few years, his sentence having expired, he divided his time between the two worlds: the bush, where he went naked but for a possum cloak in winter, and the settlement, where he made only trifling concessions to modesty.

At this time there was a persistent tale among the convicts that some kind of oriental Shangri-La could be found just beyond the mountains. In fact, some Aborigines with a mischievous sense of humour encouraged them, offering to pass them on to their adjoining compatriots who would guide them there.[6] In an effort to put paid to the canard, Hunter engaged Wilson to lead a small expedition of convicts and marines to the south-west and assigned his young secretary, John Price, to accompany and record it.

Leaving on 24 January 1798, they soon encountered very rough going and after 10 days the convicts and soldiers abandoned the exercise and returned home. Wilson, Price and two unnamed companions ventured as far as the junction of the Wingecarribee and Wollondilly rivers near Mittagong before returning via Prospect ten days after setting out. Price's journey is notable for the first description of a 'whom-batt' and a number of lyrebirds. He also reported the discovery of salt pans, which intrigued the governor.

But the venture did little to explode the Shangri-La myth. By the time Hamilton was expanding his horizons in the Hawkesbury district and surrounds, 'bolting' was rife. According to bushranger historian Charles White, 'Hundreds of unfortunate men who slipped away into the inhospitable wilds in the end died off in such numbers that an early explorer declared he had counted on one trip fifty skeletons.'[7]

Wilson's association with the Aboriginal people ended in a way typical of many other European interactions with the Indigenous population. When he tried to take a tribal girl against her will, according to the official report, another native speared him 'at a time when he was unable to defend himself'. Unsurprisingly perhaps, the gulf between the two worlds was almost unbridgeable. The European intruders with their alien coverings, monstrous beasts and incomprehensible practices began as a curiosity. But as they showed no sign of leaving – and even expanded into tribal lands without seeking permission – conflict was inevitable.

Estimates of the Aboriginal population at the time vary widely, ranging from about 300,000 to one million, depending on which side of the 'history wars' is reckoning. But recent publications strongly suggest that there were more than sufficient for the 250 individual Aboriginal 'nations' to develop and control a highly sophisticated system of land management throughout the continent.

Their principal instrument was fire, which they used to manage their food supply by directing game to locations where it could be harvested. They cleared enormous areas, eliminated destructive bushfires and exploited a great variety of vegetable 'bush tucker'. In coastal and riparian settlements they trapped fish and discarded vast mounds of shellfish shells. Indeed, according to the acclaimed academic researcher and author Professor Bill Gammage, they had created 'the biggest estate on earth'.[8]

However, by the time Hamilton encountered his young Aboriginal neighbours in the Hawkesbury, the diseases that accompanied the convicts and their jailers were already taking a terrible toll. The smallpox epidemic of 1789 is believed to have killed 90 per cent of the numerous Darug clan in the west of Sydney Town. There are even suggestions – albeit unproven – that with ammunition running low 'British officials probably spread smallpox as the only means left to defend the colony'.[9] Certainly measles and tuberculosis followed spontaneously and in short order.

Governor Phillip had set the tone of the colonial engagement with the first Australians. At first he attempted to sooth their natural concerns. But when they resisted the intruder and speared one of his servants in 1790 he sent a military detachment to punish the tribe he considered responsible. He instructed

Watkin Tench to take 50 men and kill and decapitate 10 tribal people and capture two others.

Tench suggested less strident measures: six Aborigines captured, of whom two would be hanged and four transported to Norfolk Island. If they couldn't be taken alive they would be shot and beheaded. The governor agreed. Tench explained to his diary that Phillip was 'determined to strike a decisive blow in order, at once, to convince them of our superiority, and to infuse a universal terror in Aboriginal society'.[10]

Both marines and settlers regarded Aborigines who stood in their way as fair game. The so-called frontier wars, begun when the first shot was fired from an English musket, would eventually reap a death toll of no fewer than 60,000 Aboriginal people – a figure directly comparable to all the Australian soldiers killed in World War I, but from a much larger population of almost 5 million.[11]

However, Hamilton and John Hume – no doubt encouraged by their mother – were remarkable exceptions to the rule. They and John Batman not only mixed with the Eora people of the area, they learned their language and customs, and were relaxed in their company.

CHAPTER THREE

Troubles of a Fledgling Colony

Governor Macquarie struggles with a colony in chaos, Ann Morley survives the tragedy of the Boyd, *and Andrew Hume is granted 100 acres of land.*

When Governor Lachlan Macquarie succeeded Bligh in late 1809, he brought his own military unit, the 73rd Regiment, and was at last able to curb the power of the Rum Corps. Acting Governor Paterson, having granted an astonishing 67,000 acres of land to almost anyone who asked him, departed with the corps on the *Dromedary* in May 1810. He died at sea off Cape Horn just four weeks later, reportedly from cirrhosis of the liver.

Macarthur and Johnson were by then in London defending their actions against Bligh. Johnson would be cashiered and return as a new man to his beautiful convict paramour, Esther Julian and family in 1813. Not only was he more amenable to the governor's authority, he would marry Esther the following year and live out the rest of his life on his prosperous farm. Macarthur would remain in England until 1817. His wife Elizabeth would run the grazing properties and in the process take a leading role in founding the Australian wool industry.

Macquarie was faced with a colony in shambles. Firm action was required to remake the settlement and to navigate the vested colonial interests, not least in Whitehall. But his relatively low-ranking social status meant he was not well placed to deal with the panjandrums of the Colonial Office. Macquarie had come to the position of governor as a last-minute replacement without the kind of support the Admiralty gave his naval predecessors. And his all-important family connections to the British power structure were tenuous at best.

Born in the isolated island of Ulva in Scotland's Inner Hebrides, his father was a share farmer on the estate of the Duke of Argyle. He joined the army at 14 and pursued an extraordinarily active career seeing action in America, the West Indies, India, East Indies, Egypt and Russia. But while he occupied several staff positions, promotion came slowly. By 1808, aged 46, he reckoned he was the oldest lieutenant-colonel in the army.

His one brush with the ruling class was his marriage, at 31, to Jane Jarvis, the youngest daughter of a former – and very wealthy – chief justice of Antigua. It was a genuine love match but lasted only four years before she died of tuberculosis. After a long period of mourning he married his kinswoman, 29-year-old Elizabeth Campbell, in 1807. While it too was a loving partnership, it brought no preferment from the privileged classes.

The following year they confronted the death of their first born and it was then that the government announced that his 73rd Regiment would be posted to New South Wales and its commander, Major-General Miles Nightingall, would become the colonial governor. Macquarie applied for the post of lieutenant-governor and wrote directly to Viscount Castlereagh, the secretary of state for the colonies, outlining his qualifications. He was supported by the Duke of York whom he had met in the official military social interaction with the royal family, and Sir Arthur Wellesley, the future Duke of Wellington.

It was an unexceptionable appointment for a lieutenant-colonel and would, he hoped, improve his financial position over the next four or five years. When Nightingall then changed his mind about accepting the governorship of the distant colony, citing 'serious illness', Macquarie in a flush of ambition wrote again to Castlereagh. This time he put himself forward as the colonial viceroy.

At first, his ploy seemed to have failed and shortly afterwards he dutifully attended a royal levee as the prospective lieutenant-governor. He was disappointed but philosophical. However, the next day he happened to meet Castlereagh in Berkeley Square and the minister broke the news that he was to go as governor. He departed 'on winged feet' to tell Elizabeth.

A week before his embarkation, Castlereagh gave him confidential instructions, emphasising that:

> The Great Objects of attention are to improve the Morals of the Colonists, to encourage Marriage, to provide for Education, to prohibit the Use of Spirituous Liquors, to increase the Agriculture and Stock, so as to ensure the Certainty of a full supply to the Inhabitants under all Circumstances.

A Protestant Irish reactionary from County Down, Castlereagh had very little conception of conditions in the colony. His subsequent career suggests he had a tin ear for political developments at home as well as abroad. So while Macquarie did his best to comply, he was soon forced to abandon most of the moral strictures – particularly the ban on spirituous liquors – but remained determined to increase the agriculture and stock.

During the voyage out on the *Dromedary* he shared the ship's modest facilities with a well-connected lawyer, Ellis Bent, who would become the colony's deputy-judge-advocate, in effect the chief law officer. At first they would work well together but after Ellis's Tory brother Jeffrey joined him in 1814 as the first Supreme Court judge they fell out spectacularly.

But that was well into the future. As Macquarie disembarked and threw himself into his task, he found he was dealing with an insurmountable problem. The European population, including Norfolk Island and Van Diemen's Land, amounted to about 7,000, the vast majority of whom were convicts whose treatment had alienated them from any engagement with the fortunes of the colony. Sydney Town was 'a slovenly little place'[1] and Macquarie was deeply shocked at its condition. The hospital, the barracks, the wharf, Government House and the few civic buildings were all in a state of decay. Even the church was unfinished.

The only flashes of colour were the shops, of which David Mann, a schoolmaster, wrote in 1809:

> They are particularly respectable and decorated with much taste. Articles of female apparel and ornament are greedily purchased, for the European women in the settlement spare no expense in ornamenting their persons and in dress each seems to vie with the other in extravagance.[2]

But the roads were in a parlous state and the few bridges even worse. Pigs and goats browsed among the rubbish thrown into the narrow lanes and crooked streets. All town land was crown property and was only leased for short periods to private individuals who had no incentive to build for the future.

Macquarie's first task was to regulate the administration and raise morale. On his orders, streets were widened and cleared of stumps. Gangs of convicts were engaged to clear the detritus and build fences 'in a neat, regular and desirable manner'. New streets were laid out and old ones rejuvenated and renamed. Sergeant Major's Row became George Street after the king; Windmill Row became Hunter Street and Chapel Row Castlereagh Street. Plans were made for a program to repair and replace the derelict public buildings.

The society of which Macquarie and Elizabeth were the titular heads was strictly stratified and this was reflected in the layout of the town. Government House, albeit in its dilapidated state, remained the social centre. The merchants and the 'sterling' occupied the slopes while the swill made merry at The Rocks. According to Macquarie's biographer Marjorie Barnard:

> Rum ran like blood in the veins of the body politic and gave a touch of fever to life. Officers of the regiment went marauding and rioting through the town, taking part in the rough pleasures of The Rocks and sometimes there was trouble. Ships' officers came ashore and indulged in drinking and horse-play. The same needs drove them both – the sailors were reacting against the empty confinement of their ships, the soldiers against the emptiness of too little confinement.[3]

Although the gentry might descend, when sufficiently undone by drink, to the shadowy temptations at harbourside, it was strictly one-way traffic. The hoi polloi were separated by an unbridgeable social gulf from their betters on the hill. Of course, the exigencies of the penal settlement often breached the vocational barriers between them. Government officers had no choice but to employ convict clerks; private houses were staffed by convict servants and served by emancipist tradesmen. Military popinjays secretly established their convict mistresses within their households then bowed to their demands for introduction to a widening circle of their guests. Poor free settlers who found themselves on the same economic level as ticket-of-leave men amalgamated into a single, if ill-defined, class.

Moreover, a new group of which Hamilton Hume would become the most celebrated was now coming to adulthood – the native-born Australian, often with at least one parent a convict, but also from among the less privileged free settlers forced to rely on their own resources. According to Barnard, 'They were well set up, on the average taller than their parents, good looking, especially the girls, vigorous, fine but reckless horsemen, exhibited no criminal taint, had a pride of their own and showed no readiness to marry back into the convict class.'

Macquarie quickly turned his attention to the best – indeed the only – means of communicating with the colony: the *Sydney Gazette* created by printer and editor George Howe in 1803. Howe was a Creole, born in the West Indies and who learned his trade at *The Times* of London. Convicted of shoplifting in 1799, he was condemned to death, later commuted to transportation for life. However, he secured his ticket-of-leave in 1806 and would make his permanent home in New South Wales.

His was the first newssheet issued in the Southern Hemisphere and dealt mainly with government orders and florid accounts of local happenings together with whatever advertising he could muster. By 1810 the paper was on its last legs with Howe actually facing starvation. Macquarie was its saviour. He put Howe on an annual salary of £60 and poured his General Orders into its columns. Its circulation rose to 300 each week and it was soon widely read.

He also established the settlement's first post office in George Street, run by an ex-convict, Isaac Nicholls. Until then Nicholls had collected letters from newly arrived ships and charged a shilling each to those who came to collect them from his tumbledown office near the wharf. For a small payment a letter could be put aboard the government boat to Parramatta while constables carrying dispatches might take private letters to the more distant settlements. In the new system, a list of letters received was published in *The Gazette* and could be collected for payment of eightpence each. The same charge applied to letters heading back to Britain. There was no regular delivery to the country but the postmaster would entrust letters to friends and associates heading bush.

Another of Macquarie's priorities was the 24-kilometre road to Parramatta, the only route out of the settlement. It was practically impassable in the wet and bone crunching for horse-drawn travellers the rest of the time. It had originated as an Aboriginal track and had been used by the newcomers since the days of Governor Phillip. Now it was a main road and already bustling with traffic – gentlemen on horseback going to and from their estates; detachments of soldiers en route to their tours of service in the outlying settlements; farmers driving their carts in with produce in the mornings and returning at night (often drunk and prey to thieves); constables on government business; and convict gangs on the way to work.

Macquarie and his party travelled its length on his first tour of the colony's outlying districts in November 1810. Their destination was to the south where he would name Campbell Town for the birthplace of his wife Elizabeth who accompanied him. He was particularly concerned for her morale. Shortly before her departure from England she had suffered a miscarriage and in August 1810 experienced yet another tragic loss. In fact, she would miscarry six or seven times during her ten years in the colony. But by now she was taking an active interest in developments and was regaining her lively sense of humour.

On their journey along the Parramatta Road, they passed the splendid property of the pompous Dr John Harris of the New South Wales Corps who had named his land grant 'Ultimo' (later adopted for an inner Sydney suburb). In her diary, Elizabeth recalled their first meeting. 'With the air of utmost importance,' she wrote,

> Dr Harris strutted up to me and said, 'I was once summoned to attend a Court Martial; the gentleman in reading the charge happened to say this court being convened on the 12th *ultimo*, instead of *instant.* They were not classical; but I, Madam, *being* classical, immediately perceived the mistake. I ridiculed them and wrote verses on the subject and afterwards called my home Ultimo Place.'[4]

Other properties that could be seen from the thoroughfare would also be remembered in the city's suburban nomenclature, including Annandale (George Johnson), Burwood (Alexander Riley) and Mount Druitt after Major Druitt, the government engineer. The Parramatta township was in many ways the rival of Sydney itself. In November 1788, Governor Phillip had chosen it for the government farm as it was the nearest good land with a freshwater river. The following year he granted it to the Cornish farmer, James Ruse, who had been transported for breaking and entering. His orders were to grow crops to feed the starving settlement on pain of surrendering the land. Happily, Ruse was up to the task. He produced the first successful wheat harvest on the continent and later grew up to 600 bushels of corn in a single year.

By Macquarie's time he had exchanged his grant for more fertile land on the Hawkesbury River flats. But there he shared the fate of the Humes and found himself bankrupted by repeated floods. He subsequently sold his property to the 'classical' Dr John Harris and found work as a seaman.

On arrival at the Parramatta township, Macquarie, like Phillip, with whom he was corresponding, was greatly taken with its rural serenity and settled briefly in the official country residence – The Crescent – that his predecessor had established there. He would later rebuild and expand it as a retreat to be variously used by his successors until the 1850s.

From Parramatta he turned south on the track that would become the Liverpool Road to the only other township of any size, Liverpool on the George's River. Then a little further to the south-east he called the district Appin after Elizabeth's family estate in Argyllshire where she spent her childhood. A few kilometres to the west were the Cowpastures, where in 1788 four cows and two bulls had settled after making good their escape from the confines of Sydney Town. They had been discovered in Governor Hunter's time after the Aboriginal people, astounded by their unheralded arrival, incorporated their appearance in a tribal dance.

No effort was made to capture them. Instead they were preserved by successive governors as a symbolic last resort in time of famine. No one could enter the area without express permission. Governor King had been furious when he was ordered by the Colonial Office to give John Macarthur a portion of the pastures to run his sheep. But while the Aboriginal people gave them a wide berth, the expanding herd became a source of food for the early bushrangers.

This first journey took the form of a military reconnaissance mission, and Macquarie was impressed with the potential of the Appin and Airds district. Thanks to the Aboriginal people and their managerial fires, much of it was lightly timbered with park-like areas suitable for grazing. Other parts were scrubby but the soil was good and well watered. So the following year he made the first land grants in the area beginning with 1,000 acres to William Broughton, which the grateful recipient immediately named 'Lachlan Vale'.

Broughton was Macquarie's commissary in charge of the all-important government stores. He had arrived on the First Fleet as a servant of surgeon John White and was appointed storekeeper at Parramatta in 1789, a post he maintained until 1799, during which time Andrew Hume held the same position (off and on) at nearby Toongabbie. In 1800, Broughton transferred to Norfolk Island as storekeeper and assistant commissary and four years later returned to Sydney Town as deputy-commissary of stores in New South Wales. In the wake of the Rum Rebellion, he took over as acting commissary and Macquarie confirmed him in his post. Between 1792 and 1807 Broughton fathered five children to his convict mistress Ann Morley.

But then he decided to marry Elizabeth Charlotte Kennedy, Eliza Hume's widowed sister-in-law. Ann departed for England, taking her two-year-old Betsy with her. They sailed in the *Boyd* to a seaborne tragedy more shocking even than the wreck of the *Guardian.*

With them was Te Ara, the son of a Maori chieftain being returned to New Zealand; but when he refused to work his passage the British Captain John Thompson had him flogged and starved. When they reached Whangaroa, and Te Ara told his people of the Pakeha outrage, his father determined to avenge the insult. They armed themselves and waited their moment.

Thompson and several crew members went ashore the following day to inspect a stand of kauri for felling. The Maoris held back until they were clear of the beach and out of sight of the ship, and they then killed and ate them. At dusk they disguised themselves in the crewmen's clothes and, with other tribesmen, rowed their canoes to the ship. Once aboard, they killed everyone they could see but for the few who scaled the rigging in terror and clung for dear life. Ann Morley cowered in her cabin below with her whimpering child.

Next morning a friendly chieftain from a neighbouring clan arrived and rescued the two females. He also saved the second mate, who had remained all night out of reach on the rigging, and Tom Davis, the cabin boy, who had smuggled food to Te Ara and tended his back after the floggings. The second mate was put to work making fish hooks from barrel hoops but when he proved incompetent he too was killed and eaten.

Three weeks later, Captain Alexander Berry, en route to England, arrived in his *City of Edinburgh* on a rescue mission. By then the *Boyd* had been accidentally blown up by the curious

Maoris in the ship's powder room and he quickly secured release of the survivors. However, on the northerly voyage Ann Morley contracted a fever and died. Tom Davis would remain with Alexander Berry, who in time would return to New South Wales and become a powerful patron of Hamilton Hume. But at Rio de Janeiro Captain Berry put Betsy on a ship bound for Sydney Town, where in 1812 a grateful William Broughton took her home to 'Lachlan Vale'.

In that same year, Governor Macquarie granted Andrew Hume 100 acres at Appin adjoining Broughton's property. This was good pastureland, lightly timbered and between the coast and the Cowpastures. He christened it 'Hume Mount'. It signalled the beginning of a remarkable sea change in the Hume family's fortunes.

CHAPTER FOUR

To Cross the Great Divide

Hamilton Hume's explorations are extended, and Blaxland, Lawson and Wentworth attempt to cross the Great Dividing Range.

Andrew Hume's restless spirit would at last find an outlet in developing 'Hume Mount', which would be enlarged by a grant of a further 150 acres two years later. He and his assigned convicts built a stone cottage and eventually a small convict barracks also of local stone. The family ran a small herd of beef cattle, grew their own vegetables and kept two milkers for home consumption.

'Hume Mount' was in the mid-range of properties in the district. The largest, William Broughton's 1,000 acres, was supplemented with a further 700 in 1816 to which he gave the name 'Macquarie Dale'. This was followed by Alexander Riley's 1,250-acre 'Hardwicke', so called after his wife Sophia's maiden name.

Riley was a free settler, born in Ireland's County Cavan, who had arrived in the penal colony in 1805 and struck up an immediate friendship with Lieutenant-Governor Paterson. At the time, Paterson was acting governor and with his open-handed generosity – particularly when on the drink – he gave Riley a substantial grant at Liverpool. When Paterson was appointed to head the settlement in Van Diemen's Land, Riley followed him as magistrate and storekeeper at Port Dalrymple. And when Paterson returned to Sydney after Bligh was deposed, Riley again accompanied him, this time as his secretary to the colony. Riley settled on his Burwood estate off the Parramatta Road and devoted himself to the infant wool industry. He also expanded his interests to international trade and in time would become one of the richest men in the land.

Eliza Hume's nephew John Kennedy received 200 acres near 'Hume Mount', which he named 'Teston Farm', and it too would be supplemented with a further grant of 80 acres in 1816. Other much smaller grants, ranging from 30 to 80 acres, were distributed to a mix of new settler arrivals and emancipated convicts.

Andrew Hume curbed his drinking and would never again be hauled before a court. Indeed, he was one of the first to contribute to the building of a new courthouse at Liverpool. It was a symbolic assertion of his newfound respectability. Courthouses were designed as an imposing physical proclamation of colonial rule. To the convicts and the less favoured emancipists they would become the symbol of repression, while they were irrelevant to the Aboriginal people since they had virtually no rights under the imperial regime.

By now Hamilton was 15 years old, tall and rangy with a shock of red hair. He had yet to reach his full height but was getting bigger and stronger by the day. His mother had ensured that under her tutelage he and his siblings were well educated. He would become a lifelong reader with a wide range of interests – from history to poetry – and a forceful writer in a firm and legible hand. She had also instilled in him a rare respect for the Aborigines who surrounded the new settlement in considerable numbers.

For much of each week Hamilton and 12-year-old John would work the 'Hume Mount' stock with the assigned convicts – eight men drawn from the nearest muster – but there remained plenty of time for the youngsters to explore their surroundings. In these early expeditions, they were accompanied by Dual, a young Aboriginal man of the Dharawal people. Usually they travelled by foot since horses in the early days were both rare and expensive and only now were becoming more freely available.

Governor Macquarie went about Sydney Town in a splendid carriage drawn by four horses. The 'sterling' followed suit. And in October 1810 the first race meeting was held at Hyde Park. But among the 'currency', coaching and medium-weight harness horses were being imported and bred to haul wagons and coaches at moderate speed to outlying areas such as Appin. They were generally unsuitable as saddle horses.

Gradually, the young Humes' ventures extended from three- and four-day hikes into the Dharawal country, with its deep gullies and tumbling streams, to week-long expeditions to the borders of the Shoalhaven in the south-east towards the sea, and the rough and often impenetrable country of the south-west. Dual was not only an indispensable guide; his presence ensured the safety of his white companions from interference by his clansmen.

The Dharawal were more favourably disposed to the intruders than many of their compatriots, either through an innately trusting nature or an inability to appreciate the magnitude of the occupation to follow. They were not alone in this, though Aboriginal resistance had flared intermittently from 1794 when settlers first moved out to the fertile Hawkesbury River flats. Conflict then moved south and west with the spread of settlement.

The biggest uprisings were led by Pemulwuy of the Bediagal clan, who in 1797 attacked Toongabbie with 100 warriors in what later became known as the Battle of Parramatta. He was shot seven times but survived for another five years until Governor King ordered him taken dead or alive. In 1802, he was shot to death by Henry Hacking who had been quarter-master of HMS *Sirius* and after whom Port Hacking is named.

King had Pemulwuy's head preserved in spirits and sent to Sir Joseph Banks. The tribal leader's son Tedbury continued to harass the occupiers until he was killed in 1810. Isolated incid-ents continued between settlers, convicts and Aborigines, usually as 'payback' by spear or mutilation when settlers fired on the native people as they raided crops and stock for food. But the first major hostilities after Macquarie's arrival took place at Appin.

On his initial visit to the area, the governor and his wife had been welcomed by two or three small parties of Dharawal who, he noted in his journal, 'performed an extraordinary sort of dance'. He would establish a Native Institution in Parramatta in 1814 at the instigation of his wife, where children were taught English, stories from the Bible and trained as domestic servants or farm labourers. However, Aboriginal parents resisted the idea and the children often absconded.

Macquarie would be the first to 'honour' Aboriginal leaders by awarding them breastplates and titles of his own design as 'chief' or 'king' of clans or ill-defined areas. In classic mutual misunderstanding, he also encouraged annual celebrations in

Parramatta when tribal people made corroboree before a crowd of bemused spectators.

While the Dharawal people were relatively cooperative, the neighbouring Gandangara people, their traditional enemies, had a well-merited reputation as being hostile to intruders, particularly those who misused their people. However, it was beyond the capability of most whites to distinguish between the two.

The Humes' arrival in the area coincided with a series of drought years, and this brought parties of Gandangara down from the mountains and into the district in search of food. Some settlers were killed, and in response farmers prepared to defend themselves and even to take the offensive. Early in 1814 an Aboriginal woman and her children were murdered by whites whose names, perhaps unsurprisingly, are lost to history. Macquarie's threat that such 'inhumanity or cruelty will be punished' was soon shown to be little more than empty air. The perpetrators were never arrested, much less brought to justice in the new Liverpool courthouse. However, it is known that John Kennedy took the bodies and buried them with a respectful service on his Teston Farm.[1]

The settlers were sharply divided in their attitude to the original inhabitants. While some regarded them as little more than vermin, others like the Humes and the Kennedys developed a co-dependency with them based on Aboriginal labour and protection in return for food, tobacco and 'sitting down' on their properties. So when in 1816 the Gandangara were joined by other groups from around Jervis Bay in raids into Dharawal country, the local tribespeople sought refuge among the friendly settlers and stood with them against the outsiders. The situation was complicated by similar divisions among the Aborigines

– some Gandangara people sided with the Dharawal and chose coexistence above conflict.

As the hostilities escalated, Macquarie authorised an armed reprisal against five identified Gandangara men accused of attacking cedar cutters; and in April 1816 the governor bowed to rising settler demands for military intervention. This quickly became a de facto declaration of war on all Aborigines as the former soldier oversaw a three-pronged military strike throughout the settled districts of the colony.

His instructions were clear: the soldiers were to take prisoner all Aboriginal people they found, to shoot any who refused to surrender and hang their bodies in trees. They were also to bring back 18 small children for the Native Institution at Parramatta. There was to be no distinction between 'hostile' and 'friendly' Aborigines and it was accepted that women and children were likely to be collateral damage.[2]

The British raiding party split into two at Bent's Basin on the Nepean River north of Campbell Town, with one group moving south-west against the Gandangara and the other under Captain James Wallis moving south-east against the Dharawal. Wallis was accompanied by a former convict-cum-bush guide, John Warby, and two reluctant Dharawal men, Budbury and Bundle, who sent the soldiers on an exhausting wild goose chase, then escaped at the first opportunity.

At John Kennedy's farm, Wallis noticed two of the outlawed Gandangara men among those 'sitting down' on his property. Kennedy and Hamilton Hume argued for their lives, saying they were protecting the farm. Hume even lied that he had seen the governor erase their names from the 'wanted' list. Wallis left in confusion and was soon abandoned by John Warby. However, not to be denied his chase, the officer located an Aboriginal camp of men, women and children on Broughton's property above the Cataract Gorge on the night of 17 April 1816.

According to Wallis's report, a little after 1 am his soldiers arrived in the shadows of the bush leading to the camp. 'The fires were burning but deserted,' he wrote.

> A few of my men heard a child cry. I formed [mounted] line ranks, entered and pushed on through a thick brush towards the precipitous banks of a deep rocky creek. The dogs gave the alarm and the natives fled over the cliffs. It was moonlight . . . some were shot and the others met their fate by rushing in despair over the precipice. Fourteen dead bodies were counted in different directions.[3]

The true number killed in what became known as the Appin Massacre is unknown. No action was taken against the commander or his soldiers. Indeed, the following month Captain Wallis was promoted to become commandant of the Newcastle convict settlement, a post he held until 1818 when he was relieved by one of the more notorious and sadistic of the imperial commanders, Captain James Morisset.

Hume's friend Dual was among five prisoners subsequently taken in the Aboriginal round-up, and in August 1816 he was sentenced to death but immediately reprieved and banished to Van Diemen's Land. Whether even that sentence was carried out is highly unlikely. The young Hamilton was totally opposed to the military response and unafraid to intervene on his friend's behalf. There are later uncontested reports that Dual became a well-regarded interpreter in the colony,[4] and he undoubtedly continued, at least for a time, to accompany Hamilton Hume and others as the newcomers explored the land that had been appropriated to the Empire.

The young Hume's exploratory journeys from 1814 to 1816 are not well recorded. In a letter he wrote to the *Sydney Monitor* in 1826, he simply says that, 'In the year 1814 I discovered the tract of country now called Argyle. I was [also] there in the years 1815 and 1816.' In these he was certainly accompanied by Dual and at least on the first venture by his 14-year-old brother John. But when they returned from an exhausting journey through the Bargo scrub, their mother banned the younger Hume from further journeys until he was at least 17.

Hamilton was unstoppable. His ambitions ran more deeply than personal pride, for by now the colony was desperate for more arable land and the role of pathfinder was highly valued.

From the earliest days, expansion was restricted by the Great Divide, which confined the settlement to the coastal strip. Time and again attempts to scale the Blue Mountains by men as varied as George Bass, Ensign Francis Barrallier and Paterson himself had ended in abject failure.

Like the rest of the community, the teenaged Hume was intrigued by the quest to find a way through the mountain barrier, and he had the advantage of Aboriginal intelligence. The local people knew at least two routes across the mountains – along Bilpin Ridge or via Cox's River – but they were unwilling to volunteer the tribal songlines, and the authorities now regarded them with implacable distrust. Moreover, Governor King had not only ignored the observations of the 'vagabond' John Wilson, who did make the crossing, he had pigeonholed Price's report that recorded it. It would not be rediscovered for a century.

In 1813, the 35-year-old 'sterling' stock-breeder Gregory Blaxland, hungry for more grazing land, received approval from Macquarie to tackle the barricade. He approached William Lawson, 39, a former officer in the New South Wales Corps who had married a convict on Norfolk Island and taken up an extensive grant on his return to the mainland, to mount an expedition. Third of the trio was Hume's family friend, 23-year-old William Wentworth. They had known each other from Andrew Hume's early association with D'Arcy Wentworth on Norfolk Island and later when the Wentworths settled on a property in the Parramatta district. But they'd had no contact with William from 1802 when he had been sent to school in England until he returned in 1810. He then took up a government post as provost marshall and received a grant from Macquarie of 1,750 acres on the Nepean River.

The trio's expedition was much better prepared than those that had gone before. Not only were they equipped with four pack horses, five kangaroo dogs – usually greyhounds crossed with local breeds – and supplies for six weeks; they were assisted by four convicts. They also had the detailed observations of George Caley, a naturalist appointed by Sir Joseph Banks to collect specimens in New South Wales. Nine years before, he had climbed Mount Banks and made detailed sketches of the main ridges on the mountain spine.

On 11 May 1813, they set out to climb the ridge running from Emu Plains and followed a route similar to that of today's Great Western Highway to Mount Victoria, before traversing a finger ridge to Mount York, arriving late on 28 May. From there they could see the upper section of Cox's Valley, with the Great Divide blocking the view to the west. They descended into the valley then pressed upward to the forbidding slopes of yet another eminence they named Mount Blaxland, still some 20 kilometres short of the Divide. And there they called off the attempt.

They returned to Emu Plains in only five days and reported to Macquarie. They made no claim to have crossed the barrier and he took no immediate action to exploit their efforts. However, three months later he sent for the assistant surveyor at Port Dalrymple, George Evans, to complete the task of penetrating to the interior.

Born in 1780, Evans had arrived in New South Wales in 1802, having served a short apprenticeship with a London engineer – including some elementary surveying – before migrating to the Cape of Good Hope in 1798. Initially he took up a position as grain storekeeper at Parramatta but in 1803 acted as surveyor-general before being discharged by Governor King in 1806.

He farmed land adjacent to the Humes' property in the Hawkesbury and, like them, was flooded out. Then with Alexander Riley, he joined Lieutenant-Governor William Paterson as assistant surveyor at Port Dalrymple in 1809. But before he could take up the post officially he was recalled to New South Wales, where he surveyed the shores of Jervis Bay and led a party overland to Appin in 1812. This was no small achievement and was undoubtedly behind Macquarie's decision to choose him for the final conquest of the Blue Mountains.

It was a felicitous choice. Evans took up where the land-hungry graziers had left off and forged a track through the final barriers to the western plains. Only then did Macquarie approach William Cox, a former paymaster of the New South Wales Corps who had left the regiment under a cloud of unpaid debts. He had redeemed himself as a magistrate who dealt fairly with the emancipists, and in July 1814 he answered the governor's call to build a road to consolidate the breakthrough.

Cox had no particular road-building skills but was an able supervisor, and the 30 convicts under his command were promised their freedom if they performed their tasks well. Over the next six months they made 101 miles (163 kilometres) of road through rugged mountain country, building more than a dozen bridges and splitting hundreds of posts and rails without loss of life or serious accident. The result was a very hazardous passage from the coastal confines to the western plains. The climb from Emu Plains to the first range summit exhausted the horses while the descent from Mount York was 206 metres of terrifying, precipitous track down to Prince Regent's Glen. Cox admitted it was too steep for safety or convenience, and logs had to be attached to coaches and drays as land anchors to prevent them plunging to the bottom. Nevertheless, Macquarie and his wife (on horseback) led a parade of dignitaries over its length to Bathurst on 15 April 1815.

Among them were three designated 'surveyors' – John Oxley, George Evans and James Meehan – all of whom would subsequently engage Hamilton Hume as a pathfinder. None of the three had more than a nodding acquaintance with the formalities of surveying. Oxley was a junior naval officer who first arrived in 1802 as a master's mate and undertook some coastal surveys of Western Port two years later. He returned to England in 1807 and was promoted to first lieutenant, returning the following year as government agent on the convict transport *Speke*. He brought with him £800 worth of goods for resale to the colony and an order for a grant of 600 acres near William Wentworth's property on the Nepean.

The bibulous William Paterson increased it to 1,000 acres, but Macquarie required him to surrender the additional portion in 1810. Meantime, he had accompanied the deposed William Bligh to Van Diemen's Land after Paterson freed the governor from house arrest, and while there wrote a lengthy report on the island's penal settlement, which he submitted to the Admiralty. Back in England, he applied for the post of naval officer in Sydney and became engaged to John Macarthur's daughter Elizabeth. He then attempted to 'buy' the post of New South Wales surveyor-general from the incumbent Charles Grimes, who was stranded in England in the Rum Rebellion court case.

When Macarthur discovered the extent of Oxley's debts, he broke off the engagement. But by then the eager swain – courtesy of Macarthur's patronage before the debts were revealed – had secured the surveyor-general appointment. He retired immediately from the navy and returned to Sydney to take it up in 1812. Macarthur wrote that he was 'no more fit to make his way in the midst of the [colonial] sharks among whom it will be his fate to live than he is qualified to be Lord Chancellor'.[5]

Meehan was an Irish ex-convict who had gained his surveying experience when assigned as a servant to Charles Grimes in 1801. He accompanied him and Francis Barrallier on an exploration of the Hunter River the following year. When Grimes took leave in England from 1803 to 1806 and Evans acted in his place, it was Meehan – now pardoned – who undertook most of the departmental duties. And when Grimes again left to appear in the Rum Rebellion court case in 1806, Meehan was officially appointed acting surveyor-general until Oxley bought the office in 1812.

However, while Oxley was attracted to the more grandiose aspects of the position – especially the highly publicised expeditions to uncover new grazing land – it was Meehan who honed his surveying skills and did the hard graft to give settlers clear title to their land. He was also a great improviser in the bush. On one occasion, when faced with the task of moving a cart of supplies without leather tack, he made hames, collar and harness from green timber and a hammock. On another, Hamilton Hume assisted as he devised a punt to cross a flooded river using the tray of a dray enveloped in a sheet of canvas.

Hume learned quickly and well. His many bush skills would prove essential to the success of his great expedition with William Hovell.

CHAPTER FIVE

Hume Hits His Stride

Hume comes to Governor Macquarie's attention, obtains a patron, and carves out an overland route from Sydney to the South Coast.

Hamilton Hume's early forays had not gone unnoticed among the official community. In 1815, Governor Macquarie visited 'Hume Mount' and discussed his journeys with the rising young bushman–explorer. Later that year John Oxley sent his superintendent, John Fletcher, to ask Hume for help in locating grazing land for his mob of 500 cattle that were starving in the Bargo scrub. The 18-year-old Hamilton told him: 'Follow my marked line of axe cuts on trees to Toom-bong [later Mittagong].'[1] Oxley took his advice and Fletcher easily accomplished his mission.

His official involvement was remarkable in one so young. But it was the private settlers and landholders who continually importuned the young bushman for assistance in carving out the tribal land for their own use. He was generous with his time and knowledge. According to a contemporary, 'He was a clean-living young bushman of healthy tastes, in contrast to the rum swilling officials of the period. He held himself to be a gentleman. He had a pre-emptory directness of speech and opinion, was hot-headed but warm-hearted and genial.'[2] Another reported, 'Tall, thin and bony [as a youth], he grew into a massively built man of genial disposition, untiring activity and wholly unselfish.'[3]

His first private patron – and sometime rival – was Dr Charles Throsby who, like most early landowners, arrived in the colony as a military officer in charge of convicts. Born in 1777 at Glenfield in Leicestershire, he had joined the navy in his teens and become a well-regarded surgeon. He arrived in the colony on the convict transport *Coromandel* in 1802 and was congratulated by Governor King on the health of his charges.

Throsby's early experiences in New South Wales found him at the centre of colonial mayhem. He was appointed medical officer and magistrate at Castle Hill, 30 kilometres to the northwest of Sydney Town, where the Aboriginal leader Pemulwuy had recently been killed, and his son Tedbury was leading a series of scattered reprisals. Then in 1804 came the Castle Hill uprising of Irish convicts who torched the prison farm huts and marched on Parramatta. Throsby was then sent to Newcastle, where many of the rebels were being punished, as superintendent of labour. On arrival, he discovered that the commandant, Ensign Cadwallader Draffen, had gone insane. Throsby declared him 'a helpless lunatic' and was briefly given command of the settlement himself. Draffen, however, recovered his wits sufficiently to become one of the officers who would overthrow Bligh in 1808.

During the Rum Rebellion Throsby resigned on grounds of ill-health, and in 1809 the ever-generous Paterson granted him

600 acres at Minto. He also confirmed Throsby as a magistrate despite a debilitating stutter. Macquarie, in his attempts to regularise Paterson's wild profligacy, required Throsby to surrender the grant but he then replaced it with 1,500 acres (607 hectares) in the Moss Vale district. Henceforth Throsby devoted himself with an unbridled energy – at times verging on the manic – to increasing his colonial landholdings.

In 1817, he engaged Hamilton Hume to show him his earlier discoveries in the Argyle area. They made congenial travelling companions. Throsby's stepson George Barber would marry Hamilton's sister Isabella. And while Throsby was a 'sterling' by birth, they shared an abomination of the treatment meted out to the Aboriginal people. In fact, Throsby made his feelings known to Macquarie and the two men fell out.

Throsby's particular bête noire was a Macquarie favourite – William Broughton, on whose property the Appin Massacre took place. This would remain an impediment to harmonious relations in the district. It would take a full generation before they were finally restored when Throsby's son Charles Jr married Betsy Broughton, the charmed survivor of the Boyd Massacre in New Zealand's Whangaroa Harbour.

The estrangement with the governor was also eventually repaired. Macquarie had an unbounded admiration for the pioneers, like Throsby, who were engaged in the gradual transformation of Australia from a penal settlement perched on the edge of an Aboriginal continent to a more self-sustaining extension of the British Empire.

In a second 1817 expedition, Hume led Throsby and his bushman employee Josh Wild to the rich pastures of Toom-bong. They travelled down the track Hume had marked on previous

Once again the rain returned, this time in a tropical deluge. Nevertheless, they struggled onward to Wingelo and on 24 March came upon what Meehan called 'the deep ravines running to Shoals Haven'. The chasms were an almost vertical fall of no less than 400 metres with a tangle of foliage blocking the way. Again they were forced back, so turned to the north-west through bare, stony country, crossed a small stream and reached a gently forested area that had been managed by the Aboriginal people in their meticulously networked 'estate'.[4] The Indigenous man Bundell called it Moorooaulin (Marulan).

Soon afterwards they again came to impassable gorges, so they agreed to divide the party with Throsby taking the Aborigines, one convict and a servant towards Kangaroo Valley; Meehan and Hume took the others and made southwards until they reached the Shoalhaven River. It was running a banker and Meehan wrote, 'I am satisfied that any attempt of mine to head it would be ineffectual.'[5] The only alternative to yet another retreat was to attempt a crossing.

Unfortunately, while Hume was searching for a way across, two horses escaped into the scrub and the convicts were unable to locate them. Hume later tracked them for eight kilometres through the bush, but it would be a further day before he found them. Meanwhile, Meehan had been visited by two Aboriginal men in camp and on Hamilton's return as 'a special favour' – and among much hilarity – he and Hume gave them a shave. The following day, according to Meehan:

> I went with Hamilton Hume and another in order to try if we could pass the river. Hume, who is a very good swimmer, found he could not ford any part of it, the stream is so rapid

> it cannot be withstood . . . I have determined on penetrating into the interior of the country, thinking I shall be more likely to make useful discoveries than by returning . . .

On Wednesday, 1 April they turned west and after three days of solid travelling they came upon the broad waters of Lake Bathurst. Meehan and Hume rode around it. The surveyor took its measurements and named it after the secretary of state for the colonies, unaware (or unconcerned) that the Aboriginal people had long named it Bundong after the local clan in whose country it resided.

They continued on a north-westerly course to a point where the present Goulburn–Braidwood road crosses the Mulwaree Ponds, and there they made an utterly unexpected discovery. Meehan wrote: 'Found the head and small pieces of a skeleton of a large animal which I suppose to be amphibious. Hamilton Hume found another of the same a little behind . . .' Further on, about ten kilometres from the current site of Goulburn (which he called the Goulbourne (sic) Plains after Earl Bathurst's under-secretary, Henry Goulburn) he discovered the head and thigh bones of other large and ancient animals. They were never properly identified but joined other remains that gave support to rumours of 'bunyips' in the unfamiliar wilderness.

By now they were running short of supplies and so turned for home, as did Throsby at about the same time. He had reached Jervis Bay, but further penetration south was beyond his resources. Hume and Meehan set a north-easterly course and rode the ridges until they were about three kilometres from Mount Towrang, which had been climbed 20 years previously by the wild white native, John Wilson. Hume was probably unaware of his predecessor but he seemed to possess the remarkable instincts of a homing pigeon, for on 11 April they reached the spot near Exeter where they had arranged to rendezvous with Throsby. As it happened, the doctor had arrived earlier and left the day before. They caught up with his party on the home stretch.

They had failed in their vice-regal mission, but Hume and Meehan had discovered a great deal of open country, the product of many thousands of years of Aboriginal management. And while the original inhabitants had employed their skills to nurture and harvest the native wildlife, the new occupants would capitalise upon them to introduce their own alien cloven-hoofed animals. Together, the settlers and their livestock would begin the long process of degrading a land that, until then, had been preserved for millennia by their custodial antecedents.

Hamilton Hume was rewarded for his efforts with four head of cattle. They arrived 'on credit' from the government store and had to be paid for 'in kind'. However, Meehan, Throsby and others with the ear of the governor pressed for a greater reward, and Macquarie let it be known that some 300 acres could be selected by the young explorer at Appin. The deeds would arrive 'in due course'.[6]

By then, Macquarie was under fire from their Lordships in the Colonial Office. He might have been suitably tough on Aboriginal insurrection, but he was patently soft on convicts. This raised the ire of the Conservatives in Westminster and Macarthur's confederates in New South Wales, now known as the 'exclusives'. The division in colonial society between 'sterling' and 'currency' had been joined by a deeper and more persistent split between the exclusives and the emancipists. The

British class system had been transported, taken root like some exotic weed and entangled Macquarie in his attempts to put the colony on a firmer economic footing. Indeed, it called his continuance as governor into question.

In Britain, the end of the Napoleonic Wars brought high unemployment and this together with public anger at the Corn Laws that were keeping food prices artificially high – and the Act of Union with Ireland – brought forth a rash of political rioting. One result was the so-called Peterloo Massacre in which 60 cavalrymen charged into a crowd of protestors at St Peter's Field in Manchester with sabres drawn. More than a dozen fell fatally before the slashing blades, and between 400 and 700 were injured.

Much of the blame attached to Lord Castlereagh, whose brief had set Macquarie on his colonial venture. While the Earl of Liverpool was prime minister, Castlereagh was easily the most prominent of the Tory ministers and had negotiated the Act of Union. The poet Shelley reflected the public anger when he wrote, *'I met Murder on the way/He had a mask like Castlereagh . . .'*

The government's next response, also initiated by Castlereagh, was to relieve the domestic pressure by doubling and redoubling the ships taking the protesting 'convicts' to the Antipodes. Macquarie was inundated with new arrivals. He had closed the Norfolk Island satellite colony in 1814 on orders from Whitehall, and the Van Diemen's Land penal system was already overcrowded. So he put the newcomers to work in a massive mainland building program, much to the displeasure of the 'exclusives' who wanted them divided among landholders as slave labour.

Once they had served their sentences, he granted them land, permitted them to return to their former trades and professions, and engaged experts among them, such as Francis Greenway, to design his major buildings. The brothers Bent refused to hear emancipists in the courtrooms. Samuel Marsden haughtily declined to sit on a magistrates bench with former – now very wealthy – convicts Simeon Lord and Andrew Thompson; and D'Arcy Wentworth had to take his place. Then, to add insult to injury, Macquarie even entertained them at Government House where Elizabeth by now was taking a very active and supportive role in the administration. After presenting the 52-year-old governor with a son in 1815 she had quickly resumed her official duties.

In 1819, Castlereagh's under-secretary Earl Bathurst responded to the exclusives' protestations by sending a rock-ribbed Tory, John Thomas Bigge, to conduct an inquiry on the ground. Macquarie learned of it only five days before the commissioner arrived on 26 September 1819. At first the governor welcomed the inquiry, believing 'his report *must* be favourable to my administration of the Colony and highly honourable to my character'. He was soon disabused of his illusions.

Bigge's high-handed attitude spread the impression that the governor was on trial, and his secret dealings with the 'exclusives' revealed that his real object was to disparage Macquarie's inclusive policies and prepare the ground for his ignominious recall. He took statements from selected landholders recommended by Macarthur who had finally returned to the colony 'on the strict condition that he take no further part in its public life'.

In fact, Macarthur had barely settled back into his Parramatta homestead when he demanded more land from the governor.

Macquarie refused. Macarthur was outraged, and thereafter the man who would end his days in an Australian lunatic asylum employed all his wiles to undermine the governor's standing. He volunteered as an official witness to Bigge's inquiry and regaled him with complaints that Macquarie was preventing big woolgrowers like himself from putting the colony on a sound economic footing.

Bigge also interviewed convict supervisors and singled out the Newcastle commandant James Morisset for special praise. Morisset had been hideously disfigured by an artillery shell in the Peninsular Wars and treated his convict charges mercilessly. He invented a treadmill at Newcastle as a punishment for the more defiant, with special attention to the Irish politicals.

Elizabeth Macquarie was not spared the exclusives' displeasure. The Rev. Samuel Marsden, born in the most humble circumstances and patronised by the abolitionist William Wilberforce, was now a wealthy landholder and spiritual leader of the reactionaries. He told Commissioner Bigge: 'Both profane and sacred history has taught us that it is very dangerous to offend a Lady in Power. John the Baptist lost his head for this.'[7]

By 1820, tired and unwell, Macquarie saw the writing on the wall and sent several letters to Castlereagh asking to be relieved of his duties. Finally his official resignation was accepted, though it was not until 12 February 1822, at age 60, that he and his small family embarked on the *Surry* bound for a well-earned retirement on his beloved Isle of Mull. He was farewelled by 'a Harbour full of people' and was much moved by the spontaneous gesture.

When Macquarie reached England, he was presented to King George IV by Castlereagh, ironically on the same day that Bigge's first damning volume was tabled in the House of Lords. It was a fearful blow to his reputation among the ruling class and the rest of his life would be spent in penury. Macquarie's application for a title was rejected. He was granted a pension in 1824 but died before he could take comfort from it on 1 July the following year.

Sadly, on the family's return to England Lachlan Jr would slowly break his mother's heart with a life of dissolution. It ended at 31 when he fell downstairs in a drunken stupor and broke his neck. Providentially, by then she had been dead for six years and, while her passing was unremarked in Britain, she is permanently memorialised in one of Sydney's main streets and at Mrs Macquarie's Chair, a carved rock overlooking the harbour and its beautiful Elizabeth Bay.

Castlereagh died by his own hand soon after he recalled the man who had laid the foundations for a self-sustaining Australian polity. On 9 August 1822, he confided to the king that he thought he was being blackmailed for homosexuality. By then he was descending into a wild insanity. Three days later, despite his wife removing his razors – and with a doctor in attendance – he managed to find a pen-knife and cut his throat.

He was honoured in death by his aristocratic confederates, but his many detractors were less forgiving. Shelley's friend and fellow poet Lord Byron wrote a savage quip about his final resting place:

Posterity will ne'er survey
A nobler grave than this:
Here lies the bones of Castlereagh:
Stop, traveller, and piss.

CHAPTER SIX

Overland to Jervis Bay

The young explorer's fame spreads, he journeys with Meehan to Jervis Bay, and there arise the first hints of controversy.

Hamilton Hume became well known throughout the infant Australian colony as he completed each new expedition into the unknown. His expeditions were frequently applauded in *The Gazette*. And in the small, tight community word of mouth carried his exploits from one end of the expanding settlement to the other, no doubt gaining in romantic detail along the way. In 1819, at the behest of surveyor-general John Oxley, Hume and Meehan set out once again towards the south coast, while Oxley himself reverted to the sea, his natural haunt, in the small ship *Emmaline*. They would survey the coastline from both vantage points in preparation for a further advancement of the settlement.

Accompanied by several convicts and his friend Dual, Hume and Meehan again tackled the Shoalhaven gorges but with the same result – they were forced to their summits to make a crossing before turning back to the coast. Meehan marked a big ironbark on the peak of Nowra Hill as a start point for the survey, then plunged down the steep slopes, and on 9 October they made a rendezvous with Oxley just south of Gerringong. It was a brief meeting before they parted and drove south to Crookhaven where their men hauled a boat across the isthmus to Comerong Island at the entrance to the Shoalhaven River.

They continued through the tidal flats and sandbars to the white sand and clear waters of Jervis Bay. This was relatively easygoing, and they set up camp on the beach, where they were joined by Oxley who came ashore with two of his men. While Meehan and Hume were suitably impressed with their surrounds, the ever lugubrious Oxley remarked that there was 'no place a cabbage could grow' on the entire coastal strip. In fact, there was a veritable rainforest at their backs with soil so deep it hosted a multitude of cabbage tree palms. Their return journey is not recorded.

In a letter to the governor the following year, Throsby said Hume had kept a journal but, if so, it is lost to history. Throsby appropriated Hume's enthusiasm for the area in his determination to expand his own holdings to the district. He soon persuaded Hume to lead him and a group of eager landseekers to the south-west along the track he had forged with Meehan in 1818. Included in the party was John Macarthur's 16-year-old son William. They set out on 25 March 1820 and made straight for the Goulburn Plains and onwards to the Breadalbane district and Taralga. Some years later young Macarthur and his brother James established a large property there.

The pace of exploration was by now verging on a land rush, and the restless Throsby seemed to be everywhere. Even when he was beaten to new discoveries, he attempted to claim them as his own. When he wasn't writing to Government House, he was sending letters to the *Sydney Gazette* to support his claims. And since the editor Robert Howe, son of the founder, was always eager for exploration stories and had no way of checking the facts, he usually accepted them at face value.

On 15 December 1821, *The Gazette* reported

> Charles Throsby, to whom the Colony is infinitely indebted, in company with Mr William Kearns [a neighbour and small landholder], has been on discovery to Jervis Bay. They set out on the arduous expedition on the 6th inst. Mr Throsby proceeded direct from Sydney through the County of Argyle, passing his own farm. He is decidedly of the opinion that a good road may be cut from Sydney to that harbour, and he moreover reports the land to be extremely rich and promising; and that all the lagoons and rivers, at this season of the year are fordable.

Hume was decidedly unimpressed, and for the first time responded publicly. Two weeks later the paper made amends with a correction that obviously emanated from the young pathfinder:

> The discovery of [a route to] Jervis Bay . . . had been previously [made], so we are now informed, by Mr Hamilton Hume, of Appin. Mr Hume had set out from Appin on the 17 November last, for the express purpose of accomplishing this most desirable and grand object, taking with him two natives and returned on the 5 December. Mr Hume reports that he could, without much trouble or difficulty, cause a road to be cut from Sydney to Jervis or Bateman's Bay; and also that the country is fertile and easy of access. Mr Hume

> further reports that the distance from Lake Bathurst to these two Bays, does not exceed fifty miles.

The controversy casts a new light on the earlier expedition with Meehan. The issue was not the discovery of Jervis Bay, which was well known from seaborne explorations, but its access from the productive plains west of the mountains. A third report in *The Gazette* on 11 January 1822 provides a much more detailed context, which, it says, 'we have received from respectable authority'.

'Mr Hume,' it says,

> left Appin accompanied by Mr John Kennedy, Mr Edward Simpson, John Moon servant to Mrs Broughton [William Broughton having died in 1821], and two black natives named Dual and [his brother] Cowpasture Jack, for the purpose of selecting land [in] the County of Argyle . . . When near Mr Jenkins' establishment [near Tallowa] they were joined by a third native, Udaa-Duck who accompanied them to Lake Bathurst.
>
> At [this] place Mr Hume suddenly left the party and accompanied by the natives [Udaa-Duck] and Cowpasture Jack, on the 25 November, set out on foot with nine pounds of flour and went to the top of a high hill some miles to the south-east of Shoalhaven River but more than 30 miles from the coast at Jervis Bay. Mr Hume left a mark of his being there and returned near Mr Jenkins' establishment on the 30 November and to Appin about 5 December.
>
> Jervis Bay and Bateman's Bay are 30 miles apart and separated by a very high range of broken rocky mountains; Mr Hume's exertions must therefore have been wonderful in having discovered a track capable of being made a good road

> to the two bays as mentioned in *The Gazette* and in so short a time and with so scanty an allowance of provisions.

According to Robert Webster, 'The trip probably resulted from word passed to Hume from Udaa-Duck that Throsby was making his journey to the same destination at the same time.' Hume and his companions blazed their trail with axe marks on the trees and Throsby's own diary reveals that he followed Hume's tracks and complained bitterly that Hume was using his own Aborigines for the task.

On this occasion, neither man actually reached the limpid waters of Jervis Bay, both satisfied they had achieved their goal. Unusually, Hume himself kept a journal of the trip, which clearly shows his descent from the 'high hill' to the approaches to Jervis Bay. And since his contemporaneous records are so sparse it provides a rare insight into the young Australian's adventurous spirit and his love of country:

> Tuesday 27 November 1821
> At 9 o'clock set out from Lake Bathurst in a S.E. direction towards the sea coast. At 10.30 passed the High Stone Range called by the natives Quangem, from thence proceeded down a long valley of rich land with a chain of ponds running in the northerly direction.
>
> The surrounding hills are low and scrubby, the soil not very good. At 12.30 crossed a small stream running to the Southward and appearing to fall into some part of the Shoalhaven River. At one place ascended a high hill called by the natives Cowenbullen and commands an extensive view of the surrounding country from S.E. to S. The country to the S.W. 10 or 12 miles distant from Cowenbullen appears

to be good and extensive; I was confident I should avoid the Shoalhaven in the direction I was going.

At 3 pm a violent storm of wind and rain accompanied with lightning and heavy claps of thunder – many trees were blown down near the place where I had taken shelter. At 4 pm I proceeded along the banks of a rivulet running through extensive meadows of rich land thinly wooded; kangaroos here in great plenty.

At 7 pm arrived at Shoalhaven River, it running northerly. This river has been considered by many to be impassable for a horse and cart. In 1818 when I accompanied Mr James Meehan we endeavoured to cross it towards 10 or 15 miles to the north of the place where I now crossed . . . Jervis Bay, though an extensive country and possessing many advantages for a seaport, was thought useless as no road for wheeled carriages had been discovered to it. That evil is now remedied for a loaded cart can pass over here without much difficulty.

Crossed over with great ease on a pebbled bottom, the water being about three feet deep and the river not exceeding 30 yards in width. The banks are rather low and many pieces of good land either for cultivation or grazing. A loaded cart may here pass over with safety. Remained here for the night, distant from Lake Bathurst E. by S. 21 miles.

Wednesday 28 November

At 6 am I proceeded from the river about two miles when I came to another branch. This stream, though not so large as the former, is a much handsomer piece of water; a boat might row or sail a considerable distance on either side of the [water] fall. It is 20 or 30 yards wide and well stocked with such water fowls as ducks, black swans etc. On the banks are numbers of what we call in this country wild turkey but the European name (I believe) is Bustard. There are several kinds of them. I killed one of the biggest kangaroos I ever saw, weighing 300 pounds and upwards. Also running in a northerly direction one rocky bottom water about two foot deep; the banks are low and the grass grows close to the water edge. There are several good meadows along this stream and from what I learned from the natives they are very extensive.

At 12 o'clock [we] fell in with a tribe of natives who were much surprised at seeing a white man. They were by no means timid or inclined to be hostile but appeared to be friendly. I determined to stop the remainder of the day to gain from them what information I could respecting the country I intended to pass on my way to the coast. They assured me there was not the slightest difficulty or obstacle to prevent me from accomplishing my design. They also described to me a high hill called by them Coorook, a few miles to the southward of where I then was.

[This area] abounded with the animals called Roombat [wombat] and caolers [koalas] beyond which was a very fine country with extensive plains, but they were at variance with the tribe of natives belonging to that place. I caught them several kangaroos with which they were much pleased but I could not prevail on any of them to accompany me owing to their terror occasioned by the Coast natives.

They wore coverings made of the opossum and koala skins sewed together with the lining of the kangaroo tail. I showed them the use of firearms by shooting several birds near their huts. My piece being double-barrelled I fired twice which confused them. They seemed much astonished how I could kill without putting something in the barrel.

The men are in general tall, well made and stout in proportion, with a great quantity of hair on their heads which they let grow to a considerable length. Polygamy is common among these people; men in general have three wives and I took notice of one man having six. Their weapons are much the same as the [other] natives of this part of the country, except that they are much longer – their spears being from 12 to 14 feet in length and some longer. I travelled on this day about 14 miles from last night's station.

Thursday 29 November

At 7 am set out in an easterly direction and passed over some bushy hills covered with quoits [flat stones] at 8.30. Came on good forest land, fine grass and a quantity of herbage at 9 am. Ascended a forest hill from which I saw at the distance of 6 or 7 miles in an easterly direction a high hill in the form of a sugar loaf which I then supposed to be Pigeon House. At 10 am crossed a pretty rivulet, called by the natives 'Toon'. It abounds in eels, which is the origin of its name. The stream is similar to the rivulet that runs through Mr Throsby's farm in the new country, running northward and winding through some fine meadows. At 10.30 am entered a thick brush which continued for three miles; at 11.30 was clear of the brush and passed over some clear barren hills in appearance resembling the Surry Hills near Sydney.

At 12 o'clock made the high sugarloaf hill. It commanded a very extensive view of the country in every direction, particularly to the N.W. and N. As far as the eye can reach it is without timber or grass of any kind. It being so barren I gave it the name Mount Barren. It is 3 or 4 miles due west of the Pigeon House. I erected a pole on the top previously affixing a white cloth to it as a mark or flagstaff.

A branch of the Shoalhaven river takes its rise in the gullies on the west side of this hill, from which I could see the sea apparently 10 or 12 miles distant and the Pigeon House 3 miles to the eastward. The country towards the N. and N.E. is high, mountainous and a more promising appearance as far as I could see, my view being constricted by hills and ranges.

At 2 pm arrived at the Pigeon House, saw Port Jervis bearing N.E. distant 10 or 12 miles. About 3 or 4 miles from Pigeon House I also saw a piece of water, whether a lake or river I could not discern but the surrounding country appeared to be good. Saw smoke of native fires in various directions along the Coast. Finding no obstacle of any consequence to prevent a road being made from the interior to Jervis Bay – to discover which was the object of my tour – and my provisions exhausted and being a long distance from home surrounded on the otherwise by natives of the most ferocious description, I thought it most expedient to shape my course homeward as I had succeeded in my undertaking. It being late in the evening I stopped that night about 3 miles to the southward of the Pigeon House, on the banks of a small rivulet. (The native name of Pigeon House is Tidgell.)

Most of the country I had passed over from Lake Bathurst to Pigeon House is well adapted for grazing and many parts for cultivation. It is well watered by running streams and quite easy of access – distance from Lake Bathurst to Pigeon House E. by S. 45 miles.

Friday 30 November
At daylight set out from the Pigeon House homewards in a N.N.W. direction. The country for the first 10 miles was poor but well watered. At 11 am crossed over a deep creek and passed through some good grazing ground. At 1 pm crossed a stream running to the N.W. and came to a beautiful place of forest land called by the natives Nalagoo [now Nerriga]. A road can be made through this forest to Port Jervis by going part of the track I went with Mr James Meehan in 1819 [returning from the Oxley journey]; it is partially wooded and well watered and in my opinion well adapted for sheep, covered with a thick sward of grass and abounds with wild herbage such as trefoil, burnett and clover. These herbs being all in bloom gave it a very romantic and pleasing appearance. Kangaroos are here very numerous and large, as also the wild turkey.

At 4 pm came to a large creek. The water had risen to a great height owing to the heavy rains that fell a few days before. There being no trees that could afford bark to make a canoe, I was obliged to swim across with my clothes and gun above my head. It ran so very rapid that it swept me down over a rocky fall and I with great difficulty escaped from being drowned. I found about this creek great quantities of limestone.

At 5 pm I ascended a high rocky range resembling a mountain into a thick brush, passing through several gullies which were very thick and troublesome. I travelled till dark and stopped that night in a thick barren brush quite destitute of grass. Distance from Pigeon House – 25–30 miles.

Saturday 1 December
At 6 am set out through very thick brush, in some places almost impenetrable with vines and underwood. At 9 am came to a deep creek the sides of which were quite perpendicular and 100 feet in depth. Consequently was obliged to travel 5 or 6 miles along the side to find a crossing place which I happily effected. After crossing the creek I proceeded along a high stony range for several miles. The brush still very thick and deep gullies on each side.

At 2 pm fell in with a party of natives at a place called Toolwong. At 6 pm arrived at the banks of the Shoalhaven River opposite Mr Jenkins' farm in the new country. To cross this river was one of the more arduous tasks I have ever undergone. At 6 pm I began to descend the bank and it was 8.30 when I arrived at Mr Jenkins' hut on the other side.

The country through which I passed these last 30 miles is totally impossible for a horse and performed with extreme difficulty by a man. It is entirely barren and full of gullies and creeks. I took with me two natives Nullanan [also known as Cowpastures Jack] and Underduck, native of Lake Bathurst. The behaviour of both these natives during the whole of my tour exceeded all my expectations.

Journal from Lake Bathurst to the Sea Coast, 1821.[1]

Foremost in Hume's mind was obviously the value of the land to the agricultural pursuits of the settlers and the way in which the country could develop into a going concern. It is highly doubtful that Hume, any more than his black compatriots, understood the manner in which a European influx would totally transfigure the continent on which he travelled. The land seemed limitless, more than enough to accommodate any number of newcomers as well as its Aboriginal population.

That he referred to his Aboriginal companions at all in his journal – however fleetingly – was itself remarkable for his time. But it was never clear to him that their existence as a race might be endangered by the white colonists. In his firsthand experience they were warring tribes. And in the Social Darwinist values of the day they trailed far behind the mechanically astute and socially sophisticated Britishers, whose superiority was self-evident. It had fashioned them an empire that enveloped half the known world. The Aboriginal people would simply adapt themselves to the new reality.

At the same time, however, he stood emotionally apart from 'the Europeans', as he called them, who insisted on naming the edible native bird a Bustard, 'what we call in this country wild turkey'. And the ease of his interactions with the tribal people was unfeigned. They were equally at home in the country of their birth.

CHAPTER SEVEN

In Search of Captain David Stewart

Thomas Brisbane becomes governor, Hamilton Hume joins an expedition to Bateman's Bay, and the Hume–Hovell expedition is proposed.

As Hamilton Hume was heading home in summer heat through the dangerous terrain of the Argyle, another figure of Scottish ancestry was beginning a very different but equally hazardous endeavour in the colony's major settlement. The British imperialist Sir Thomas Brisbane, exactly twice Hume's age at 48, had entertained the ambition for many years to become governor of New South Wales. However, he was much more interested in the colony's location than its imperial potential. For Brisbane had two obsessions, both centred upon the heavens.

In early childhood he had fallen under the religious spell of his paternal aunt, Lady Maxwell of Pollock, whose Christian piety knew no bounds. And during his university years he became entranced with the study of astronomy. Together these obsessions provided a powerful motive for the aristocratic descendant of Robert the Bruce to journey to the Southern Hemisphere where the stars were in need of catalogue, and the colonial inhabitants in even greater need of his Christian credo.

Brisbane's ancestors had attained high office in defence of the realm at sea and on land and he followed them in the profession of arms as an ensign in the 38th Regiment, which he joined in Ireland. There he began a much closer friendship than his predecessor with Arthur Wellesley, the forthcoming hero of Waterloo and Duke of Wellington.

Brisbane had applied unsuccessfully for the vice-regal post in 1815 and three years later Wellington pressed his case with the secretary for the colonies, Henry Bathurst (3rd Earl Bathurst). At the time Wellington and Brisbane were in British-occupied Paris where Brisbane had prevented his soldiers from looting and destroying an astronomical institution. Wellington met him on the street and reported that Bathurst, a model Tory politician, had replied: 'He wants one that will govern not the heavens but the earth in New South Wales.'[1]

Brisbane was outraged at the perception that he had allowed his scientific interests to interfere with his military duties. Wellington sympathised: 'I shall write to his Lordship that, on the contrary, you were never in one instance absent or late, morning, noon or night, and that in addition you kept the time of the army!'

Notwithstanding his powerful supporter, Brisbane would have to wait until 1821 before Bathurst finally approved his mission to the colony. In the meantime, Brisbane had used his time profitably. In 1819, he married Anna Maria, the eldest daughter and heiress of Sir Henry Hay Makdougall of Makerstoun, Scotland. (He would subsequently add the surname Makdougall to his own by deed poll.) His bride was 'an unassuming, plain woman' who 'preferred to live in great retirement, devoting herself to her husband, her children and the good works of a Christian lady'.[2] She could hardly have suited Brisbane better.

Financially secure, he could indulge his passion for astronomy, build his own observatory on his Scottish estate and, on his New South Wales appointment, acquire the very latest telescopes and other devices to travel with him and Anna Maria to Sydney. Also aboard were his two assistants, German-born and astronomically trained Karl Rumker and a gifted Scottish amateur, James Dunlop, the son of a weaver who at 17 had built his own telescope.

On their arrival, while waiting for Macquarie to officially vacate his post, the three men oversaw the building of a first-class observatory beside the governor's mansion at Parramatta. Throughout his entire four-year incumbency, Brisbane would spend six days a week at Parramatta and only one (Tuesday) at his Sydney office. Much of the day-to-day management fell to his colonial secretary, Major Frederick Goulburn, the younger brother of the newly retired but still influential British under-secretary of state for the colonies. It was a recipe for administrative confusion, resentment and rancour.

Despite his physical separation from the managerial centre, Brisbane had a clear view of what was required of him. According to Bathurst, Macquarie's land grants to the emancipists and the less well connected had been altogether too generous. It was Brisbane's task to 'regularise' the system with properly conducted surveys and to restrict further grants only to those with the funds to develop the land. In other policy changes he was to offer the Aboriginal people the hand of sympathy provided they accepted Britain's colonial dominion over their country. And he was to act on Bigge's recommendations for firmer control of the convicts.

His land reform pleased no one. Tickets of occupation allowing a settler to occupy a proposed grant before it was surveyed would henceforth be issued only when a required number of stock had actually been bought. The emancipists were usually unable to produce the capital required to meet these initial demands or guarantee the required improvements once they had taken up residence. At the other end of the social scale the 'exclusives', led by Macarthur and Samuel Marsden, had an insatiable thirst for more and better land. But under Brisbane's regime no one was allowed a grant of more than 8,000 acres near any township; and the growing settlements like Sydney and Parramatta were encircled by great swathes of country reserved for the crown.

His attitude to the Aboriginal people swung wildly between the extremes of cloying patronage and violent retribution when they showed any resistance to his 'Christian principles'. If they would not turn from their wicked ways, he decided, 'They were to be put to the torments of hell, so that others, seeing their anguish, might not follow their example.'[3]

His attitude to the convict population followed a similar path. He separated an increasing number from government service and assigned them to landholding masters in the expectation that both parties would appreciate his Christian benevolence and act accordingly. Neither did. And while cruel landholders might be tapped on the wrist, recalcitrant convicts were punished mercilessly. The least brutal sentence was 100 lashes for a minor offence; then came commitment to the 'squalid filth and misery' of Sydney's Darlinghurst Gaol. More fearful was assignment to the prison farms at Emu Plains, Bathurst and Port Macquarie, where they were starved and bashed by the camp commandants.

When these deterrents failed to produce the required redemption, Brisbane oversaw the most shocking and degrading punishments of Australia's colonial era at Port Arthur and Macquarie Harbour in Van Diemen's Land, Redcliffe Point in Moreton Bay and even further north in Melville Island. But the ne plus ultra of penal sadism was reserved for Norfolk Island, which on Lord Bathurst's orders was to provide 'a secondary punishment which will not admit of mitigation'.

When the island had been abandoned in 1814, its buildings demolished and crops and orchards razed, a pack of wild dogs had been left behind to kill any remaining livestock until they turned on each other. On Brisbane's orders, it would be reconstituted as a place of deliberate terror. 'I could wish it to be understood,' he wrote, 'that the felon who is sent there is forever excluded from all hope of return.'[4] And for 20 years from 1824 (with only a single three-year period of human decency under the reformer Alexander Maconochie) it would fulfil his promise as the sink of penal depravity.

However, despite Andrew Hume's early experience on the island, the horror stories that soon emanated from it were of little relevance to his eldest son. Much more concerning was Brisbane's relative indifference to the exploration of the continent that had rated so highly in the priorities of his predecessor. In this, Brisbane was supported by his derisive surveyor-general John Oxley who was increasingly running his office in between coastal voyages.

Shortly after Brisbane took office, Oxley's naval colleague, Lieutenant Robert Johnston (son of the former lieutenant-governor) sailed south as far as Bateman's Bay where he named the tiny offshore island after his cutter, *Snapper.* He sailed it up the Clyde River – known as Bundoo by the Aboriginal people – and early the next year returned with Alexander Berry, his employee Tom Davis, the hero of the Whangaroa Massacre, and Hamilton Hume.

One of Johnston's tasks was to discover the fate of Captain David Stewart, who in 1820 had been sent by Macquarie to investigate rumours of an unlikely passage between Twofold Bay and Lake Bathurst near Goulburn. His boat was wrecked at the Twofold Bay entrance and when he and his convict party walked up the coast to Bateman's Bay they were believed to have been killed by Aborigines. This was only the latest in a series of clashes. Nine survivors of the 1797 wreck of the *Sydney Cove* had fallen to Aboriginal spears in the area, and in 1808 three members of the schooner *Fly* had also been killed when they ventured ashore.

However, when Hamilton Hume made contact with them – and Johnston distributed gifts – the visit passed without incident. Hume by now could speak and understand a fair smattering of tribal languages. And the Aboriginal people were adept at gesture and mime. Once he had gained their confidence, their colloquy became something of a performance in which several Aboriginal 'speakers' took part. However, they were not unsophisticated, and were often 'economical with the truth'. For example, while they accepted the gifts as their rightful due, Hume noticed European belongings and part of a boat's gear, and decided Stewart and his men had been killed. He made no mention of it to the natives and completed the meeting with his usual polite good humour.

The party then sailed up the Clyde for several kilometres, and while Johnston charted the estuary, Hume, Berry and Davis went bush and explored the surrounding country for four days. Hume led them up Pigeon House Mountain, and on their descent they discovered the Burrill and Conjola lakes. Heading west, they followed Aboriginal tracks almost to the present site of Braidwood.

On their return, Johnston sailed about 30 kilometres south of Bateman's Bay to Tuross Head in search of fresh water, but without success. Turning north, he and his party entered every inlet up to Shoalhaven. Hume and Berry landed about 10 kilometres north of Bateman's Bay and walked along the coast. They were joined by the local Aboriginal people, who once again were friendly and helpful to the young Australian.

Their little cutter was severely damaged in a storm off St George's Inlet. Forced ashore, it lost its rudder and false keel. Once repaired and refloated, they sailed it round the point to the now familiar Jervis Bay where the landlubbers parted company with Johnston and his crew and travelled overland to their properties.

Hume also accompanied Berry and Davis on a similar journey later that year. By then Berry had formed a partnership with a fellow merchant, Edward Wollstonecraft, and they funded the expedition. They were on the lookout for good grazing land, and in June 1822 he and Hume set out from Sydney in the 15-ton half-deck vessel *Blanche* with Tom Davis as skipper. They made for Crookhaven and on 23 June found themselves in rough weather off Shoalhaven. Davis launched a boat to cross the bar and climbed aboard himself. Tragedy struck when the boat broached and overturned. Despite their best efforts, Davis and a crewman were drowned. It was a shocking tragedy for the young man, who had survived the horrors of the Maori massacre only to fall victim to the whims of nature.

After a brief but heartfelt ceremony they landed and continued the expedition. Berry appreciated Hume's 'eye for good country', and he chose 10,000 acres surrounding a hill the Aborigines called Coolangatta, meaning 'fine view'.[5] He would pay the government an annual rent of £10 and receive 100 convicts to work the property that he had named after the hill. The local Aboriginal people supplied them with fish, and over the next month with three convicts under Hume's supervision they built a hut and cut a 200-metre canal across the spit of sand between the Shoalhaven River and Crookhaven. This allowed boats to reach the river without crossing the bar that had taken Davis's life.

Berry would settle on the block and five years later would marry Wollstonecraft's sister Elizabeth, a cousin of Mary Wollstonecraft Godwin, wife of the poet Shelley and author of the classic novel *Frankenstein*. Many years later, Berry wrote to Hume, 'The canal which I commenced under your auspices still exists and even now is the only safe entrance to Shoalhaven River.'

No sooner had Hume returned home than he accepted another commission, this time from Wollstonecraft, to drove a mob of cattle from Oxley's and Throsby's properties at Bong Bong down to the Five Islands. Hume had earlier marked the track and followed it with the 93 head of cows, steers and three working bullocks. Wollstonecraft provided two convicts and Hume enlisted the younger William Broughton to give a hand.

By this time, Berry had developed a mutually respectful relationship with Governor Brisbane who with Anna Maria and his entourage had travelled to Sydney on one of Berry's ships, the *Royal George*. Berry himself was aboard and it was a long and pleasant journey. While Brisbane was certainly no pathfinder in the Macquarie mould, he did have a natural curiosity about the vast tracts of country beyond the settlement. Moreover, Commissioner Bigge's report included a section on 'Agricultural and Trade in New South Wales', which recommended an expedition from the south coast of the continent north to Lake George.

In early 1824, Brisbane raised the matter with Berry. His preference, he said, was for the government to sail a party of convicts to Wilson's Promontory, from whence they would make their way back to Sydney. He would offer pardons and rewards 'appropriate to their station' should they make it back alive. Berry's immediate response to the madcap scheme is lost to history, but easily imagined. However, he tempered his reply in a letter with the suggestion that if the governor were to pursue it he might consider putting an 'ardent and experienced traveller' in charge. And he had just such a man in mind: Hamilton Hume, who had already proven himself a natural leader of men with the bushman's ability to roll with the country's punches and a unique capacity to engage with the native people.

Brisbane saw the wisdom of Berry's argument and, when he formally agreed, Berry relayed the offer to his young protégé. Hume was interested, but he had already learned the hard lesson that any such expedition should start from a large settled area, so that if disaster struck they could make a quick retreat, even if a different return route had to be taken. He made a counter-offer: he would lead an expedition from Lake George south to Bass Strait. He knew the country they would first encounter since by now he owned and occupied the grazing run furthest out, and he was confident in his ability to see it through. As he later wrote to Brisbane, 'Presuming myself (altho' an Australian) capable from experience of understanding such an expedition . . .' He needed only six convicts in his command, he said, and was prepared to set out forthwith.

Brisbane was convinced and gave the orders to outfit the operation. However, his enthusiasm was short-lived. A combination of Goulburn's interference, Oxley's pessimism, and his own pinchpenny attitude to official spending meant that within the month he had modified his commitment. He would no longer supply the rations and equipment from government stores; instead he offered only his 'sanction and protection', a meaningless assurance to a pathfinder in the vastness of the Australian bush. But by now Hume's blood was up; it was the challenge he might have been made for; the opportunity was too great to pass up; somehow he would make it work.

It was a bigger task than he could have envisaged. He had never planned anything as far-reaching with all the logistical demands involved. But at 26 he was at his best physical condition – big and strongly built, with a maturity and confidence beyond his years. He had been a trusted and sought-after co-leader with the best surveyors, explorers and bushmen of his day. He was honoured and respected by the community, revered for his ability to find new and productive pasture for the land-hungry gentry; and a legend among the hardy settlers who followed in his wake. He was energetic and tireless, hot tempered with the incompetent but quick to cool down and make amends. Deafness in one ear from a childhood accident gave the false impression of his being unduly aloof. In fact, he was open to suggestion but single-minded once he had decided on a course. He had earned his fame the hard way, and he enjoyed it. But while he was confident the journey would add immeasurably to his reputation, his deeper motive was the lure of discovery in his native land.

Berry was aware of his young protégé's weaknesses as well as his strengths. He counselled Hume to curb his impetuosity, and used the colonial grapevine to seek out a fellow traveller with the skills and temperament to complement his abilities. It was at just this time that another man ambitious for the fame that would attend such an expedition made contact with Berry – one William Hilton Hovell.

Born in Yarmouth on Britain's east coast to a merchant seafaring family in April 1786, he went to sea aged only ten after his father, the captain of a trading vessel, was taken prisoner by the French. He rose from cabin boy to foremast hand, then rejoined his father in trading ships on his return two years later. By the age of 22 he had become a mercantile marine captain. In his travels he had met the surgeon Thomas Arndell who had sailed with the First Fleet and returned several times to New South Wales supervising the transport of convicts. In 1810, Hovell married Arndell's daughter Esther and they produced a boy and a girl.

By 1813, Hovell had decided to follow his father-in-law to New South Wales, where he had established a property on the Hawkesbury. Hovell and his family arrived in October that year, and he had soon joined the operations of the wealthy emancipist Simeon Lord. He captained several of Lord's trading vessels along the coasts of Australia and New Zealand but the voyages were rarely free of incident. One of his vessels ran aground in New Zealand; and in June 1816 his 40-ton schooner *The Brothers* was wrecked on the Kent Islands in Bass Strait. The cargo of 20 tons of salt and 800 bushels of wheat was lost overboard and one seaman, Daniel Wheeler, was drowned. For ten weeks the survivors lived on wheat washed ashore and whatever else they could scavenge until they were rescued by the brig *Spring* under the command of Captain William Bunster. The survivors arrived in Sydney on 6 September 1816. Hovell abandoned the sea thereafter.

He had earlier been granted 600 acres by Macquarie at Narellan, just beyond Campbell Town, and he and his family settled there. He made short exploratory journeys in the surrounding country and on one trip in 1823 came upon the Burragorang Valley. By then he had used Arndell's family connections to establish a social position among the 'exclusives'. But at 38 he was anxious to make a greater mark, so when word reached him that Berry was looking for a person of substance with navigation experience, he put himself forward.

Berry arranged a meeting with Hamilton Hume and the two men seemed to get along well. Hume later wrote, 'Mr Hovell agreed with me to find jointly the men and equipment and necessary cattle.' It would be one of the very rare occasions when they found themselves in comradely accord.

CHAPTER EIGHT

Hume, Hovell and the Great Expedition

The party sets out from Appin to journey to Western Port.

Governor Brisbane appears to have had only the vaguest notion of the extraordinary potential of the journey to Western Port. His obsession with the heavens – in both their physical and spiritual incarnations – and his daily administrative squabbles with Goulburn left little time or inclination to speculate on the great unknown beyond the settlement's boundaries. And, of course, his perceptions were constrained by his background in the relatively compact farmlands of the British Isles.

Not so the young pathfinder and the eager landgrabbers within the colonial community. There was a palpable excitement in Hume's household and among his neighbours as preparations got underway. It was easily his most ambitious undertaking, and he was impatient for the challenge. But even he could not know what a transformative experience was in store for him and his infant nation.

In his parsimony, Brisbane made only the most modest contribution to the expedition in the form of six pack saddles, one tent, two tarpaulins, several suits of 'slops' for the convicts, a few bush utensils, a small quantity of arms and ammunition and two skeleton charts on which Hume and Hovell could trace the journey. Hume says, 'With the exception of [these articles] we were thrown entirely on our own resources. I had to dispose of a very fine imported iron plough to help raise money to purchase my supplies for the journey. We also took with us two carts which were our own private property.'

Their livestock included two horses and a bullock from Hume as well as one horse and four bullocks from Hovell. The carts would be loaded with their supplies and drawn by a span of bullocks. They would use two horses for riding hacks with a spare horse and bullock. Each man had a musket or fowling piece, and Hume brought along his kangaroo dogs – including two purebred greyhounds – to help keep them in meat.

The party included six convicts of which Hume supplied three: Henry Angel, James Fitzpatrick and Claude Bossawa.

Angel was a nuggety, athletic little sparrow, born in Salisbury, England in 1790. He had been accused of stealing £40 and transported for life in 1817. In fact, the crime was committed by an uncle who would confess on his deathbed in 1840. Angel would then be offered a pardon and a free passage back to England. He would take the pardon but decline to return. He had worked on the road gangs in the Blue Mountains before being assigned to Hume, and had a droll sense of humour.

James Fitzpatrick was a powerful figure, a well-read Irish 'political' convicted of 'attacking a dwelling' and transported for seven years. He too was assigned to the road gangs, but escaped, and on recapture was returned to the roads until offered the assignment to Hume.

Claude Bossawa was a cocky little character who, according to Hovell, had been a pugilist. However, when William Broughton heard of this he was highly amused. He'd personally given him a thrashing, he said, and found him 'chicken-hearted'. Henry Angel agreed. On one occasion, he would lie down in the dirt rather than continue the journey.

Hovell's three men were also a mixed bunch. William Bollard and Thomas Smith came from his own property, and Tom Boyd was provided by Hume's relative John Kennedy. Hume knew Boyd to be a courageous and capable hand, and probably organised his enlistment. Born in Dublin, he was 26 and physically robust. He'd been transported for 'highway robbery' and would show himself fearless in the face of danger. William Bollard had great stamina, and would become a very useful member of the party; but Thomas Smith would fail to rate a mention in either Hume's or Hovell's accounts of the expedition.

Both Hume and Hovell made contemporary records of the expedition, each of which raises problems for the historian. Hume kept a very detailed chart of their progress, though his written narrative at the time is to be found mostly in reports to the governor. He would not publish the full story until much later.[1] Hovell's account is even less reliable, since it passed through the hands of a partisan editor in Dr William Bland and became a rambling tale designed to highlight Hovell's sound judgement and superior British common sense. It was not published until 1831, seven years after the event.

It is not in doubt, however, that they set out from Hume's Appin property on Sunday, 3 October 1824 accompanied by

Hume's brother John. Hume says, 'The instructions given us were to take our departure from Lake George and push on, at all hazards, to Western Port; and in the event of meeting any river not fordable we were further instructed, if practicable, to trace its course to the sea, or as far as our means would permit.'

They took it easy over the first few days as the bullocks pulling the carts settled into their rhythm and the expedition developed its modus operandi. Claude Bossawa was put in charge of the perambulator that Meehan had lent Hume for the journey to measure their daily progress, and it quickly became known as 'Claude's wheelbarrow'.

They camped outside the boundary fence of a Spanish settler, and spent the second night at Klensendorff's Inn on Myrtle Creek. Their route took them down the southern road, which crossed the Mittagong Range following Hume's markings from ten years before. They then stopped at a blacksmith's for minor repairs to the drays while Hume and Hovell had breakfast with Mr Atkinson at his 'Oldbury' station at Sutton Forest. They then negotiated the rough Wombat Brush and camped at Paddy's River before pushing on to 'Glenrock', the property of George Barber, who had married Hume's sister Isabella. Here Hamilton's brother John left them, no doubt to his older brother's later regret.

Barber had his own interesting past. While he was still a boy, his father had been lost at sea and his widowed mother had married Dr Throsby. George himself ran away to sea, was shipwrecked, captured by the French and kept a prisoner in a monastery in Portugal for a year.

'We remained there on the 9th,' Hume says, 'and Mr Hovell and I visited Dr Reid, of *Inverary Park* near Bungonia who kindly furnished me with medicines for the use of the party, especially a remedy against snake bite. The carts, in the meantime, were despatched by the short road to Goulburn.'

The surveyor William Harper was at 'Inverary Park', so Hume and Hovell took the opportunity to check their compasses and Hovell his other navigational instruments. Unfortunately, while Hume's compass worked perfectly, Hovell's implements were either defective or their operator incompetent. Throughout the expedition he was never able to determine their exact whereabouts or the precise course of their journey. Hume says, 'On the skeleton chart I then drew a line from the point of departure to Western Port to serve as a base on which to act throughout the journey.'

The crossing of the first river the party encountered provided one of the lighter moments of the journey, and a story that pursued James Fitzpatrick for years afterwards. Like most of his compatriots he had never learned to swim, and when crossing Hume told him to hang on to the tail of one of the bullocks. He followed the leader's orders but was just enjoying the triumph of his arrival on the opposite bank when the beast showered him in excrement, much to the amusement of his fellow travellers. Later in the journey, Henry Angel's sense of humour was the source of another amusing anecdote. When one of the men (probably Claude Bossawa) complained of illness, Angel rolled some fish eyes in flour, telling him Mr Hume had prescribed the 'medicine' for his ailment. The patient took the 'pills', pronounced himself cured and thanked his benefactor profusely.

On Wednesday 13 May, they reached Hume's distant holding with the Aboriginal name Wooloobidallah, the most southerly station then surveyed. He had claimed it jointly with

William Broughton after their 1821 expedition, and the grant was pending. 'We took our final departure from my station on the 17th,' he says, 'and that day travelled about twelve miles.'

They had now established a routine in which Hume and Hovell occupied the tent while the men slept under the two tarpaulins. Each evening, Hume would mark their journey on his chart while Hovell would make copious notes in his journal.

At this stage, they would travel as a group, but as the country got rougher Hume and one of the men – usually Tom Boyd – would scout ahead for stock feed and water for the next day's trek. They had hoped for an Aborigine of Hume's acquaintance to guide them into this part of the unknown, but he failed to arrive, so they pressed on.

The dogs ran down a big kangaroo as they traversed good grazing land and the boggy country at the headwaters of the Lachlan. Having crossed the dividing range between what would become Gunning and Yass, they camped for the night in the vicinity of the land on which Hume would later spend most of his life.

> About three o'clock in the afternoon of the 19th we made the Murrumbidgee River at Marjurigong. The river was flooded and to ford it was impossible. The current was running at three or four miles per hour. From the day of our arrival until the 22nd there was no abatement whatever in the height of the water. As our time was precious and further delay out of the question, it was determined to make an effort to cross on this day.

This decision was Hume's alone, and it would mark the first serious split in the expedition's leadership. At first he attempted to make a canoe from the bark of a box tree, but it was the wrong time of year and the sap was down; this meant that it quickly cracked and filled with water. It was at this point that Hovell quailed. According to Tom Boyd he said, 'We shall never get on with our expedition; we cannot cross these rivers.'

Undeterred, Hume then drew on his earlier experiences with Meehan. 'I took the wheels off my cart, covered the body of it with my tarpaulin and made of it a very excellent and serviceable punt,' he says.

He then called on Boyd, who was 'a very excellent swimmer', and the two of them braved the torrent, each with a fishing line between their teeth and with the line secured to a rope. Pummelled by flood debris in the ice-cold water, they made it across well downstream. Hume says, 'We thus established a communication between either bank. Then, with much trouble and not a little danger, the whole party with cattle and stores were safely landed on the other side.' Boyd says, 'Mr Hovell could swim, but gave us little or no assistance in getting across.' By evening, despite a storm at sunset, everything was repacked and they settled in for the night just beyond the southern bank.

Hovell passes over the incident as a lucky chance in which he took a positive role. 'We were fortunate enough to succeed far beyond our expectations,' he says. 'Thus did we accomplish in a few hours and without loss or injury, what we before thought impracticable.' Hume was unforgiving but generous: 'My associate, had he been dependent on his own resources and left to his own shifts, would not under any circumstances have crossed the Murrumbidgee,' he said, 'though he might have proceeded to trace it downwards and by doing so he would have acted, so far, according to the instructions furnished for our guidance.'

On Saturday, 23 October, they travelled through broken country until they crested a range and came upon the lush Narrangullen Meadows below. They camped there for two nights as they sought a way out of what seemed an endless series of steep hills in the area that now hosts the Burrenjuck Dam. Probing for a way through, they split the party with Hovell and Tom Boyd heading one way, and Hume another with two men.

The dogs with Hovell ran down and killed an emu, which Boyd hung over a tree fork. As they pressed on, Hovell asserted his leadership, and in spite of Boyd's protests they were soon totally lost in wild country around Narrangullen Creek. They spent an uncomfortable night. Boyd says he told Hovell to his face that he would 'not be out another night with him'.

Next morning, he says:

> I heard Mr Hume firing guns for us on which I remarked to Captain Hovell that we were out of our latitude altogether. He asked me how? I replied that I judged from the direction the guns sounded. We made in that direction and shortly met Mr Hume looking for us. We returned with him to the camp.

Hume says, 'When I found him he was actually, but unsuspectingly, travelling back in the direction of Yass.'

Henry Angel was even more caustic: 'I know well from our own talk among ourselves that none of the men [from that point] had any confidence in Captain Hovell. We had no dependence on his taking us through. In fact, he was the worst man in the party, excepting Claude.'

On Monday the 25th, they resumed the journey by following Hume's recent track along the rocky valley of Sugarloaf Creek until it met the Goodradigbee River. By now the going had become so rough that Hume decided they would have to leave behind the carts and some of their gear. Hovell agreed. They found a good camp site, and that night the livestock grazed on a patch of green feed. Next morning after crossing a shallow stream they sorted out the equipment to be left behind.

Hume took his trusty tarpaulin, but to his surprise Hovell decided to leave his behind. This became a bone of contention, the more so when Hovell claimed in his account that it was Hume who discarded his own tarp despite his obvious reliance on it for river crossings. Hume says, 'Had I not taken mine, as will be seen, the expedition must have been forced to return. One cause of our success, simple as it may appear, was my sticking to my tarpaulin, and lugging it along all through our weary journey.'

The pack saddles were then strapped on to the cattle and loaded with their gear. 'Not being accustomed to them, they gave us great trouble,' he says, 'as well as occasioning great delay.' Nevertheless, with careful handling they settled down and Hume scouted west to find a way through the brutal terrain. He again came upon the Murrumbidgee and beside it a track his Aboriginal compatriots had previously described to him. He returned to the camp with a big kangaroo he and his dogs had hunted down.

On Wednesday the 27th, they started late as some of the bullocks had strayed in the night, but they made nine kilometres into an area they named Limestone Valley, where once again they met the meandering Murrumbidgee. They followed the Aboriginal track Hume had discovered the day before and passed abandoned gunyahs. The path narrowed to overhanging cliffs, where the bullocks were unable to pass without risk to their lives and their precious cargo.

The narrowing track then petered out completely, forcing them to retrace their steps to within a few kilometres of their previous camp. They remained there overnight and it was here that Hovell made the remarkable accusation in his journal that it was Hume who had left his tarpaulin behind. Hovell had been marking their wildly zigzagging route with axe cuts on trees. Now he complained that his arm was too sore to continue doing this, but Hume refused permission for any of the men to take over what he deemed a useless exercise.

On the 29th, they began to struggle through the high, rough country that was to tax their strength and determination for many days to come. Hume still scouted ahead with one of the men, but because they were travelling over sharp ridges they were simply doubling their efforts, so for a time he remained with the group and selected the likeliest looking peak as it hove into view. The limestone formations they were traversing were crippling the feet of man and beast alike. The bullocks were carrying up to 120 kilograms in their pack saddles and came under great stress.

They camped by rushing mountain streams and for the next two days they veered away from the ridges and followed gullies south-west until they reached the boggy headwaters of Tomoorama Creek. Progress slowed even further as they struggled through soft earth riddled with half-hidden wombat burrows. Twice in a single day, the packs had to be unloaded from the bullocks and carried by the men, who staggered under their weight.

On the last day of the month, they again found themselves surrounded by sharp ridges and a precipitous cliff that plunged so deeply that even the steadiest horses reared back from it. However, there was no other way out, so they dismounted and slithered and scrambled their way down its slope. At the base they gathered themselves before striking upwards again to another crest. From there they could see the towering peaks of the Bogong Range to the west and south-west, and a sparkling stream dead ahead. But they first had to rest by a rocky creek and it was not until evening that they reached the Goobraganda River where it spilled over into a waterfall.

Here at last they could briefly spell the stock on the grassy flat on the first day of November. They also killed a kangaroo and caught a crayfish that Hovell pronounced the equal of an Old World lobster. He also noted in his journal that they were planting European peach stones and clover seeds wherever they camped.

The next day they made five kilometres north-west along the riverbank, then turned up Walls Creek Valley over another ridge and down to the gap at Log Creek through which the present Snowy Mountains Highway passes. They were confronted by a picturesque valley with clear evidence that the Aboriginal people of the area also valued its natural attractions. Kangaroos abounded. A little further along they spotted lyrebirds that Hovell took for pheasants, then walked marvelling through a bellbird glen.

They reached the main stream that flowed through the valley – known by the Aborigines as 'Tumut' – on Wednesday, 3 November. They were now in the area that would later be inundated by the Blowering Dam. They rested for one night before following the east bank of the river southwards until it turned into the rocky hills and valleys of the Bago Range.

In the summer heat, the bush flies during the day and the mosquitoes at night did little for their morale. In his journal, Hovell claimed that his legs, from socks to knees, were 'one raw sore'. The explorers began to rise earlier to advance a few miles before the heat of the day and the steep hills took their toll. Hovell says that as they climbed one particularly sharp ridge:

> within one furlong of the top we found it necessary to unload the beasts, to take them to the top empty, and for the men to bring up their loads . . . the cattle [were] in danger every minute of their rolling down the side. Had this been the case they must have been dashed to pieces, it being at least 1½ miles to the bottom.

On Sunday, 7 November, the animals were so exhausted that Hume called a rest day. The bullocks recovered quicker than the horses, but both benefited from the breather. They pressed on the following day, and in the early afternoon they sighted the snow-covered peaks of the Australian Alps.

Hume immediately took his own counsel and came to a decision. 'I proposed that we should take a direction more westerly in order to avoid the formidable barrier which threatened to intercept our way,' he says. 'But Mr Hovell dissented from my proposal.' A furious row erupted. Tom Boyd reported: 'When we came in sight of the Snowy Mountains . . . Mr Hume and Mr Hovell had a great difference about the course they should go.'

While Hovell later made light of the argument, even suggesting in his journal that it was he who suggested a change of course, in truth the dispute became so heated that they decided to separate and continue independently towards their goal. However, to do so they had to divide the equipment evenly, and this proved wildly impossible, since at the Goodradigbee they had reduced their gear to one of each item. And as both lay claim to the single tent, they were on the point of cutting it in half when Hume realised the futility of the act and let Hovell have it. However, in the fight over the only frying pan they managed to tear it apart.

'We did separate,' Hume says. 'Mr Hovell held his course south; I steered mine west.' Each took his three assigned convicts and poor Tom Boyd was again caught on the wrong side. 'I had to go with Mr Hovell,' he says. However, 'after travelling some distance, I represented to him that the course we were steering led us right among the Snowy Mountains and if we once got among them we could not get out and all must be lost.'

Not too long afterwards, Hovell realised his mistake. That, Boyd says, was when 'he agreed with me; and at his desire I sought and found Mr Hume's track'. Hume says, 'When my party turned into camp and lighted the fire for the night, great indeed was my surprise to hear one of my men call out, "Here comes Mr Hovell," and sure enough, there he was, with his man Boyd running down our tracks.'

CHAPTER NINE

The Great Expedition Continues

Hume finds a way to ford the 'Hume', Captain Hovell incites rebellion, and the party appears to reach its goal.

The following day, an uneasy peace prevailed. The cooperative mood was enhanced by the open country through which they were passing. Keeping west by south, they had their best day's run since leaving the Yass Plains. Their dogs killed two kangaroos but, in the fierce struggle before the riders reached the scene, one of the greyhounds was severely injured. Hume dressed its wounds but thereafter it was no longer a leader in the chase.

Soon afterwards they found themselves again in wild mountain terrain, and on 11 November they climbed a vertiginous peak in the Yarrara Range. It took three hours to reach the summit, then another hour to scramble down the other side, where they rested themselves from the midday heat. But there was no escaping the clouds of flies and mosquitoes determined to feast on their flesh and blood. Hovell was despairing. 'I have no plan to adopt unless it is to be like the natives themselves,' he wrote, 'go naked and lie on the dirt and smoke.'

The next day, they broke free of the mountains and travelled more than 20 kilometres. But they were unable to bring down any fresh kangaroo meat and were reduced to feeding boiled flour to the dogs. They camped on a rise now known as Mount Pleasant and the following day saw a pinnacle they called Battery Mount, later renamed Mount Tabletop. Its surroundings were fine pasture country so reminiscent of the Cowpastures they called the area Camden Forest.

They headed towards the range, but camped about four kilometres from the peaks and spelled the livestock. Hume and Hovell climbed the mountain while the men brought down a kangaroo and briefly restocked the meat larder. On Monday, 15 November, they continued the journey through rich open forest. Here the birdlife was abundant – from plain turkeys and mallee hens, to the smaller quails and plovers – and Hume was a dead shot. All would help to fill the pot over an open fire. Some of the men were in such good spirits at the prospect they sang songs of their native homelands as they walked. And they killed another kangaroo as they followed the Bungambrawartha Creek where it tumbled down a gentle slope to the grassy plains ahead.

Hamilton Hume was scouting well ahead of the main party on foot, and about noon on Tuesday, 16 November he returned in great good humour. He had discovered a mighty stream, far bigger even than the Murrumbidgee. Tom Boyd says, 'We hurried on and were soon sharing his joy at the swirling waters. A cheer went up when Mr Hume said he would name the river after his father.'

The accounts of the next few critical days differ remarkably. Hume passes over the extraordinary efforts involved in overcoming this immense natural barrier to their progress. It is left to Tom Boyd and William Hovell to fill the gaps. 'Here,' Boyd says, 'it was 70 or 80 yards wide. Downstream it grew wider and upstream we could find no ford. There was no tree that would serve as a bridge and we had no cart now to turn into a boat. Captain Hovell urged Mr Hume to return to Sydney.'

However, before crisis point was reached, Hovell's journal records the travails of the next two days as they ranged back and forth over the area until Hume decided to build a primitive 'boat' with his tarpaulin over a timber frame to cross the stream. To Hume's later outrage, Hovell claimed it was *his* tarpaulin that provided the means to continue.

Hume set to work, and according to Boyd, '. . . with my help made the frame of a boat with wattle-tree poles and branches. The tarpaulin was put under these, brought up around the basket-like sides and behold! We had a fair boat. I had the honour, and the risk too, of being the first to cross the river.'

That was just the beginning of their ordeal. Once across, they pressed on, only to find another almost equally hazardous waterway (later called the Mitta Mitta), which joined the Hume upstream. It was at this stage that Hovell openly rebelled. Hume says:

> On my getting ready to cross the Mitta Mitta, to my surprise Mr Hovell objected and volunteered an address to the men, in which he pointed out, as well as he could, the hazards existing in the rear, suggesting the possibility of others ahead, and appealed to their sense of personal safety, in conclusion asking would it not be the most prudent step to turn back, recross the Hume, and trace down its nearest bank, according to part of our instructions.

Hume responded and Hovell redoubled his efforts claiming that the tarpaulin was fast wearing out and could not be replaced. Now Hume's blood was up. 'I do not think it necessary to point out the defects of the tarpaulin to the men,' he shouted. 'If they don't like to risk themselves in it they can stop and be damned.'

Hovell appealed directly to Claude Bossawa, one of Hume's own men but the weakest link in the chain; and the little fellow agreed with the sea captain. At that point, Hume admits, he 'got angry'.

> I told Mr Hovell I would prefer being rid of him altogether, rather than having one in his position setting such a bad example. I gave him to understand, very plainly, that for me, or all I cared, he might just remain on the side of the river he was on, but I was determined to pursue the journey as originally intended.

Now it became physical. Henry Angel says, 'Mr Hume got in a passion and I think called both Mr Hovell and Claude cowards.' Hume says, 'I also threatened to put Claude *in* the river if he did not cross it with me.' In fact, he picked him up by the scruff of the neck and shook him. And, he says, 'I frightened the fellow into crossing with me.'

The split party again divided the remaining equipment and supplies. Boyd says, 'I was obliged to remain with Mr Hovell.'

However, Hovell's nerve soon quailed before the prospect of a leaderless return across the alien landscape. Hume says, 'After I had crossed the Mitta Mitta, taken my wattle boat to pieces and made a start onwards, Mr Hovell called after me, pressing me to stop and assist him over, and that he would accompany me. I did so.' Boyd swam across to collect the rebuilt boat and over the next hour men and supplies were floated over in the increasingly waterlogged canvas coracle. They set off south once more but then, says Hume, 'To [Hovell's] horror, on the very same afternoon we made the Kiewa River, bank high.' However, they were lucky enough to find a fallen tree to span the torrent.

Years later the events of that day remained crystal clear to Hume and indeed the convicts whose lives could well have been lost in the vastness of the wild. From his Cooma Cottage at Yass, Hume wrote:

> Had I at this time become in any way discouraged, or had I yielded in the least to the reluctance of Mr Hovell in crossing the Hume, and his refusal to cross the Mitta Mitta with me, our expedition must have ended on the north bank of the Hume. I can here safely affirm that only for my own fixed determination to go on at this point, Bass Strait would never have been reached by any of the party.

Astonishingly, Hovell's journal entry claims that in negotiating both crossings he was at one with his co-leader in his determination to forge ahead. He does wonder, 'How we are to contrive to make a boat to take our provisions across (having no cart with us now) I am, as yet at a loss to say, as the only tarpaulin we have is going to pieces and the bark [for a canoe] will not strip off the trees this time of year.' Nevertheless, he rises to the challenge:

> Having determined overnight to cross the [Hume] river, if practicable, we commenced first to patch up my tarpaulin, the only one we have with us . . . we then made a frame . . . something after the shape of one I had before made when wrecked at

> Kents' Group, Bass Straits, in the year 1816. We then put the tarpaulin over the frame . . .

In his disingenuous account, the raging confrontation at the Mitta Mitta might never have occurred.

By now the expedition was coming under severe physical stress. The men's clothes were fast wearing out and several of the livestock were lame. Fortunately the country was well stocked with kangaroos and they were able to catch a brolga for the pot. They also became increasingly aware of the Aboriginal presence for, while none came close enough to converse, their fires were ever present before them and to both sides of their course.

Hume was naturally cautious in his dealings with previously unknown tribes, but he welcomed their presence for the signs their tracks gave to waterholes and flowing streams. He had developed the ability to 'read' the bush, to avoid the impassable and go with the Aboriginal flow as indicated by their abandoned camp sites and gathering places.

Hovell, the relative stranger to the land, tried to heal the rift between them and on Wednesday, 24 November he wrote, 'My friend has just ventured an opinion that he is sure all those rivers empty themselves into the sea, but he does not say whether an inland sea or the ocean. My opinion is that they empty themselves into one immense lake, and the waters of the lake are carried off into the ocean in the N.E. or S.W. coasts.' Hovell's vision, of a vast inland sea – which he shared with other European-bred venturers in the great south land – would become one of the enduring myths of the early colonial experience.

They camped near the junction of the Buffalo River near the site of present-day Wangaratta. Continued dry weather worked in their favour and they had no problem finding a ford. They climbed yet another range and spied to the south-east a peculiarly shaped snow-capped eminence they called Mount Buffalo. This was well-watered country, and they were soon crossing their ninth river since leaving the Murrumbidgee.

Each day the heat was increasing and the Aboriginal fires were stripping away the feed for their livestock. Then on 27 November, according to Hovell's account, 'When we were crossing one of the creeks the bank gave way and Mr Hume's mare fell upon her back into it and her load, which was flour, was not half way in the bags before we could get her on her legs again.' Hume was using his mount as a pack horse to lighten the load of the footsore bullocks and this was a serious loss since not only were their supplies running low, the hunting dogs were either wounded or almost exhausted.

The next morning they started early to seek food and drink for the stock and happily came upon a small valley they called Norton's Meadows. The livestock filled their bellies but when the men saw a mob of kangaroos in the distance the dogs were too weak to bring them down.

The nights were relatively cool and they now had to pass over the Strathbogie Ranges, a barrier of very rough, high country in the next two days hard travelling. One night in the mountains it was so cold they couldn't sleep. Their clothes were wearing through and they had to keep a roaring fire to prevent themselves from freezing. On the first day of December, they made their way down the range and at the base the dogs spotted a kangaroo. Three of them gave chase but two didn't return. The third was ripped by its quarry and crippled. Thereafter he would be a passenger they could ill afford to keep. However, the following day the two errant hunters returned to their camp on a small creek just north of the present-day Molesworth.

They were now in a lush valley fed by a sparkling stream they named the Goulburn River after Governor Brisbane's colonial secretary (though landmarks commemorating Brisbane himself are notable for their absence). They crossed it on a fallen tree but had to cut a way down the steep banks for the cattle to reach the water. That evening they caught a feed of cod and Hume shot a kangaroo. They rested a day and the men used the time to mend their clothes as best they could. Some went looking for a lost dog but without success.

On Monday, 6 December, they started early and made an assault on the series of ranges that hemmed them in. Water was scarce, as, to their dismay, the creeks and rivulets they had relied on were nowhere to be found. Fortunately it rained that afternoon, and towards evening they found a watercourse they named King Parrot Creek after the flashing scarlet, green and blue passerines that populated the area.

Soon, however, the beauties of the Australian bush were replaced by the torments of a seemingly endless ripple of stony ridges where the brush became so dense they could see no more than ten metres ahead. Two men had to take the lead and cut a path for the cattle. By nightfall they were exhausted, and according to his journal Hovell rewarded them with a nip of brandy with their nightly damper. Unfortunately that only made them thirsty, and they spent the night fending off leeches and March flies.

Next morning they had just returned to their thankless task when a potential tragedy struck Hume. 'I was walking along the barrel of a fallen tree looking intently ahead,' he says, 'when a vine or some other obstruction caught my foot and tripped me, causing me to fall upon a jagged limb which entered my groin.' A terrible pain took his breath away as the sharp spike speared into him. 'Fortunately,' he says, '[it] took a superficial direction which [otherwise] would have finished my journey there and then.'

However, it was bad enough to cause him intense discomfort and he could not continue. They returned briefly to their camp site until he partially recovered. He named the peak Mount Disappointment, and from there they retraced their steps towards the slightly easier going at King Parrot Creek. 'From this point,' he says, 'we got on very well upon the whole until we came to Sunday Creek' (near the present site of Kilmore).

By Saturday, 11 December, they were on the move before 5 a.m., following the creek to the west, when they were suddenly surrounded by the smoke from Aboriginal fires as the native Australians worked their country as they had since time immemorial. Late in the afternoon a sudden wind change sent the flames in their direction and they had to retreat. Next day they retraced their steps and set a course for Mount Piper in the Plenty Ranges. But now their condition was becoming critical. They had no fit dogs left and their provisions were almost exhausted.

On Monday, 13 December, Hume left camp early and scouted ahead. He was relieved that his wounded groin was healing without infection and he made good progress. He reached a muddy creek and traced its course until he found a ford, then returned to the rest of the party, only to find that once again Hovell had stirred the men to rebellion.

Hume was shocked and outraged. They had travelled so far in previously unchartered country; they had surmounted all the obstacles and obstructions nature could place in their way; and now, just when one final effort was required to reach their goal,

Hovell had spread such fear among them that they had lost heart. 'I found a strong disinclination to proceed further,' he says in the euphemistic circumlocution of the day. 'And while I was reasoning with them, Mr Hovell stood aloof and mute.' Hume would not be swayed. 'On my map I pointed out to the men our position – the distance we had come and how far we had to go.' He argued and cajoled. Gradually, he won them round. 'At last I came to a compromise with the party,' he says, 'that if we had no decided prospect of making the coast within the next two or three days, I should give up the journey and return with them.'

Once again, they loaded their gear on the aching shoulders of both man and beast, and struggled on. At first it was hard going. 'That same day,' he says, 'we crossed the Dividing Range.' But then, 'being some distance in advance of the party, I observed an opening and a fall of land far to the south.'

It was not unexpected. This was an area of great Aboriginal significance. It not only possessed a powerful spiritual dimension for the local people; it was a trading hub for the exchange of stone implements. The signs of Aboriginal activity were all around. And for Hume the topography indicated a natural sloping towards the coast. That was exactly what he'd been searching for. 'Thinking the struggle at last won,' he says, 'my heart rose, and I cheered long and loud. Most of the men left their cattle and rushed towards me.' Hovell had been trying to fix the perambulator, which Claude Bossawa had run against a boulder. But then he too joined in the rush. Hume pointed them to their goal. Even Hovell briefly felt the sense of triumph in the moment.

The next day was literally all downhill. Hume said he could see water in the far distance. But then, according to Tom Boyd, 'Mr Hovell ridiculed and said it was smoke.' The next day, Boyd says, 'we came upon a blackfellows' camp, with the mud-oyster shells lying about it. Mr Hume pointed out these to Mr Hovell and asked where they came from. He replied, from the sea, of course . . . and we made the sea that day.'

It was 16 December 1824.

Hume says it was about four o'clock in the afternoon when they finally reached their goal. 'We camped that night near the beach, without [fresh] water,' he says. But before they bedded down, both Hume and Hovell cut the letter 'H' into the only tree large enough to contain the mark. Some of the men caught sea bream and all enjoyed a change of diet.

Hovell makes no mention of the triumph in his journal. His main concern is the prospect of their returning with only five weeks rationed food for the trip, which had taken 11 weeks so far, and the ten rivers they would have to cross if they were to make it safely home.

However, the day was not yet done. Fitzpatrick says, 'I went shooting ducks about half a mile or a mile from the camp, when five blackfellows ran me for my life. I sang out as I ran towards the camp; the blacks got close up and had thrown some spears at me, when Mr Hume and Boyd came to my rescue.'

Boyd says, 'Mr Hume had thrown off his boots, but hearing the shouts he started up, took his gun and called upon us to take ours and follow him. Captain Hovell did not stir.' The two armed men frightened the Aborigines off; but then Hume decided that if they were to make a successful return journey, he needed their help.

'I went afterwards to the blacks,' he says, 'had a palaver with them, and brought them to our camp.'

CHAPTER TEN

The Homeward Journey

There is dissent over the party's end point, and Hume leads the perilous journey home.

By Hovell's calculations they had arrived – in perfect accord with Brisbane's instructions – at Western Port. Hume was not so sure. His friend James Meehan had been along that coast with surveyor-general Charles Grimes and had told him that there were islands in Western Port, but none in Port Phillip. And there were certainly none visible from the shore or indeed the high ground as they approached. Moreover, he knew that Matthew Flinders' map located 'Station Peak' directly beyond Port Phillip, and this coincided with his own observations.

So while his official navigator was adamant, the bushman continued to harbour doubts, and in an expedition with Captain Sturt three years later he was firm in his view that their southern terminus had been Port Phillip, near the present city of Geelong. This would become very significant in time, but for the moment Hume's principal concern was the safety of his party and the hazardous cross-country return journey that stretched before them.

The Aborigines had told him by signs and actions that there were white men in the south-west who were sawing timber. 'They described the sailors and vessel under sail,' he says, 'and [they] made use of English expressions.' Fitzpatrick was fascinated by their miming, 'pulling boats, cutting trees and rolling logs.' Hume says, 'I was very desirous to proceed [there] but I could not prevail on Mr Hovell to accompany me.'

The Aborigines also urged him to go with them to meet a white man who was living with them. This was undoubtedly William Buckley, a former English soldier transported for 14 years on a trivial offence and who had been among the convicts sent by ship to Port Phillip in 1803 to form a new settlement. When it failed the following year, Buckley and some of his companions escaped to the bush. And while the others perished, the very tall and rangy Buckley was adopted by an Aboriginal family group. He would later make contact with Hamilton Hume's boyhood friend John Batman when he established the Port Phillip Association to found the city of Melbourne.

However, Hovell was particularly anxious to start the return journey. So on 18 December they set off, initially retracing their steps, but with some helpful suggestions from the Aborigines. Indeed, Hume's 'palaver' was almost certainly more extensive than his single reference would indicate. In his journal, Hovell describes (somewhat disapprovingly) that they pulled Hamilton's beard and nose and opened his shirt. He even suggested that later Hume 'sulked' whenever this incident was retold. But this probably says more about Hovell's attitude to the Aboriginal people – whom he suspected of waiting in ambush – than it does of Hume's demeanour.

At about 8 am the following day, a Sunday, Hume says:

> the report of a cannon was distinctly heard in the direction of the place pointed out by the natives the day before . . . down the harbour fifteen or sixteen miles. So convinced were we that the report was that of a cannon that one and all agreed to turn back to Geelong [the local Aboriginal name for the area, formally adopted in 1827]. In a short time, however, doubts and difficulties were started [and] I was out-voted.

Hovell's man, Tom Boyd, puts it more succinctly: 'Mr Hume was very desirous to return, expecting to find some ship there, but he could not prevail on Mr Hovell. They had some difference about it, which made matters go stiff for some days again.'

On that note, they resumed their journey and held to what Hume called their 'lonely course across the downs to the north-east'. By then their remaining supplies consisted of only 150 pounds of flour, six pounds of tea and no sugar or salt. And before them was a trek of at least 700 kilometres across country stripped by fire and in the baking heat with ten formidable streams and a serried barrier of punishing mountain ranges.

Reluctantly, they killed and butchered their lead bullock, 'Captain', who could barely walk. It was a tough decision. The ageing oxen had served them faithfully and well, but he was totally played out and Hume had no heart to continue the torture. They had no salt to pickle the meat so could only dry it as best they were able, knowing it would not last long in the summer heat.

They camped that night on the right bank of the Werribee rivulet, which Hovell named the Arndell after his wife's family. They could see in the north-west the mountain range that Matthew Flinders had called Station Peak. They called the highest point Mount Wentworth after Hume's friend William, but it was later redesignated Mount Macedon.

In his later account, Hume gives only the most perfunctory description of the extraordinary feat of bushmanship he performed in leading them home. Hovell continued to write up his journal every second night, and though it bears all the marks of an editor, it paints a vivid picture of an increasingly desperate journey. On Monday, 20 December, they camped at Broughton's Creek, the same site they had used the previous Tuesday on the way south. Keeping Mount Wentworth (Macedon) on their left, they reached the Plenty Ranges. In the hundreds of kilometres of dividing range, there is only one natural low pass in south-east Australia, and assisted once again by the heavy Aboriginal traffic evident in the bush tracks and markings, Hume had found it, at the current site of Kilmore.

Once through, they stayed overnight at Sunday Creek, which had figured so dramatically on their downward trek, but next morning Hume swung west of their original course. This allowed them to avoid a forest of tangled gullies and steep ridges; and their new route was almost exactly where the Hume Highway and the interstate railway run today. Indeed, it is this homeward journey that really represents the transport thoroughfare that subsequently permitted the opening up of the most productive country on the Australian continent.

But first the party had to survive the many perils ahead. By Thursday, 23 December, they had reached the Goulburn River some 30 kilometres west of their earlier crossing point. Though it was still a substantial stream, it was now easily fordable. And the following day – Christmas Eve – they camped on its north bank and indulged in a fishing session that produced a fine catch of native cod. The remaining animals also took advantage of the good grasses on the fertile river flat.

On Christmas Day, the men ate the last of the beef courtesy of their lead bullock. And then began a catalogue of endurance that would test every man and beast to his limits and some beyond. The livestock would suffer terrible torments, not least Hume's saddle horse, which was bitten on the nose that day by a snake. Hume used the snake bite 'medicine' provided by Dr Reid at the beginning of the journey and, whether it helped or not, the horse survived to endure the sufferings of the trek.

Despite the hardship, morale among the men was good. Against the odds, they had achieved their first goal; now at least they were homeward bound, and if they reached it they would have carved their names into the colony's history. As a gesture of fellowship Hume named the Goulburn Valley Esther's Plains after Hovell's wife.

They passed over the Wombat Ranges on 27 December and camped briefly near the site of today's township of Euroa. They were now travelling over 'the sunlit plains extended', and the magnitude of their discoveries was becoming apparent. Soon Mount Buffalo was on their right, and they rejoined their outward course at Hurdle Creek. On Wednesday, 29 December, they crossed the Ovens River, and fortune remained with them as they hauled in an excellent catch of native fish. Hovell killed a death adder but decided not to eat it.

Once again they found themselves in the midst of Aboriginal fires as the native Australians followed their complex annual management schedule. But Hume's resolution drove them on as thunderstorms threatened. He knew too well that a downpour upstream of the rivers they had still to cross could send unbridgeable torrents across their path. And for the moment his luck held.

They began the new year with a forced march of 35 kilometres in a single day despite their failing condition. They rested just below the site of Yackandandah and pushed on next day. It was here they first contacted an Aboriginal group on the homeward journey when they came upon about 30 women and children who scattered at their approach. Hume gradually induced them to return and when they settled down the youngsters showed their skills at throwing small reed spears at a target of bark while the women resumed their spinning of native flax.

By 3 January 1825 they had reached the Hume and were greatly relieved to find it very much lower than on their outward journey. They were able to ford it comfortably about two kilometres further upstream from their earlier crossing. This came as a tremendous relief to Hamilton; he had been deeply concerned until then that they might find themselves stranded by an insuperable barrier, one that in bitter irony he had named for his own father.

Once across he relaxed the pressure on his party and allowed the hard-pressed horses and cattle to eat their fill. The men by now had become expert fishermen, and hauled in a mighty catch including a 40-pound cod. But from now on the baking heat was unrelenting, the food scarcer by the day, their clothing falling from them in rags, the flies almost unendurable and the livestock increasingly footsore and lame.

On Wednesday, 5 January, they followed the river until it turned south-east and Hume broke away from his earlier track again to avoid the hardest going. They travelled beside Battery Mount Creek upstream and passed about 15 kilometres to the east of Mount Tabletop. That day, despite their deteriorating condition, they were still able to advance almost 30 kilometres towards their goal.

Here they again made contact with an Aboriginal group but they were uncommunicative and Hume urged his party on. However, the Aborigines returned the following day and approached cautiously because of the utterly unfamiliar bullocks with their unblinking stare. It took all Hume's persuasive powers to induce three of the men to remain with them overnight, and he took the opportunity to question them about the country ahead. Once settled into the camp on Little Billabong Creek they were more than happy to respond. They knew the country well. In fact, one of them had travelled as far as Lake George.

Next morning they awoke to find the horses had strayed, and the Aborigines helped to find them. They begged Hume and his friends to come with them so they could show them off to their women and children camped about five kilometres away. Hovell spurned them and set off on their planned course, but Hume took his three men and accepted the invitation. 'We went with our friends of the forest to their camp,' he says.

> We found about thirty to forty natives awaiting us, a special messenger having been sent to inform them of our coming.
>
> Among them I observed a very tall, white-coloured young man, several inches higher than myself. The number of women and children inspired me with confidence, being a sure sign that they were peacefully disposed. Many of the children took hold of my hands and knees, at the same time patting me. I had nothing, however, in the shape of presents to give them except an old tin pot and a broken knife.

The group performed a corroboree in honour of their guests.[1]

> At the request of the old man I named one of them and some of their children. The three who had remained in our camp overnight gave me their names as Nowingong, Cooradoc and Wowhely . . . on leaving our sable friends they pointed out the direct line for Tumut and I at once started into my proper course, fully expecting to overtake Mr Hovell. But to my surprise I found he had been waiting by for me and after a good deal of beating about he came across my trail and overtook me in the afternoon while [we were] resting.

After the single meal of Aboriginal bush tucker, they returned to a starvation diet. When travelling alone, Hume could survive for days on a ration of native insects, berries, roots and other vegetation. But the time and effort required to gather and prepare them made it an impractical alternative for an eight-man party with no previous experience of their tastes and texture.

Now the kangaroo dogs were lame and Hume's ammunition was almost expended. On Saturday, 8 January, they served out the last of their travelling rations – six pounds of flour to each man and a little tea, which had to last at least 220 kilometres to the nearest outstation hut. The stock were crippled and all but exhausted. The men were little better – their boots were worn through and they could barely hobble behind the leaders.

Hume had to manage his scarce resources with the greatest care. And on the morning of 9 January he knew that in order to reach the gear – including a single cask of salt pork – they had left behind by the Goodradigbee River he would have to turn the party east and into the mountains. There was no other way. By now Hovell had lost any inclination to argue and they plodded through clouds of flies until Sunday evening, when they camped near the site of Adelong.

Prolonged malnutrition was now taking its toll, and on Monday, 10 January the position was becoming critical. They had reached the Tumut area below the junction of the Tumut and Goodradigbee rivers, roughly 40 kilometres north of their crossing on the outward journey. Once again, the mountain streams delivered a reprieve, with fish to provide a little protein. And on Tuesday they crossed the river into fine grassland where a mob of kangaroos was lazing in the summer heat. However, Hume's dog could no longer raise a trot and the 'roos quickly retreated beyond the range of his rifle where they watched cautiously as the travellers pressed on.

Hume would have preferred to follow the Tumut downstream but since it was unknown country he was concerned that he would lead the party to a dead end. So he had to assault the craggy Brindabella Ranges as the only certain route to their supplies. But by Wednesday, as they struggled upwards, their progress had slowed to a crawl. The one saving grace was a plentiful supply of clean, fresh water as they discovered the upper reaches of the Goobraganda and followed it about five kilometres. Hovell noted three waterfalls at a ravine before Hume turned the party to the east.

The next day, he used his last ammunition to stalk and shoot a kangaroo. The meat was a welcome relief but so also was the hide that the men used to wrap their feet and that Hume fashioned into moccasins for the lamest bullocks. They camped at what they called Dinner Time Creek, and next afternoon they passed the place where they had fed and slept on the last day of October.

Now Hume turned them south-east, searching for a better track, and that night they found a flat, stony area on a ridge to light a fire and cook the last of their tasteless damper. The next morning, Friday, 14 January, they travelled along the ridge through very rough country. Hovell says that by now their progress had become 'a journey which for fatigue and intricacy, and even danger to the cattle, it is impossible adequately to describe, sometimes over steep crags, loose stones slipping under their feet, gullies and deep ravines traversed by small streams'.

By sunset they had reached a break in the bush that would lead them down towards the Goodradigbee flats, but they were so exhausted they had to camp on the slope two-thirds of the way to the valley floor. There Hume's dog had to be put down.

Next day they rejoined their outward course in the valley, caught some small fish and used the final scrapings of flour. They staggered on through a long, blistering day in the hope that the equipage they had left behind – and which was now almost in reach – had not attracted the Aborigines nor been damaged by the weather.

Hovell's journal never names the convicts who were the mainstay of the party after Hume, but it is clear that Bossawa, Smith and Bollard were little more than walking skeletons, Bossawa virtually naked and at the limit of his endurance. They dropped behind while Hume and Hovell, accompanied by Angel and either Boyd or Fitzpatrick, went ahead while the others shuffled forward with the equally exhausted bullocks.[2]

The leaders urged themselves on over the treeless plains and through a ghostly stand of eucalypts until there it was, just ahead of them and almost as they had left it, the drays with their cache. As they gathered around it, the only damage visible was a hole in the tarpaulin that looked to have been made by a tomahawk, and a small keg of spirits that had rotted away and leaked out. However, the cask of salt pork was untouched. It was a moment of triumph for Hume, but there was still a way to go before they reached the safety of colonial settlement.

The rest of the party with the bullocks finally caught up with them at one o'clock in the afternoon, and after a feed they gathered their resources to cross the river. Once again luck was with them. The summer rains still held off and, though the bullocks were so weak and crippled that they had to be manhandled up the bank, they successfully forded the Goodradigbee.

The stock had come to the end of their road, so Hume decided to turn them loose on the good valley pasture. Hovell ordered Bollard and Boyd to stay with them and to have them haul his cart on to the Murrumbidgee later if they were able. Hume's reaction to this is not recorded. The rest of the party then moved on with the horses and Hume's cart. Bossawa and Smith could no longer walk, and they travelled to the Murrumbidgee in the back of the dray.

On Monday, 17 January, they confronted the river that had first caused Hovell to doubt the wisdom of the expedition and the determination of his leader. Now it was a placid stream and they passed over it with barely a murmur of concern. Hume could practically smell the welcoming wood smoke of his outstation hut as they advanced on the Yass River. It too parted before them and on Tuesday, 18 January 1825 they finally sighted the slab hut on his station's outskirts. He was home.

His first action was to collect supplies to be sent back to Tom Boyd and William Bollard, but they had given up all hope of the cattle recovering before they died of starvation themselves and were heading homeward. By 24 January after 16 weeks hard travelling – only five of them on the homeward journey – they had all returned. It was over. It was done. He had brought them through.

James Fitzpatrick later wrote, 'Mr Hume was always the leading man of the party; he was always ahead with his gun on his shoulder. We followed him, and Mr Hovell amongst us.' Tom Boyd was even more direct. 'But for Mr Hume we would never have come back at all; we would all have died in the bush had we depended on Mr Hovell.'

It is difficult to overstate the magnitude of Hume's achievement. At only 26, he had challenged and overcome the almost insuperable natural barriers of an unforgiving landscape. He had done so against the faint-heartedness of his co-leader and in the face of exhaustion and dissent from other indentured members of his party. He had rallied them to press on, and given the lead in spite of an injury that would have felled a lesser man. He had defied the implicit threats of the Aboriginal fire makers, and used the signs and routines of the Aboriginal people to guide him through the endless maze of the Australian bush.

And in so doing, he had swept aside a curtain to reveal a potential cornucopia upon which a nation could be firmly founded – without a single loss of life.

CHAPTER ELEVEN

The Triumphant Return

Hovell tries to steal Hume's thunder, Governor Brisbane's Aboriginal policies stir up trouble, and differing accounts of the great journey appear.

Despite their differences on the track, in the euphoria of the day the Australian bushman clearly felt a sense of camaraderie with the British sea captain in the wake of their remarkable achievement. They had made it through against the odds, and he and Hovell, together with their hard-working fellow travellers, deserved all the official recognition available. When they arrived at Hume's station the two leaders agreed, he says, that they would present themselves jointly to the authorities in Sydney with news of their triumph.

The following day, he wrote, 'Mr Hovell left me, alleging that he had some important business to transact with a Mr Forbes, but promised, should he reach *Glenrock*, my brother-in-law's place, before me, he would await my coming up. On arriving at [*Glenrock*] I was surprised to find that Mr Hovell had left for Sydney the day before. As may be supposed, I was again a little annoyed at such treatment.'[1]

In fact, he was furious and, after seeing to his men, set out in pursuit. 'I overtook him at the residence of . . . Mr James Atkinson, near Berrima,' he says, with obvious relish. They then rode in tandem to deliver their news to Major Goulburn in Sydney. Hume sent a brief personal note written at Appin to Governor Brisbane, in which he reported that he'd arrived

> safe home in company with Mr Hovell who accompanied me in the Expedition Your Excellency was pleased to entrust to my Care, for the purpose of exploring a passage thro' the interior to Western Port.
>
> I feel much pleasure in informing Your Excellency that we have discovered, adjoining to that extensive Harbour, one of the finest parts or tracts of Country Yet known in Australia. It is chiefly immense Downs and Forests partially wooded, the whole of which is easy of access and well watered by the different streams that run into the Tweed – I have so taken the liberty to name that river which falls into Western Port . . .

In fact, it was the Yarra making its way to Port Phillip. He then describes their river crossings on the outward journey (without any reference to Hovell's recalcitrance) and gives Hovell's calculations for their arrival on the southern coast.

He concludes:

> I beg leave to recommend to Your Excellency's notice and favourable Consideration, the men who accompanied us on the Expedition, as they have undergone a great deal of fatigue, and have been very attentive to all orders given to them. I will

> do myself the honour of waiting on Your Excellency in a few days and trust I shall be able to render a satisfactory account of our Journey to Bass's Straits.

Whether the meeting actually took place – either at Sydney or at the Parramatta Observatory – is unknown. But certainly Hovell tried to use his sterling contacts to secure an audience with the governor.

By then Brisbane was preoccupied with his own difficulties. Major Goulburn had lost patience with his absentee managerial style and was arrogating control of the colony's administration to himself. At the same time he was complaining to his influential friends in Whitehall and urging Brisbane's recall.

The governor's Aboriginal policies were proving absurdly provocative, and in mid-1824 an uprising in the Bathurst area could only be put down after he declared martial law and sent 75 additional soldiers to the district. He actually received an official 'rocket' from Bathurst for having sought a troop of cavalry without sending an estimate of the cost. His response was to raise a patrol of colonial youths, armed, mounted and dressed as light dragoons. He put them under the orders of Major Morisset, who sent punitive raids to all the Aborigines' known camping areas. Brisbane reported to London that Morisset's tactics of 'keeping these unfortunate people in a constant state of alarm soon brought them to a sense of their duty. And "Saturday", their great and most warlike chieftain, has been with me to receive his pardon ...'

Further disturbances in 1825 were also ruthlessly put down and by then Morisset had travelled to Westminster, where his reward – direct from Lord Bathurst – would be command of the Norfolk Island penal colony, where he could exercise his sadistic urges without restraint. But that would not occur during Brisbane's incumbency. For by mid-1825 the administration of New South Wales was falling into disarray.

The governor had been at loggerheads with his commissary-general, William Wemyss. Brisbane believed some of the leading merchants were making undue profits on imports, and ordered Wemyss to introduce the Spanish dollar as the colony's standard currency. Wemyss was unimpressed, and though the government initially set its value at five shillings sterling they devalued it at least twice to the detriment of the colonists.

Moreover, as the grain crops in both New South Wales and Van Diemen's Land looked set to fail, wheat rose from six to more than 30 shillings a bushel. In September 1824 the government chartered the ship *Almorah* to sail to Batavia for a cargo of rice and flour. But now the farmers with a decent crop worried that they would be undercut by the imports, and started a petition through the Rev. Samuel Marsden, who in addition to his other mercantile interests was now acting president of the Agricultural Society.

Then came reports that the *Almorah* was also bringing £30,000 worth of Spanish dollars, which would further devalue the currency, and ten of the leading merchants petitioned the governor, who hotly denied it. When the ship arrived on 17 February, Brisbane was appalled to discover that Wemyss had not only acquired the 5,000 bushels of rice as requested, he had also ordered 53 chests of tea, 288 bags of sugar and 106,000 Spanish dollar coins. And to Brisbane's intense embarrassment he'd added six cases of wine, some spirits, and some seeds and plants expressly for the governor.

Brisbane called his senior official 'obnoxious', and claimed he had set out deliberately to annoy the public and put the governor in a bad light. If so, he certainly succeeded. The merchants of Sydney set forth on a mission that recalled the Boston Tea Party of 1773. They conspired with Captain Charles Mitchell, master of the brig *Slaney,* to take command of the *Almorah* and seize the tea. But instead of dumping it in Sydney Harbour they would hold it as contraband, since it infringed the East India Company's monopoly of the tea trade. (And when the fuss died down they would sell it themselves.)

Brisbane's Attorney-General Saxe Bannister gathered a party of constables and attempted to board the *Almorah* to serve a writ on Mitchell, but was fired on with muskets and had to withdraw. The piratical Mitchell threatened to sink the ship with the loot aboard, and for a time there was a Mexican stand-off. It was resolved only when Mitchell hired William Wentworth and his senior law partner Robert Wardell to oppose the writ, then slipped out to sea in the *Slaney* under cover of darkness, never to return. The tea remained in the *Almorah's* hold. Brisbane wanted Wemyss dismissed, but by then he had sniffed the breeze and was in London defending himself and traducing the governor's reputation.

Meantime, Hovell was also engaging Wentworth's services as part-owner of *The Australian* newspaper to assert his leadership of the expedition. On 27 January 1825, the paper reported:

> We have just room to announce that Captain Hovell and Mr H. Hume have returned from their excursions to the southward. It appears that they penetrated as far as Western Ports [sic], Bass's Straits, where they discovered a river of considerable

Part of the crew of His Majesty's Ship Guardian *endeavouring to escape in the boats* by Robert Dodd, 1790. Hamilton Hume's father, Andrew, was aboard HMS *Guardian* heading from the Cape to New South Wales when it struck an iceberg. (*National Portrait Gallery, Canberra*)

Governor Lachlan Macquarie (1762–1824) by Richard Read, 1822. Macquarie led the transformation of New South Wales from a penal colony to a free settlement and encouraged the explorations of Hamilton Hume and others. (*Mitchell Library, State Library of New South Wales*)

Alexander Berry (1781–1873), 1856. A friend and patron of Hamilton Hume, Berry accompanied him on two expeditions to the south coast of New South Wales, and introduced him to William Hovell. (*Mitchell Library, State Library of New South Wales*)

Dr Charles Throsby (1771–1828). Hume's first patron and sometime rival in exploration. (*Berrima District Historical Society*)

View of Lake George, New South Wales, from the north east by Joseph Lycett, 1825. In the previous year, Hamilton Hume and William Hovell were instructed to find a path from the lake to Western Port. (*National Library of Australia*)

Hume and Hovell crossing the Murray in 1825 by F. A. Sleap, 1888. (*State Library Victoria*)

The tree marked by Hume and Hovell near Albury in 1824 on their journey of discovery to Port Phillip, ca. 1880–89. (*State Library Victoria*)

Captain William Hilton Hovell (1786–1875), 1866. The former sea captain was nominally joint leader of the great expedition, but soon proved inept. The leadership and bushcraft of Hamilton Hume saved the expedition on many occasions. (*Mitchell Library, State Library of New South Wales*)

Captain Charles Sturt by J. M. Crossland, 1853. Born in England, he was a great explorer of Australia's interior and a friend of Hamilton Hume. (*Art Gallery of South Australia*)

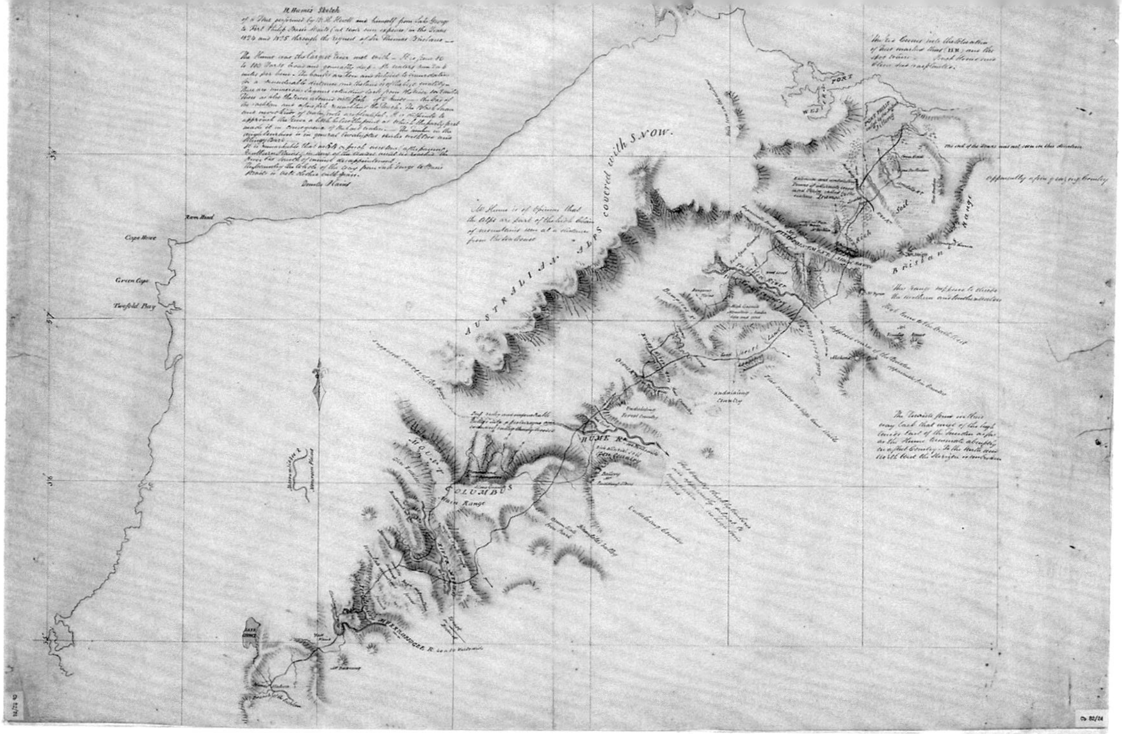

The trail of William Hilton Hovell and Hamilton Hume from Appin to Port Phillip. This map of the journey is believed to be a copy, possibly sketched by Thomas Mitchell from a rough sketch provided by Hume. (*Mitchell Library, State Library of New South Wales*)

The Darling River in 1838, from a drawing by Thomas Mitchell. Hume and Sturt discovered and explored the great river in 1829 whilst searching for an inland sea. (*From* Australian Discovery By Land, *1929*)

Sir Thomas Mitchell (1792–1855), ca. 1830. Born in Scotland, Mitchell was another great explorer of Australia's interior and friend of Hamilton Hume. (*Mitchell Library, State Library of New South Wales*)

Sir Henry Parkes (1815–1896), photo by H. B. Solomons, 1887. Administrator, reformer and Seventh Premier of New South Wales, later called the 'Father of Federation'. (*Mitchell Library, State Library of New South Wales*)

The bushrangers Michael Bourke (i.e. Burke), Ben Hall, Frank Gardiner, Johnny Gilbert and John Dunne (i.e. Dunn) by Patrick Marony, 1894. *(National Library of Australia)*

Explorer Hamilton Hume (left) and his wife Elizabeth, with an unnamed horseman at Cooma Cottage, ca. 1870. (*National Trust of Australia, NSW*)

Hamilton Hume (1797-1873), ca. 1869. (*Mitchell Library, State Library of New South Wales*)

> magnitude . . . they represent the country to be remarkably rich and much superior to the country of Argyleshire or Bathurst . . .

On 10 February, the same paper printed a short description of the journey and in an editorial spoke of 'Mr Hovell and his party'. It also contained the warning: 'Four mountain ranges will prevent exploitation . . . we suspect that all carriages must be laid aside. All inland commerce, we fear, will have to be carried in packs and panniers on the backs of mules . . .'

This caught Hume's attention, and he quickly penned a reply to be published the following week: 'I observed that you endeavoured to give an account of the country through which I lately passed to Western Port and the Bass's Straits,' he wrote, and took the editorialist to task for suggesting the country was impassable. Indeed, he bet £500 that he could take a cart and a pair of horses down the entire track from Appin and would set out the moment the bet was covered. Happily, no takers were forthcoming.

A further letter followed, either from Hume or one of his supporters, signed 'Truth and Justice' that fixed upon the phrase 'Mr Hovell and his party'. The writer asked:

> Pray Gentlemen, may I inquire, where did Mr Hume go to? We have seen most of the men who were on the expedition with the above gentlemen, and they have positively declared to us, and are ready to make oath if required, that had it not been for the perseverance and abilities of Mr Hume, the object of the journey would never have been accomplished . . . We regret much that ever Mr Hume allowed such a person as Mr Hovell, who possessed such poor abilities as an explorer, to be of his party.

The opposition paper, *The Gazette*, sniffed a controversy and was quick to stir the pot on Hovell's behalf, asking:

> Where was the justice in Mr Hume writing a letter to His Excellency the Governor immediately on his return, with scarcely adverting to his friend and companion and principal, Mr Hovell? Mr Hume, we question not, possesses superior abilities as a bush ranger, but whether Mr Hume is possessed of abilities equal to Mr Hovell in other respects, is what also should come under consideration.

These 'other respects' were not listed. In a community divided so indelibly by 'class', there was no need. The jumped-up currency lad should have had proper respect for his sterling 'principal'. The native Australian must always give precedence to his English betters.

Hume's friend and patron Alexander Berry, who mixed freely with the bunyip aristocracy in Sydney, could see where Hovell's self-aggrandisement was heading. He wrote an urgent note to Hamilton in Appin on 2 June 1825:

> Come down to Sydney in receipt of this, and bring along with you the rough copy of your journal,[2] the map, and all the papers belonging to it. I should wish to see you derive some advantage from your labours, and unless you act with promptitude I shall be unable to assist you, and you may lose your reward.

It is unclear whether Hume took his friend's counsel. But it does appear that Hovell retired from the field, at least temporarily, knowing that the other members of the party were more than willing to tell the true story. It may also be that the influential Berry, who'd had long conversations with Hume about the trip, was happily regaling Sydney's dinner tables with some of the more engaging stories of the journey.

Either way, the colony's eager landseekers were more than happy to back Hume's report with action. They would swarm over the rich river valleys, the well-watered plains and the foothills of the newly discovered pasture lands. And in the process Hume's 'friends of the forest' would be dispossessed of their country without a backward glance.

On 24 March 1825, Brisbane wrote a rather confused note to Under-Secretary Robert Horton:

> I have to announce to you the discovery of new and valuable country of great extent, extending from Lake George towards Western Port in Bass's Straits by two young men, Messrs Hovell and Hume, *the latter colonial.*[3] They [were] directed by me to reach Spencer's Gulf in the hope of interrupting any rivers that might run south. The above persons appear to have performed their duty well.

Not well enough, it would seem, for the government to recompense them for the hire of their own horses and bullocks as agreed before the expedition. In fact, the commissary made an official complaint when they returned only the muskets, the rest of the government equipment having have been worn out on the trek.

Nevertheless, Hume was sufficiently encouraged by Brisbane's response to seek a grant of land in a letter penned on 26 April 1825. Coincidentally, it was on this day that Dr Bland announced that he intended to edit and publish Hovell's journal of the expedition. In the event, it would not be completed and released to the public, nor to Hume, until 1831.

However, Hamilton Hume was preoccupied by more personal matters. He had built his cattle herds to the point where in June he was able to tender successfully to supply 1,000 pounds of beef to the government. He was also planning a return to the Hume River to trace its westward course in the belief that it probably emptied into Spencer's Gulf. But most importantly, he was courting the beautiful, if rather delicate, Elizabeth Dight, the second daughter of John and Hannah (nee Hilton) Dight.

Like others before and after him, John Dight was a ship's surgeon who abandoned the sea for the colonial life in 1801. Elizabeth was born the following year and raised on her parents' 'Durham Bowes' and 'Mountain View' properties at Richmond. And though it had been widely expected that Hamilton would marry one of the Broughton girls, the Humes and the Dights had long been friends. Hamilton and Elizabeth tied the knot at St Phillip's Anglican Church under the patient ministry of the Rev. William Cowper on 8 October 1825. Hamilton postponed indefinitely his return to the mighty Hume, and in so doing would lose the opportunity to confirm the family's name upon the country's greatest river.

Meanwhile, Brisbane had received the shattering news from Westminster that he was recalled. The only saving grace was that his administrative tormentor Goulburn had also received his marching orders. The governor's last months were plagued by one slanging match after another.

He was at odds with the Presbyterians led by the volatile Rev. John Dunmore Lang when he required them to share their place of worship – a schoolroom – with the Catholics. When he refused them a grant to build a church, Lang sailed back to England and enlisted Lord Bathurst himself in the cause. He claimed that Brisbane 'spends the greater part of his time in his observatory or shooting parrots'. In response, Bathurst scolded the governor for his 'ill-advised and extraordinary' action towards 'the members of the Church of Scotland, the established church of one of the most loyal and intelligent portions of Great Britain.'[4]

However, it was the Anglicans led by Samuel Marsden who would scrape the bottom of the moral barrel with a manufactured tale about Brisbane's (and Goulburn's) friend, the assistant-surgeon, Dr Henry Douglass. Marsden and his confederates alleged that Brisbane, Goulburn and Douglass were somehow involved in sending female convicts to the government farm at Emu Plains as prostitutes for the male convicts and passing travellers. This was one step too far for the 'flogging parson'. When a board of inquiry cleared Douglass and the others of all charges, Bathurst fired off an official letter debarring Marsden from any prominent public office and describing him as 'a very turbulent priest, with somewhat more of malignancy in his character than will allow him ever to be quiet, or let another person do so'.

Nevertheless, Brisbane's fate was sealed. He would leave the colony with a heavily pregnant Elizabeth and their son Thomas in November 1825. One of his final acts was to grant Hume and Hovell about two square miles of land each in recognition of their achievement. But both had to sell their land to repay the debts incurred in outfitting the expedition. And given the bounty to be delivered to government coffers from their discoveries, they had every reason to feel short-changed.

It was a sad departure. Brisbane's administration had been erratic and indecisive. His re-establishment of the Norfolk Island penal settlement and his treatment of the Aboriginal people were acts of a man totally in the thrall of an imperious religious code. His one notable achievement had been mapping the stars of the Southern Hemisphere. By late 1825, he and Dunlop, his Scottish compatriot, were able to publish a catalogue of 7,385 stars.

Brisbane endured a tragic journey home during which he and Elizabeth lost their newborn son. Indeed, they both witnessed the death of their four children – their two daughters in 1849 and 1852 and their only surviving son Thomas, the victim of plague, also in 1849. At the time he was serving in Gibraltar with the 34th Regiment, of which his father was colonel.

Brisbane died on 27 January 1860 at his Scottish home, in the room where he had been born 87 years before.

CHAPTER TWELVE

Not Western Port?

Governor Darling's controversial reign begins, he asks Hume to find a better way over the Great Divide, and Hovell jumps at the chance to return to Western Port.

When the new governor, General Ralph Darling, sailed through the Sydney Heads in the *Catherine Stewart Forbes* to take up his appointment on 17 December 1825, he had already performed an important vice-regal task. On the way through Bass Strait, the ship's captain had turned to starboard and sailed down the east coast to Hobart Town. There Darling and his family disembarked, and with a ceremonial flourish proclaimed the independence of the colony of Van Diemen's Land from New South Wales.

Administration of the new polity was entrusted to Lieutenant-Governor George Arthur, though Darling remained his superior as governor-in-chief. The two men shared a common military background and had similar conservative – not to say reactionary – political attitudes, though Arthur was the more approachable of the two.

Darling had been born in the slave colonies of the West Indies in 1775, the eldest son of a British Army sergeant-major in the 45th Infantry Regiment. Indeed, his life had been steeped in slavery. He enlisted at 14 in his father's regiment where his first job was a minor post in the Grenada Customs House. But at the outbreak of war against the French he was immediately involved in putting down a slave revolt on the island.

At 18 young Ralph was granted an officer's commission as an ensign in 'an act of charity' without having to make the usual payment. He then alternated between frontline fighting in the Napoleonic Wars and administrative duties among the staff officers. This bred 'a belief in the value of hierarchy, formality and obedience'.[1] It also confirmed his view of the essential superiority of imperial Britain and the men who made it so.

A year in India from 1805 was followed by the Peninsular Wars with the 51st Regiment as a lieutenant-colonel, after which he found a congenial billet at the Royal Horse Guards in London, where for the next decade he was responsible for army recruiting. On 4 June 1813, he was promoted from brevet colonel to major-general and by now he numbered himself among Britain's upper classes. Four years later, at 46, he confirmed his social position by marrying the 19-year-old Eliza Dumaresq, daughter of a wealthy Shropshire squire, and embraced his extended family. When he attained minor vice-regal status as acting governor of the tiny slave colony of Mauritius in 1819, he engaged both his brothers-in-law, Henry and William Dumaresq, in substantial administrative posts.

His predecessor on the island, Major-General Gage Hall, had tried to stop the smuggling of slaves into the colony, particularly from Madagascar; but he was outflanked by the sugar planters. When Darling took over, he paid the Madagascan chief, Radama, £2,000 a year in a futile attempt to at least slow the traffic. Then in a novel twist he actually imported 'convicts' – slaves by another name – from India and Ceylon. But at least he was able to create a slave 'register' and for that Lord Bathurst expressed his 'entire approbation'.

By the time he departed in 1823 he was deeply unpopular with the islanders, not least because of his decision to permit a British frigate to breach quarantine regulations, thereby starting a cholera epidemic. But since it was essentially a French colony temporarily under British military command, Whitehall was forgiving. Darling was 'efficient', according to the panjandrums, and after Brisbane's chaotic administration a dose of military efficiency was very much in order in the white slave colony of New South Wales.

They were also worried that a resurgent France might be tempted to claim at least part of the vast Australian continent. Between 1801 and 1803, Captain Nicolas Baudin had led an expedition of two ships down the west coast, across the Great Australian Bight to Van Diemen's Land where they charted the length of the east coast and engaged in extended contact with the Aboriginal people. They then turned north to the continental coastline and Baudin's compatriot in the *Naturaliste,* Captain Jacques Hamelin, headed for Sydney as he was short of food and water.

En route he explored Western Port and named an island in the bay Ile des Français. Then in early 1825, reports reached London that another French ship, *L'Astrolabe*, had visited the area. The Colonial Office took this as an indication that the southern inlet might well become the site of a French intrusion.

When Darling learned that Hume and Hovell had reached Western Port he asked Hume to return there by ship to survey it in more detail in preparation for a British settlement. He mounted a naval flotilla of two vessels, the *Fly* and the *Dragon*, to advance on the port and proclaim that all of 'New Holland' was under British sovereignty. Moreover, he ordered the commander Captain Samuel Wright to begin construction of the settlement.

The newly married Hamilton Hume declined the offer. He was fully engaged in developing his new Appin property. However, when Darling then turned to Hovell he jumped at the chance. On 9 November 1826, they set out accompanied by a detachment of the 3rd Regiment and 21 convicts. The weather was bad and the journey took 16 days. When they attempted to berth the ships they encountered great stretches of mudflat. They landed on Phillip Island, where they cleared a site for gun emplacements, which they named Fort Dumaresq after one of Darling's brothers-in-law who had followed him from Mauritius and now occupied top posts in his new administration. On 3 December, they fired a 21-gun salute and proclaimed the entire area for the British crown.

Once ashore it was immediately clear to everyone – with the notable exception of Hovell – that they were in the wrong place. Unlike the area that Hume had reported upon so favourably, Western Port was scrubby, muddy and with no fresh water stream to support a settlement. Though provided with horses and men to explore the area, Hovell was reluctant to admit the error, and recommended to Darling that Western Port was suitable for a substantial outpost.

However, his was a lone voice. Captain Wetherall of the *Fly*, who accompanied him on one of his expeditions, wrote, 'It is very evident that [Western Port] is not the country described by Messrs Hume and Hovell and that they could never have been there, as their accounts are not applicable to a single point in it or to the anchorage.'[2] Nevertheless, a reluctant Darling permitted the construction to continue. Captain Wright remained there into the new year when he handed over to Lieutenant Basil Burchell, who developed a timber mill and brickworks, barracks, a blacksmith's shop, a house for the commandant and a hut for a hospital. However, their efforts were in vain, and early in 1828 – with no further sign of French interest – Darling ordered the settlement abandoned.

Though he wrote to Secretary of State for the Colonies, Viscount Goderich, that, 'Nothing could have been less satisfactory than the information obtained from Mr Hovell,' Darling rewarded him for his participation with 1,280 acres of land, which Hovell claimed was 'on such conditions [that] it was no better than outright purchase'. When he complained and sought further grants, Darling's colonial secretary Alexander Macleay didn't bother to mince his words: 'His Excellency considers you have been amply remunerated for any public service you may [have] performed . . . your application cannot be complied with.'[3]

Meantime, Darling turned to Hume to solve the critical need for a more practical and efficient route over the Blue Mountains in place of Cox's perilous goat track. By 1827 there were so many whole trees cut down as coach anchors and abandoned on descent that they clogged the track, and gangs of convicts had to be sent to burn them. The road was a ribbon of bogs, swamps, boulders and mud, and since it was carved through thick scrub there was no grass adjoining it to feed the cattle that travelled its route. The task had great appeal for Hume. Having opened up the vast riches to the south of the settlement, it was apt that he should assist in cutting through the final barriers to the rich western plains.

On Friday, 28 September 1827, *The Australian* reported: 'Mr Hamilton Hume set off from town on Tuesday on a new journey into the interior.' And a few days later *The Monitor* added, 'That enterprising Australian, Mr Hume, has started an expedition to the interior. The gentleman's merits as a traveller are likely it seems to be appreciated by the present government which we are glad of on all accounts, for the sake of Mr Hume, for the sake of science and the country.'

Since he was traversing familiar country, Hume almost certainly travelled alone with a single hack and a packhorse for his supplies. He apparently kept a diary, but it has been lost to history. However, he spent a full month ranging the area and seeking alternatives. He then sent a prompt report and a proposed route to Alexander Macleay (also lost) who passed it immediately to the surveyor-general, John Oxley, and suggested a surveyor should inspect it as soon as possible.

That duty fell to the new deputy surveyor-general, Major Thomas Mitchell, who set out with Hume and assistant surveyor George White. Mitchell was impressed. As he wrote to Macleay:

> Instead of descending into the valley at Mount York, Mr Hume proposed that the road should continue along the dividing range (called Darling's Causeway) which separates from the Mount York branch at about four miles eastward of that extremity and extends westward until it heads the sources of the Grose [River]. From thence the general direction is N. West to the separation of the ranges N. East of Walerawang . . . Mr Hume

> has also marked a shorter road which would pass through Lithgow Valley and to the Southward of the Sugarloaf or Mount Walker, a remarkable hill situated about nine miles South of Walerawang. It would then cross Cox's River.
>
> As a line of road to Bathurst which should also avoid Mounts York and Blaxland and also Cox's River, this line of Mr Hume's seems to me the most eligible that can be found. The straight line of direction is about midway between the present road and that marked by Mr Hume.

This was a major advance on the current thoroughfare but before recommending it Mitchell wanted to examine an even straighter line if practicable. Hume also believed the route could be refined and he set out again to do so. He returned early in December and reported directly to Mitchell. He then told *The Gazette* that:

> The range I discovered leads off three or four miles on this side of Mount York in a North West direction; it is the main leading range of that part of the country and is in general very even, lightly timbered and composed of good material for making a road – and it is the dividing range between the eastern and western waters.

He then gave three alternative descents from the range, but in the event, Mitchell opted for a slightly different route. By then they had become fast friends, and the governor recognised Hume's achievement with the granting of a further 1,280 acres of land without any of the arduous conditions attached to Hovell's grant. Hume chose Booroo, a magnificent pastoral prospect at the western end of the Yass Plains, and later called the property 'Humewood' in memory of a family seat in Ireland's County Wicklow.

His association with the Scottish-born Mitchell, who would become surveyor-general the following year, had a particularly pleasing consequence. Hume's influence was behind one of Mitchell's first instructions to his assistant surveyors that would perpetuate Australia's Aboriginal heritage. 'You will be particular in noting the native names of as many places as you can,' he wrote. 'The natives can furnish you with the names of every flat and almost every hill and the settlers [must] select their grants by these names. The names of new parishes will also be taken from the local name of the natives.'

Prior to his second trip through the Blue Mountains, Hume found himself caught up in a rising tide of bushranging activity. Darling's treatment of the convicts, whether serving their time or emancipated, was even more draconian and divisive than his predecessor's. British notions of class were observed even more strictly in the colony than in England itself, becoming as unbending as the caste system in India. But conditions in the vast interior, with its scattered population and wild redoubts, gave the rebels among them – particularly the Irish – an alternative to a life of sublimation to the system, albeit a hazardous and temporary one.

The road to Parramatta was particularly prone to hold-up and by 1828 bushranging had become so prevalent that in some areas travellers armed themselves and banded together before setting out. At the same time a 'bush telegraph' arose among the 'hutkeepers' and downtrodden emancipists with their few scrubby acres, who not only provided the bushrangers with information on police movements, but also harboured them when necessary; and others 'fenced' the proceeds of their robberies.

Most prominent was 'the Wild Colonial Boy', the Dublin-born Bold Jack Donahue, transported to New South Wales in 1825 for 'intent to commit a felony'. He was assigned to a road gang and then the Quakers Hill property of Assistant-Surgeon West, whose rank and given name (Major) were identical. After receiving two punishments of 50 lashes each he escaped and went bush with fellow convicts Kilroy and Smith.

Their gang quickly became known as 'The Strippers', as they stripped wealthy landowners of their horses, clothes, money and food. Captured while robbing bullock drays on the Sydney–Windsor road, they were sentenced to death (twice) by Judge John Stephen on 1 March 1827. Kilroy and Smith were both hanged, but Donahue escaped between the Sydney court and the jail in Sussex Street.

For the next two-and-a-half years he became the most celebrated bushranger in the country, as he and his gang ranged from Bathurst to Yass, east to the Illawarra and north to Wollombi on the approaches to the Hunter River valley. Darling put a price of £200 on his head, but there were no takers. By now he was 22 years old, and 163 centimetres tall with flaxen hair and blue eyes. And romanticised tales of his derring-do circulated through the colony.

Hamilton Hume's first brush with the outlaws occurred when his brother-in-law George Barber was accosted by John Walsh (sometimes Welsh) at Stonequarry Creek near Appin as he drove his chaise home. A musket ball struck him in the neck, but he refused to stop until Walsh overtook him and shoved a pistol in his chest. When Barber told the outlaw of his famous relation, Walsh reportedly said, 'I'm sure I'll be hanged for you,' and disappeared into the bush. Chief Constable Edward Farley contacted Hume, and with two of his Aboriginal compatriots the quartet tracked Walsh to his hideout where they surprised and captured him. Judge John Stephen extended his transportation for life but he escaped and after a series of hold-ups was finally hanged in 1842.

However, bushranging was only one of many issues that were confirming Lord Bathurst's view that as governor, Ralph Darling would prove 'a troublesome gentleman'. He zealously followed Bathurst's instructions to enforce 'discipline' among any Aboriginal people who dared to resist the colonial incursions. The secretary of state had ordered him to 'repel such Aggression in the same manner as if they proceeded from subjects of an accredited State,' virtually a declaration of war. But at the same time – and somewhat paradoxically – he was to promote 'Religion and Education' among them in cooperation with the Anglican archdeacon Thomas Hobbs Scott.

The churchman was much better connected to the English aristocracy than Darling. His father had been chaplain to George III and, though he was a confirmed bachelor, his three brothers, Oxford graduates like himself, had married well within their class; one of his sisters wed the Earl of Oxford, another married a leading conservative MP and the third was matched with Commissioner Bigge who engaged Scott – before he took holy orders – as his secretary on his New South Wales investigation and report.

During this earlier sojourn in the colony Scott had become friends with John Macarthur, and soon after his return to New South Wales Scott invested in his giant Australian Agricultural Company with its million-acre grant for grazing on the Manning

River between Newcastle and Port Macquarie. Though he nominally answered to the Bishop of Calcutta, he was granted the widest latitude and invariably dealt directly with his principals in London who sought – without success – to have the Church of England recognised as the 'Established' religious organisation within the colonial governance.

Darling's relations with him were at best formal and at worst hostile. But that was typical of the governor's interaction at all levels of colonial society save his own extended family and the loyal, 'hearty and cheerful' Alexander Macleay, with his private passion for butterfly and insect collecting. Macleay had arrived in the colony ahead of Darling, and was well regarded in Whitehall, though he would also attract a share of the hatred and animosity directed at the governor by his most virulent enemies, the newspaper proprietors William Wentworth and Edward Smith Hall.

Wentworth's fractious, idiosyncratic personality was by now well known through the columns of his *Australian* newspaper. However, Smith Hall took belligerent independence to a new level when in May 1826 he and Arthur Hill published the first issue of *The Monitor* with its motto: 'Nothing extenuate nor set down in malice.' In fact, his enemies in the Darling administration would charge him time and again with malice aforethought. And often enough the courts would agree with them.

By 1826, he had been in the colony for 14 years, during which he had made a reputation as a vigorous social leader and a poor farmer. He had been influential in setting up the Bank of New South Wales and acted for a time as its only employee, living in its tiny George Street premises to guard the daily deposits. He had received land grants from Macquarie, which he had been forced to sell, but in 1821 he resigned as coroner to try again at his 'St Heliers' property at Lake Bathurst. However, after four years and with the impending death of his first wife, Charlotte, he returned to Sydney and left the property to the management of his 19-year-old son Edward.

The Monitor quickly became the mouthpiece of the 'have-nots' in Darling's stratified society, and a clash with the military disciplinarian soon followed. The system of governance that had given successive governors untrammelled powers was due for review in 1828, and the more liberal members of the community – Wentworth and Smith Hall prominent among them – sought the rights of a representative assembly and trial by jury. They presented these claims by petition to the governor shortly after his arrival. Darling was thoroughly unimpressed; and, as was his wont, made his feelings plain. The newspapermen responded with a campaign designed to blast the vice-regal martinet out of his Georgian mansion.

Darling was uniquely vulnerable. His treatment of his own troops of the 57th Regiment was so oppressive that, according to journalist and author Marcus Clarke:

> a pernicious and dangerous feeling ran current in the garrison that to be a soldier was not always to be better off than a convict. More suicides took place in the [regiment] than in any other corps quartered there before or since – five men . . . committed robberies in order to obtain their discharge, while two had incurably mutilated themselves for the same purpose.

However, instead of 'lightening the military yoke' Darling vowed that he would 'take dire vengeance on any exponent of the rebellious doctrine'.[4]

So when Privates Joseph Sudds and Patrick Thompson robbed a Jewish shopkeeper of a length of calico with the obvious purpose of securing their discharge and sentence to a distant penal colony, Darling was outraged. On 8 November 1826, they were tried and sentenced to seven years transportation. All went to plan, and on leaving the dock Thompson smiled to the military judge, 'I hope your Honour will let me take my fire-lock. It may be useful to me in the bush.'

When Darling heard of it, he commuted the sentence, directed that they be publicly stripped of their uniforms, and for the next seven years they would work in chains on the road gangs before being returned to their regiment. Moreover, while in prison Sudds and Thompson were loaded with heavier irons than those placed upon the most desperate convicts, and round their necks were spiked iron collars attached by another set of chains to their ankle fetters. The projecting spikes prevented them from lying down and the connecting chains were too short to allow them to stand upright.

Unknown to Darling, Sudds was suffering from 'dropsy and bronchitis', and he died in prison five days later. This was journalistic manna from heaven for Wentworth and Smith Hall.

CHAPTER THIRTEEN

Sturt's Search for an Inland Sea

Darling encounters further troubles, and Hume leads Charles Sturt on an expedition to find the inland sea.

As a practising barrister, Wentworth was perfectly placed to carry the fight to the governor. He pursued it in his newspaper, and when Darling sought legal support for his actions from his chief justice Sir Francis Forbes, Wentworth put the opposing case. Forbes found that the governor had no right to commute the sentence of the two soldiers to labour in the chain gang and ordered Thompson released. However, Darling took the issue to his Executive Council, and with the support of his brother-in-law Captain Henry Dumaresq as council secretary, his actions were approved. He wrote to Lord Bathurst assuring him he had the matter well in hand.

But then came the newspapermen's dream witness. Captain Robert Robison of the Royal Veterans provided them with personal testimony of the horrific nature of Thompson's treatment.

> I was returning from the command of the Bathurst district when we stopped a night at the government station at Emu Plains. The chains that Private Thompson worked in were brought for us to see . . . I was induced to put them on my own person. I found it quite impossible while I had the collar and irons on me to lie down, except on my back or face, there being two long iron spikes projecting from the iron collar, which was riveted round the neck, independently of which there were two chains on either side extending from the collar [to] those on the legs. I guessed the weight at about 30 lbs or 40 lbs, or even upwards.

Armed with this fresh information, Wentworth succeeded in assembling a commission consisting of Alexander Macleay, Acting Attorney-General William Moore and himself on board the maritime hulk *Phoenix* to examine Thompson. The aggrieved soldier, now confident of public support, made much of the cruelties he and Sudds had endured. *The Australian* and *The Monitor* carried full reports.

An enraged Darling then ordered Robison's court-martial and dismissal from the service and hit back at the press by proposing a stamp duty on the papers and a licence to publish that could be revoked by the governor. Wentworth took the issue to the courts and once again Chief Justice Forbes – sitting with Judge Stephen – demurred.

Darling's fury was palpable, not least because prior to his leaving England he had been told that he should impose some form of press censorship, but during his first months in Sydney he'd insisted it was unnecessary. Now he believed the judiciary had joined with the journalists in a conspiracy against him.

He complained that Forbes was 'a republican, sympathetic to dreadful Yankee principles, greedy of power' and 'conducting a systematic opposition to my government'. According to his biographer, 'As the year went on Darling became more and more excited. He wrote at enormous length and very repetitively to London. He saw insults and intrigues everywhere.'[1]

Fortunately they did not extend to Hamilton Hume and his fellow explorers. Hume retained a very active interest in the field and was in constant touch with its leading figures. But even there turmoil reigned.

In 1828, when John Oxley died at only 48, partly from the 'privations' of his several exhausting expeditions to the interior, he was succeeded as surveyor-general by Hume's friend Thomas Mitchell. Born in Grangemouth, Scotland in 1792, Mitchell came from humble parentage, but had a remarkable inquiring mind and at only 19 was commissioned in the field during the Peninsular Wars. His military patron was Sir George Murray, the quartermaster-general, who in 1814 selected him to produce plans of the major Peninsular battlefields. Four years later in the wake of the Napoleonic campaign he married Mary, the 18-year-old daughter of General Richard Blunt, one of Wellington's favourite commanders. After the war he was placed on half pay and promoted to captain, but in 1827 with Murray's support he was appointed to the post of assistant surveyor-general in New South Wales with the assurance that he would eventually succeed Oxley.

He arrived in Sydney with at least four of the 12 children – six of each – that he and Mary would produce in the land of their adoption. He was appalled to discover a shockingly run-down department. Oxley had allowed his pessimism towards the colony's potential to affect his professional diligence. And he was equally lax in his own financial affairs; they were in such a parlous state that the authorities made an ex gratia grant of 5,000 acres to his grieving sons to save the family from total penury.

Mitchell had scarcely enough surveying instruments to go round; most of his surveyors were incompetent; and small areas had been surveyed without any attempt to relate them into the bigger picture. This led to violent disputes at the boundaries. When he set about making a general survey, he had to use tent poles to measure a baseline and have hilltops cleared of every tree but one to create trigonometrical points.

Happily Sir George Murray was appointed secretary of state for the colonies in 1828, so Mitchell had a direct line to the source of power. Murray would not remain long in politics and was regarded as 'an old soldier and a high-bred gentleman' who looked the part but did little more than promote his Scottish friends and relatives from his native Perthshire. Though Mitchell had to take care not to offend the irascible Darling, the secretary cast a kindly eye from the Colonial Office and in turn Mitchell's private letters kept him fully informed of his plans and progress.

Mitchell's initial trip over the Divide to Bathurst with Hamilton Hume had whetted his appetite for more journeys of discovery. But a combination of his new administrative tasks, Darling's suspicions and a very ambitious young military aide to the governor in Captain Charles Sturt, meant that he was denied leadership of the first great expedition undertaken in the new regime. Sturt was given the assignment to answer the question that Hovell had alluded to and that had bedevilled the colonisers since they first ventured beyond the Great Divide and discovered a multiplicity of streams heading west: was there a great inland freshwater sea that would provide the water required to support a thriving continental agricultural settlement?

Most believed that the answer held the key to the success or failure of the entire colonial venture, and the colonists were split fairly evenly according to their natural disposition as optimists or pessimists. But unquestionably, the leader of an expedition to confirm its existence would be hailed as an imperial hero. From the beginning, Sturt was undoubtedly a believer.

Mitchell took the governor's decision badly. Not only did he match Sturt for ambition; his middle name was Livingstone, and exploration was in his blood. He and Sturt would become sworn enemies thereafter. However, he warmly approved when on 23 October 1828 the governor's aide-de-camp, Captain William Dumaresq, wrote to Hamilton Hume seeking his engagement as the expedition's second-in-command.

The Australian pathfinder was now 31 and in excellent health. He had established his Appin farm as a base and had stocked his Yass property with both sheep and cattle. He was ready for a new challenge.

On the question of the inland sea, he was agnostic. He had crossed the Lachlan, the Murrumbidgee and the Hume, all of which were heading west, and he had surmised that the biggest of them would find its outlet to the sea at Spencer's Gulf. But since he had declined that second journey to confirm his suspicions, he was happy to let the facts decide.

The Aboriginal people provided no certain answers to the intruders' questions, but in any case by now the colonial establishment regarded them as a thoroughly untrustworthy 'enemy'. Undoubtedly Hume made his own inquiries among them, but while there is evidence that there was extensive trading between tribal groups and a general cooperative system of fire management, language and territorial barriers precluded a definitive answer.

Aware of Mitchell's 'back channel' to Murray, Darling wrote to the secretary of state justifying his decision to choose Sturt as leader. 'Though some time in the country,' he said

> [Sturt] has had but little opportunity of being practically acquainted with its character. In order therefore to afford him the assistance of an experienced Traveller, I have attached Mr Hume to the expedition, who made an excursion Southward in the neighbourhood of Western Port during Sir Thomas Brisbane's administration. He is an enterprising man, whose knowledge of the country generally and experience in conducting an establishment of this nature now employed cannot fail to promote the success of the expedition.

In fact, Sturt had first wanted the veteran botanist Allan Cunningham as his deputy since he had already experienced the rigours of the north-west in his expedition west of Moreton Bay, during which he discovered the 'Gap' in the mountains that now bears his name. And for all his bush experience, Hume was two years Sturt's junior, and the military man had led a singularly circumscribed life.

Born in India to a judicial officer of the East India Company, Sturt had been sent 'home' to England aged only five to live with relatives and at 15 enrolled in the exclusive Harrow school. His father could not afford to send him to Cambridge, but his aunt had a social connection to the Prince Regent and used it to gain him a commission as ensign in the 39th Regiment. Like so many of the military men who populate early Australian history, he too served in the Peninsular Wars. He then fought against the Americans in Canada and returned to England a few days after Waterloo. Service in France and Ireland followed before he was sent with a detachment of his regiment in December 1826 to take charge of a cargo of convicts bound for New South Wales in the *Mariner.*

Once arrived on 23 May 1827 Sturt revealed what colleagues saw as his overweening ambition and secured the plum post of 'military secretary' in the office of the governor. Within six months, the tall, slim officer with his aquiline nose and close-set eyes had pressed his case to lead an expedition to the interior to solve the riddle of the rivers. The governor gave the vice-regal nod but by then he was so caught up in his various feuds and vendettas that it was almost a year before he signed off on the detailed arrangements.

Sturt finally departed Sydney with three soldiers and eight convicts on 10 November 1828. Hume joined them in Bathurst, having left Elizabeth somewhat reluctantly as she was enduring one of her many bouts of ill-health. Before leaving he asked the governor, through Alexander Berry, to assign a soldier to keep watch on her welfare.

The explorers made for the government station in Wellington to collect their stores, livestock and equipment. The contrast with his own poorly supplied expedition would not have been lost on Hume. There was flour aplenty and enough salted beef and pork to ensure no one would go hungry. The convicts were trained farriers, carpenters and harness makers; their six horses were well broken; and their 12 bullocks in fine condition. Hume took a few days at the start to train them to pull the carts, on which they even carried a well-appointed boat.

However, in the first days of their journey they travelled through a landscape blasted by drought. This was a mixed blessing, since it meant that the rivers would be fairly easy to cross, but they would have to ration the drinking water. Nevertheless, by heading north-west they made very good initial progress. On 4 December, Hume wrote to Elizabeth's brother Lin Dight:

> The drought appears to have been very great in this part of the colony, so much so that the Macquarie River here can be crossed without wetting your foot . . . but I must say that the land and the grass around this country are equal to any I ever saw and upon the flooded lands and the banks of rivers there are quantities of very large apple trees and blue gums. The former timber I never before saw growing so far in the interior.
>
> It is my opinion that this is not the part of the country to look for rivers, for there is not a drop of water to be found in the back forest at any distance from the main streams, and they are very few and of little magnitude.

They were moving through sparsely settled country but the landholders they met were pleased to see them. Hume says, 'Dr McLeod accompanied us to the plain. He is really a pleasant, good-natured fellow.'[2]

Hume was in his element as scout, interpreter and negotiator with the Aboriginal people they encountered, and easily the best shot in the group when bagging kangaroos to complement the larder. According to Sturt, he was particularly adept when the cattle strayed 'in tracking the animals [and effecting] their speedy recovery'. Soon the military man joined him out front of the team, especially in the evenings when he probed forward to discover the best route – and the nearest water – for the following day's journey.

They met many Aboriginal people during the first weeks, and on one occasion when violence threatened, Hume strode forward and temporarily exchanged his rifle for an Aboriginal spear. Belligerence turned to fellowship in a moment. A few days later, more than 50 accompanied them. Hume was able to converse with them, and both groups soon relaxed in each other's company. Further on, Sturt found himself alone in the lead when he came upon a shady glen sheltering 'a very numerous tribe of natives' with an old man standing before them. He saluted the horseman. 'Behind him the young men stood in a line,' Sturt says, 'and behind them the warriors were seated on the ground.'[3]

> I had a young native with me who had attached himself to our party and who, from his extreme good nature and superior intelligence was considered by us as a first-rate kind of fellow. He explained who and what we were and I was glad to observe that the old chief seemed perfectly reconciled to my presence, although he cast many an anxious glance at the long train of animals that were approaching.

The warriors, by contrast were 'hideously painted with red and yellow ochre and had their weapons at their sides, while their countenances were fixed, sullen and determined'.

But Sturt had learned his lesson well. He rode to the warriors and temporarily swapped his rifle for a spear. 'They immediately relaxed from their gravity,' he says, 'and as soon as my party arrived, rose up and followed us . . . The young native acted as interpreter and by his facetious manner, contrived to keep the whole of us in a fit of laughter as we moved along.'

When they reached Mount Harris (between modern-day Nyngan and Gulargambone), which had been discovered and named by Oxley in 1818, they were at the outer boundary of settlement. 'There are some men and a native of this place,' Hume wrote, 'going with us so far to bring back letters.' So he included a second letter that has survived to ask Lin Dight to jog Alexander Berry's promise about Elizabeth's military guard. Henceforth whatever diary notes or journal entries Hume might have made have been lost. But unlike his earlier garrulous companion on the southern trip, Charles Sturt kept a meticulously accurate record of their journey; and it is filled with glowing references to his second-in-command. 'Mr Hume's experience rendered it unnecessary for me to give him other than general instructions,' he says.

They climbed Mount Harris, where Oxley had dragged a boat on rollers. The rotting shell of the craft was still there and it kindled a wave of melancholy in Sturt as he contemplated the transient nature of life. 'Only a week before I left Sydney,' he says,

> I had followed Mr Oxley to the tomb. A man of uncommon quickness and great ability, the task of following up his discoveries was not less enviable than arduous. But, arrived at that point at which his journey may be said to have terminated and mine only to commence, I knew not how soon I should be obliged, like him, to retreat from the marshes and exhalations of so depressed a country.

Once beyond Mount Harris, they expected to find the 'interminable marshes' described by Oxley but instead discovered mudflats caked dry. The company's morale was quickly sapped by an almost unbearable heatwave that sent temperatures above 43° Celsius for days on end, and on occasion soaring to 53° in the shade. On one hellish day, it reached an almost unbelievable 65° in the sun.

Having found a few billabongs on a river course, they turned further to the north-west. 'We issued at length upon a plain,' Sturt says,

> the view across which was as dreary as can be imagined; in many places without a tree, save a few old stumps left by the natives when they fired the timber, some of which were still smoking . . . on this exposed spot the sun's rays fell with intense power upon us, and the dust was so minute and penetrating that I soon regretted having left the shady banks of the river.

By now at least two of the party, Henwood and Williams, were suffering from painful eye infections; then two others, Riley and Spencer, went down with dysentery. Sturt does not make it clear whether they were convicts or soldiers, but since Riley and Spencer recovered and returned to Wellington to report the expedition's progress to the governor, we can assume that at least one of them was a military man.

On 26 November, Hume and Sturt rode forward of the party to a belt of trees where, Sturt says, 'We found an absolute check to our further progress. We had been moving directly on the great body of the marsh, and from the wood it spread in boundless extent before us.' The two leaders decided to camp there and split their resources to see if one or other could find a way through. 'It was therefore arranged,' Sturt says, 'that I should take two men and a week's provision with me in the boat down the river; and that [Hume] should proceed with a like number of men on an excursion to the northward.'[4]

Sturt's journey through the tangled web of streams, fallen trees and sudden mud banks was as exhausting as it was frustrating. They lifted the boat over one log after another, and found their legs covered in leeches. The drought broke with a downpour and at night they found a raised hump where the men cut away reeds to provide a space to unroll their swags. 'At 2 am it commenced raining with a heavy storm of thunder and lightning,' he says,

> the boat was hauled ashore and turned over to provide us a temporary shelter. The lightning was extremely vivid, and frequently played upon the ground for more than a quarter of a minute at a time . . . Notwithstanding that the elements were raging around me, as if to warn me of the danger of my situation, my mind turned solely on the singular failure of the river . . . to lead us to an open space.[5]

At dawn he made for a second channel, which took him back to camp. There he found Hume who had discovered 'a serpentine sheet of water about twelve miles to the northward', which he believed was a river channel. 'On the morning of the 28th therefore we broke up the camp,' Sturt says, 'and proceeded northward under Mr Hume's guidance, moving over ground wholly subject to flood, and extensively covered with reeds; the great body of the marsh lying on our left.'

This took them to a rich open plain. 'Crossing it in a westerly direction we arrived at the channel found by Mr Hume. The boat was immediately prepared, and I went up in it to ascertain the nature of its formation.' By now all his melancholy thoughts were cast aside. It was just possible that it led to the entrance of the great inland sea.

CHAPTER FOURTEEN

The Search for the Inland Sea Continues

Hume and Sturt encounter obstacles, including blinding sun and tormenting mosquitoes, and eventually reach the Darling.

Alas, there was no inland sea. But Sturt was just at the beginning of his quest. 'For two miles it preserved a pretty general width of from twenty to thirty yards; but at that distance began to narrow, and at length became quite shallow and covered with weeds,' Sturt says. 'We were ultimately obliged to abandon the boat and to walk along a native path.'[1]

After pressing on through fairly open country they found another running stream, so they returned for the boat and the two leaders sailed it westward until it too became 'completely lost in a second expanse of reeds'. However, it was here they discovered some remarkable Aboriginal handiwork 'with a singular scaffolding erected by the natives on the side of the channel to take fish. [We] also found a weir for the like purpose,' Sturt says, 'so it was evident the natives occasionally ventured into the marshes.' Hamilton Hume climbed a big tree to reconnoitre the area, and to Sturt's dismay discovered that the marsh extended in every direction but particularly to the north. 'I really felt at a loss what step to take,' he says.[2]

By now Christmas had passed with barely a mention in his journal. Hume set out to the north-east to discover whether they could penetrate the soggy barrier in that direction and the heatwave returned with a vengeance. Sturt decided to give his men a few days rest. However, he found inaction impossible, and on 31 December he and several men crossed the river channel and headed closer to true north than Hume. No sooner had he reached a vast, well-covered sandy plain than he was confronted by Aboriginal fire management. The area was 'almost wholly enveloped in flames,' he says. 'The fire was running with incredible rapidity.' He and his party ran hell-for-leather to escape the flames. 'It was not until after sunset that we struck upon a creek and we halted on its banks for the night.'

Hume rejoined the group and it was clear that they were in an area much favoured by the Aboriginal people since there were several 'huts' and heaps of mussel shells. The fire had burned up the feed for the expedition's livestock so they moved down the creek line and came upon a big Aboriginal camp. 'We now observed a number of huts, out of which the natives issued, little dreaming of the spectacle they would behold,' Sturt says.

> But the moment they saw us they started back . . . and each with a firebrand ran to and fro with hideous yells, thrusting them into every bush they passed. Their huts were in a moment in flames.
>
> I walked my horse quietly towards an old man who stood more forward than the rest, as if he intended to devote himself

> for the preservation of his tribe. I remarked that he trembled so violently that it was impossible to expect that I could obtain any information from him; and as I had not time for explanations, I left him to form his own conjectures as to what we were and continued to move towards a thick brush, into which they did not venture to follow us.

They travelled north for almost 30 kilometres before reaching a creek, where they watered and rested the livestock.

Once more on the move they found themselves in gently rising country leading to stony ridges and thick acacia scrub. But just before sunset they found an open space to camp.

> The day had been extremely warm and our animals were as thirsty as ourselves. Hope never forsakes the human breast; and thence it was that, after we had secured the horses, we began to wander around our lonely bivouac. It was almost dark when one of my men came to inform me that he had found a small puddle of water, to which he had been led by a pigeon.

It was just enough to sustain them.

The next day they left the sandy country and found rich red soil leading to a mountain range. Sturt and Hume climbed a peak to see what lay before them, and reached the summit just as the sun was setting. Sturt says, 'My eyes, from exposure to the glare had become so weak, my face so blistered and my lips cracked in so many places that I was unable to look towards the west and was actually obliged to sit behind a rock until it set.'

They descended to the plain, where they were tormented by mosquitoes, and several of the men complained of illness.

Then one of the convicts named Norman set out on his horse looking for water and became lost for three days, until Hume found him with the assistance of some Aborigines he met along the way. The leaders were now scouting separately and sharing their discoveries before deciding which way to proceed. This time Hume made a much longer foray than usual, returning after four days with reports of good country ahead, well watered and stocked with kangaroos and wild fowl. He had also made contact with several Aboriginal groups. It was a useful patrol, but next morning he was decidedly unwell.

Hume rested while Sturt returned to Mount Harris for more supplies and to send back reports. When he rejoined the party a week later, they had made only about 25 kilometres north of where he had left them. And now lack of water was becoming critical. 'Mr Hume, who was quite unfit for great exertion, underwent considerable bodily fatigue in his anxiety to find some,' Sturt says.

> Neither men nor animals were now in a condition to travel; and Mr Hume had endeavoured to obtain a supply of water by digging pits among the reeds. From these he had drawn sufficient for the wants of the people when I arrived. Mr Hume, I was sorry to observe, looked very unwell; but nothing could prevent him from further endeavours to extricate the party from its present embarrassment.
>
> As soon as I had taken a little refreshment, therefore, I mounted a fresh horse; and he accompanied me across a small plain immediately in front of the camp.

The quest for water took until nine o'clock that night when they discovered a small lake. But as they returned it rained and the pits Hume had dug filled with more than enough water for man and beast alike. The Australian pathfinder soon recovered, but over the next few days as they headed to the north-west they were again in danger of dying of thirst.

'Our provisions were running short,' Sturt says, 'and if a knowledge of the distant interior was to be gained, we had no time to lose. I was determined, therefore, to pursue such a course as would soonest and most effectually enable us to determine the character of the western interior.'

The great inland sea seemed as far away as ever.

On the evening of 18 January 1829, they broke camp and travelled to a creek they had crossed upstream previously. 'But both Mr Hume and I were so fatigued that we were glad of an opportunity to rest, even for a single day,' Sturt says. However, they were suddenly overwhelmed by thousands of insects he identified as 'kangaroo flies'. They were 'about half the size of the common house fly, had flat, brown bodies, and their bite, although sharp and piercing, left no irritation after it.'

During the day, he says:

> they appeared to rise from the ground, and as fast as they were swept off were succeeded by fresh numbers. It was utterly impossible to avoid their persecution, penetrating as they did into the tents. The men were obliged to put handkerchiefs over their faces and stockings upon their hands; but they bit through everything. To add to our discomfort the animals were driven almost to madness, and galloped to and fro in so furious a manner that I was apprehensive some of them would have been lost. I never experienced such a day of torment; only when the sun set did these little creatures cease from their attacks.

Next day at noon, they stopped beside a creek where the cattle were able to feed. But in the afternoon they were again in open country where, he says,

> Nothing could exceed in dreariness the appearance of the tracks through which we journeyed, on this day and the two following. The creek on which we depended for a supply of water gave such alarming indications of a total failure that I had serious thoughts of abandoning my pursuit of it. We passed hollow after hollow that had successively dried up, and when we at length found water . . . sometimes in boiling it left a sediment nearly equal to half its body; at other times it was so bitter as to be quite unpalatable . . . There was scarcely a living creature, even of the feathered race, to be seen to break the stillness of the forest. The native dogs alone wandered about, though they had scarcely strength to avoid us; and their melancholy howl, breaking in upon the ear at the dead of night, only served to impress more fully on the mind the absolute loneliness of the desert.[3]

Day after day they pressed forward from one small billabong to another, and Sturt began to have serious doubts about the fabled inland sea. 'If the rivers of the interior had already exhausted themselves,' he asked himself, 'what had we to expect from a creek whose diminished appearance where we left it made us apprehend its speedy termination.'

There was, however, one saving grace: 'the improved condition of the men'. Hume in particular was back to form. Unfortunately, the same could not be said for the cattle and horses. 'They were in a sad plight,' he says. 'I proposed to Mr Hume therefore to give them a few days' rest.'

While they were regathering their strength, Sturt, Hume and two others scouted the area and two days later came upon a gentle upland 'where the country appeared like one continuous meadow', he says. 'I never saw anything like the luxuriance of the grass on this tract of country, waving as it did higher than our horses' middles as we rode through it.'

They were now on Oxley's Tableland and, with the rest of the party, crossed the plateau in good order, leaving it on 31 January heading north through brush and across a wide plain. It was thinly covered by box trees providing homes for hundreds of topknot pigeons. On the other side, they reached a very wide, dry creek bed, which they followed with Hume leading the way in quest of water. In all their searching, they found but a single pond. 'It is impossible for me to describe the relief I felt at this success,' Sturt says, 'or the gladness it spread among the men.'[4]

Next day they left the creek line and swung to the west following an Aboriginal track with footprints indicating it had been recently in use. At sunset, Sturt and Hume crossed another broad, dry riverbed with flooded gum growing on its banks. 'We returned to the camp after a vain search for water,' Sturt says:

> and were really at a loss what direction next to pursue. The men kept the cattle pretty well together [overnight] and, as we were not delayed by any preparations for breakfast, they were saddled and loaded at an early hour.
>
> As the path we had observed was leading northerly, we took up that course and had not proceeded more than a mile upon it, when we suddenly found ourselves on the banks of a noble river! The channel was from seventy to eighty

> yards broad and enclosed an unbroken sheet of water, evidently very deep, and literally covered with pelicans and other wild fowl. Our surprise and delight may be better imagined than described!
>
> Our difficulties appeared to be at an end, for here was a river that promised to reward all our exertions, and which every moment appeared to increase in importance to our imagination. Coming from the north-east and flowing to the south-west, it had a capacity of channel that proved we were as far from its source as from its termination. The paths of the natives on either side of it were like well-trodden roads; and the trees that overhung it were of beautiful and gigantic growth.

They had reached the Darling.

The banks were too steep for the cattle to negotiate, but that didn't stop the men from flinging themselves down with joyous shouts and leaping face first into the water. Sturt says, 'I shall never forget the cry of amazement that followed their doing so, or the looks of terror and disappointment . . . the water was so salt as to be unfit to drink!'

Sturt was no less shattered than his men.

> Our hopes were annihilated . . . the cup of joy was dashed out of our hands before we could raise it to our lips. Not even the cattle would drink it, but when they reached it stood covered in it for many hours, having their noses alone exposed above the stream.

Sturt's thoughts turned to the great inland sea and the possibility that it was not only salt but tidal. But then Hume scattered sticks on the water, and if there was a current it was 'barely perceptible'. Sturt was torn between wild elation and crushing despair. 'Its fish were so numerous,' he noted, 'their leaping kept the surface in constant agitation' and the pelicans indicated 'some Mediterranean or other'; yet despite all the signs of human traffic there was not a soul in sight.

Hume took the initiative and, according to Sturt:

> with his usual perseverance [he] walked out when camp was formed and at a little distance from it ascended a ridge of pure sand crowned with cypresses. From this he descended to the west and at length struck upon the river where a reef of rocks crossed its channel. Curiosity led him to cross it, when he found a small pond of fresh water on a tongue of land and immediately afterwards returned to acquaint me with the welcome tidings. It was too late to move, but we had at least, the prospect of a comfortable breakfast in the morning.

Next day they watered the cattle in the pond and replenished their own supplies. They followed the course of the river to the south-west, and on the afternoon of 5 February they came upon a scene almost as remarkable and unexpected as the salty river. Just back from the banks was group of 70 Aboriginal 'huts' that Sturt estimated could accommodate 12 to 15 people each. 'They appeared to be permanent habitations,' he says:

> and all of them fronted the same point of the compass. In searching amongst them we observed two beautifully made nets of about ninety yards in length. One had much larger meshes than the other and was most probably intended to take kangaroos, and the other was evidently a fishing net.

> In one hut, the floor of which was swept with particular care, a number of white balls – as of pulverised shells or lime – had been deposited, the use of which we could not divine.

Moreover, a trench had been dug around the hut to keep rainwater out and 'the whole was arranged with more than ordinary attention'.

They resumed their journey, still puzzling over all of these enigmatic discoveries when 'we came suddenly upon the tribe to which this village, as it might be called, belonged'. At first they noticed three or four young men seated on a bank a fair distance away. The Aborigines were unaware of the visitors as they approached. Sturt says:

> The crack of the drayman's whip was the first thing that aroused their attention. They gazed upon us for a moment and then started up and assumed an attitude of horror and amazement, their terror apparently increasing upon them. We stood perfectly immobile until at length they gave a fearful yell and darted out of sight.

Their cries soon brought about a dozen others up from the river. They took one look at the alien creatures and followed their compatriots 'without once venturing to look behind them'. The explorers were well positioned on a rise and decided to wait there until the Aboriginal people returned. They dismounted and rested on the bare earth.

> We had not been long stationary when we heard a crackling noise in the distance and it soon became evident that the bush had been fired. It was, however, impossible that we could receive any injury on the narrow ridge upon

> which we stood so we waited very patiently to see the end of this affair.

The smoke billowed their way and rose over their heads. Then one of the older Aboriginal men reappeared from the spot where he had left them. 'He advanced a few paces towards us,' Sturt says:

> and bending his body so that his hands rested on his knees, he began to throw himself into the most extravagant attitudes, shaking his foot from time to time. When he found that all his violence had no effect, he turned his rear to us in a most laughable manner, and absolutely groaned in spirit when he found that this last insult failed of success.

That was when Hume intervened. He called out to the man and used as much language common to several groups that he could muster until he finally induced the Aboriginal elder to come forward and meet him. Once they made friendly contact Sturt joined them with the gift of a tomahawk, 'the use of which he immediately guessed,' he says. 'Mr Hume's manners had in great measure contributed to allay his evident agitation. I could see in a moment that his bosom was full, even to bursting.'

Then the others returned as the grass fire ran its course and soon the visitors followed them to the river where the Aboriginal men had been setting a net. They showed them how they'd strung it in a semicircle from shore to shore. Sturt was amazed at the speed with which they accepted the intruders. 'These men whom we had thus surprised and who, no doubt, imagined we were about to destroy them – having apparently never having seen or heard of white men before – must have taken us for something preternatural,' he says, 'yet from the extremity of fear that had prompted them to set their wood in flames they in a brief space so completely subdued those fears as to approach the very beings who had so strongly excited their alarm.'

One reason, he felt, was soon evident. Some of the people were suffering from a particularly unpleasant skin condition. The old man 'called several young men to Mr Hume and myself and nothing could exceed the anxiety of his explanations or the mild and soothing tone in which he addressed his people'. It quickly became clear that they were using the white balls found in the 'hospital' hut to treat the disease, but to no avail. 'It really pained me that I could not assist him in his distress,' Sturt says. But his mission was still incomplete and 'we pushed on to make up for lost time'.

In the days that followed, Hume finally solved the riddle of the salt water. Riding ahead of the party along the riverbank, he noticed a localised current and called out to Sturt. 'We discovered some springs in the very bed of the river,' he says, 'from which a considerable stream was gushing, and from the encrustation around them we had no difficulty in guessing their nature: in fact they were brine springs, and I collected a quantity of brine from the brink of them. Here at length was a local cause for its saltiness that destroyed at once the anticipation and hope' for the great inland sea.

At least for now.

CHAPTER FIFTEEN

The End of the Journey

The local press unites against Darling, Sturt tries for the inland sea again and Hume declines to join him.

Sturt was deeply reluctant to abandon his quest, but the combination of his disappointment at Hume's salt springs discovery and the failing condition of both men and animals left him little choice. He and Hume made one more foray down the river a little distance, but it was really just more of the same.

On their return, they experienced one of the more baffling events of the expedition. On a perfectly cloudless day, they suddenly heard 'what seemed to be a report of a gun fired at a distance of between five and six miles', Sturt says. It stunned the whole party.

> It was not the hollow sound of an earthly explosion, or the sharp cracking noise of falling timber, but in every way resembled a discharge of a heavy piece of ordnance. I sent one of the men immediately up a tree, but he could observe nothing unusual. The country around him appeared to be

> equally flat on all sides. To this day, the singularity of such a sound, in such a situation, is a matter of mystery to me.[1]

It was a curiously apposite note on which to conclude his journey into this alien land, and for Hume it must have brought back memories of the gun fired at the Geelong terminus of his expedition with Hovell. But before doing so there was one final ritual to be observed: the naming of the eccentric and contrary stream that marked the boundary of his ambition. His choice – the Darling – could hardly have been more fitting. The journey homeward was marked by several contacts with the Aboriginal people, and again Hume's intervention forestalled any open conflict. Towards the end of the expedition Sturt wrote:

> Now it is evident that a little insight into the customs of every people is necessary to ensure a kindly communication; this, joined with patience and kindness, will seldom fail with the natives of the interior. It is not to avoid alarming their natural timidity that a gradual approach is so necessary; they preserve the same ceremony among themselves.[2]

In this, he reflected a similar sentiment to that of George Augustus Robinson, the official protector of Aboriginals, who the following year said, 'God has given them the same portion of understanding as ourselves . . . I hope ere long I shall be able to prove to the world that these people are not the degraded race as they have been represented; that they have as much intellect as their opponents – the whites.'[3]

But it was not a sentiment shared by Darling who, on this issue only, found common cause with Justice Forbes, William Wentworth and the vast majority of those who were appropriating the Aboriginal homelands. Indeed, when in the New South Wales Supreme Court in 1827 Lieutenant Nathaniel Lowe became the first 'officer and gentleman' charged on overwhelming evidence with the vicious murder of an Aboriginal man in his custody, the community was aghast. However, after a five-minute retirement by a panel of officers as his jury (during which – as reported in *The Australian* – 'the utmost impatience was manifested by the auditors in court to hear the result'), they returned to announce a verdict of 'not guilty'. Lowe's 'numerous friends' crowded around him to offer their congratulations 'on the happy termination of the trial'. A second burst of applause broke out as he 'triumphantly' left the court.[4]

As Sturt and Hume made their way back to the settled areas, they explored parts of the Bogan and Castlereagh river valleys, and at times Hume left the party for several days to conduct exploratory patrols among the Aboriginal people. His reports formed an important element in Sturt's official account and consolidated the friendship between the two men. It was a bond that would endure for the rest of their lives. And though their paths would diverge as Sturt's obsession with the mirage of the inland sea took him ever further from the hard-headed, practical world of the bushman-grazier, their mutual respect would remain undiminished by time.

They arrived back in Wellington on 29 March 1829. Most of the men were suffering from exposure, dysentery and eye troubles, and Hume himself was afflicted by persistent bouts of asthma. But Sturt and his deputy had brought the entire party and their animals home without loss. Both Sturt and Darling wrote lavishly in Hume's praise. Sturt told the governor:

> I have on all occasions received the most ready and valuable assistance from Mr Hume. His intimate acquaintance with the manners and customs of the natives enabled him to engage with them and chiefly contributed to the peaceful manner in which we have journeyed.
>
> I cannot but say he has done an essential service to future travellers and to the colony at large by his conduct on all occasions since he has been with me . . . I can scarcely conclude my remarks by noticing how very inadequate has been the recompense awarded by the colony to Mr Hume.

Darling in turn wrote to Sir George Murray and combined his encomium with a touch of self-congratulation: 'I am happy to find, Sir, that Mr Hume, whom I selected to accompany Captain Sturt, proved an able assistant. His services from his general knowledge of the country and the character of the natives must have been very important . . .'

The expedition was one of the few bright spots in the governor's stormy administration. The Thompson–Sudds affair continued to bedevil him at every turn. In the four-and-a-half months since Sturt departed, Wentworth had forwarded to Murray a long Bill of Indictment against the governor. And a motion in the House of Commons criticising Darling's actions was passed on the votes. A New South Wales correspondent for the London *Morning Chronicle* using the by-line 'Miles' took up the cudgels on Wentworth's behalf, filing a series of articles highly critical of the governor. The issue then became a cause célèbre of the Opposition Whig Party against the Tories, with whom Darling was fiercely aligned.

In Sydney, Smith Hall's *Monitor* launched a barrage of attacks on all aspects of Darling's policies, particularly his treatment of the convicts and the emancipists. The governor retaliated, calling him 'a fellow without principles, an apostate missionary', and withdrew his right to graze his stock on waste land next to his 'St Heliers' property. Darling's fellow Tory, Archdeacon Scott – also the subject of Smith Hall's attacks – had him evicted from his family pew at St James's Church. Scott then charged him with criminal libel and while the judge found the offence proved, he awarded the archdeacon the trifling sum of £1 damages and released the newspaperman on his own recognisance. However, two further charges of libel against others resulted in the editor serving a jail sentence. And though he continued to edit his paper from the penitentiary, Darling saw his chance to silence his critic. He amended the *Newspaper Regulation Act* so that anyone twice convicted of 'blasphemous or seditious libel' could be banished from the colony.

But this only united the local press in their opposition to Darling and all he stood for. When Smith Hall sued Scott for evicting him from his pew and won £25 damages, they cheered him on. Darling paid the fine but by now Scott was also at loggerheads with fellow churchmen, John Thierry, the Roman Catholic priest and John Dunmore Lang, the Presbyterian minister whom he described as his 'slanderer-general'. The unrest in the religious community was no different from the tensions in the colony at large.

Under Darling's administration the English and Irish convict population continued to grow by the thousands; the chain gangs slaved on the roads; others were apportioned to their landholding masters in regimes that ranged from the relatively benign to the outright brutal. The outlying penal settlements became hellholes.

Norfolk Island continued its descent into moral destitution with his appointment of the sadistic Morisset as commandant. Darling was initially reluctant to appoint him because of the high salary he had negotiated during his trip to London to apply for the post, and instead made him New South Wales superintendent of police. But when he discovered him 'a most zealous officer' he signed the transfer and Morisset arrived on the island with his family in May 1829.

The prisoners were already in a sorry state and several attempts at mutiny had been fiercely suppressed. Under Morisset, according to reports smuggled out to Smith Hall's *Monitor*, the convicts were 'made the prey of hunger and nakedness at the caprice of monsters in human form . . . and cut to pieces by the scourge [with] no redress or the least inquiry made into their suffering.' The commandant's name would find an appropriate memorial on the mainland in a hospital for the criminally insane.

One of the more bizarre penal outposts was Fort Dundas on Melville Island off the north Australian coast. It originated from seaborne surveys by Captain Philip Parker King. In September 1824, Captain James Bremer arrived with a complement of convicts and soldiers in the HMS *Tamar*. He named the establishment after Sir Philip Dundas, the First Lord of the Admiralty, and almost immediately they were harassed by the Aboriginal Tiwi people whose island they had invaded.

Cyclones and white ants added to their trials. They had no animals to assist the convicts with the heavy work, and the water buffaloes they imported from Timor were strangers to their demands. In 1827, Darling had sent Major John Campbell to take charge, but the Tiwi were unrelenting. They repeatedly attacked the settlement, fatally spearing the surgeon John Gold and storekeeper John Green. The British retreated in disarray, and by February 1829 the Tiwi were once again the undisputed masters of their land.

A similar fate befell an attempt to colonise another outpost on the nearby Cobourg Peninsula in June 1827 with four ships, several score of convicts and a military detachment under Captain James Stirling, a headstrong Scot who had served with distinction in the Royal Navy in the Napoleonic Wars. He was replaced the following year by Captain Collet Barker, but to no avail, and that outpost, too was abandoned by Darling in 1829. Coincidentally, Collet Barker was speared to death in 1831 when swimming across the Hume (by then renamed the Murray).

Around this time, Hume received an invitation to participate in another exploration. Sturt had begun preparing for his second major expedition almost as soon as he returned from his journey to the Darling. The governor agreed that there was still much to discover but his orders were for Sturt to confine himself to the area where it was believed the Murrumbidgee would join the Lachlan. Moreover, he would send a ship to the southern coast where Flinders had mapped a riverine outlet. It would bring Sturt and his party home if they reached that distant goal. And he agreed that the captain should seek Hamilton Hume as his second-in-command.

Sturt pressed his case to Hume as forcefully as he could. But Hamilton was concerned about Elizabeth's debilitating asthma and was now battling his own bronchial condition. Moreover, Darling had formally granted him 1,200 acres of excellent country near the Crookhaven River, which reaches the sea at

Nowra. This was in the heart of Alexander Berry's holdings and he would eventually sell it to his old patron. Meantime, he was fully occupied developing his block at Yass. So, with an uneasy heart he was forced to resist Sturt's invitation.

Nevertheless, the 34-year-old army captain was able to persuade most of the initial team to rejoin him in his quest to trace down the Murrumbidgee and from there, he fondly hoped, to that vast, shimmering inland sea. Hume's replacement would be George Macleay, the son of the colonial secretary. Only 20 at the time, George had been a mere two years in the colony after his education at Westminster School so was more a companion than a true deputy in the Hume mould. But he was good-humoured and, according to Sturt, in the appalling conditions they would endure, 'He would do his utmost to lighten the toil and cheer the men.'

They set out from Sydney on 3 November 1830 and for the next 25 days travelled through scattered settlement until they left Warby's station near Gundagai. They then followed the Murrumbidgee to the west, crossing it many times to find passage for the bullock drays through the steep banks and heavy timber. It was hard going, and it took until Christmas Day to reach its junction with the Lachlan.

There they found themselves surrounded by the same kind of seemingly endless marshland that had so bedevilled the earlier expedition up the Macquarie. Sturt was torn between Darling's strict instructions and his own untameable ambition to be the first white man to stand on the shore of the great inland sea. It was really no contest. He decided to use the whaleboat they had carried with them on the back of a dray; and in addition he had his men build a small skiff from local timber. Having tested and found it relatively waterproof, he set forth with seven men in his small flotilla down the Murrumbidgee channel on 7 January 1830. The rest of the party remained to guard their stores until they returned.

Alas, while the skiff was waterproof it was poorly designed, and at the first solid puff of wind it overturned and sank. All hands were rescued and joined their fellows in the now crowded whaleboat. Undeterred, Sturt directed his craft down the firm current of the broad Murrumbidgee, stopping to camp on its banks each evening; and on 14 January they encountered what Sturt called 'a broad and noble river'. Unbeknown to the explorer, this was the stream Hume had named after his father six years previously. In his careerist ambition – and unmindful of the vagaries of political mortality – Sturt named it the Murray after the colonial secretary who even then was preparing for a life of rustication in Scotland as the Whigs swept his Tory Party from office. He would deeply regret removing his friend's family name from the colony's grandest waterway, but he was in thrall to his political superiors. If Hamilton protested, no records remain; however, it undoubtedly caused him personal anguish as yet another consequence of his native birth.

On two occasions, as they camped on its broad banks, the local Aboriginal people challenged them, and without Hume to intervene they were unable to develop a workable dialogue. However, they escaped without loss of life, and on 23 January reached another river flowing in from the north. Sturt rowed upstream and guessed correctly that it was the Darling of his earlier encounter. He then turned back and continued down the Murray until they reached Lake Alexandrina on 9 February. From there they walked over sandhills to the southern coast.

Sturt now had the evidence of his eyes that the inland rivers ran to the open ocean; but against all reason he persisted in the notion that there might still be that great inland freshwater sea with the capacity to water a limitless bounty of grain and livestock. His frustration became acute when he realised that no ship could navigate the shallows of the Murray delta, and Darling's promised vessel was nowhere to be seen. He now faced the appalling prospect of rowing the whaleboat almost 1,500 kilometres against a strong current with a worn-out crew and a distressing shortage of food.

There followed one of the more incongruous and paradoxical journeys of the colonial experience – Sturt's party almost perished from starvation while travelling through some of the most bounteous country for thousands of Aboriginal people in the entire continent. They began it on 12 February, and on 23 March arrived exhausted at their Murrumbidgee depot, where they expected to find their base party.

They were shattered to discover it deserted. By now in the advanced stages of starvation, they struggled on until 14 April, when Sturt abandoned the boat and sent two of the stronger men to seek the depot party, which he hoped had retreated to a more congenial camping area. He and the rest were utterly spent. And there they remained for almost a week until finally the two returned with supplies. The revived expedition staggered into the settled areas and reached Sydney on 25 May 1830.

They found the colony even more divided against its governor than when they left it. Bushranging gangs were in open rebellion and found support and shelter among the estranged emancipists and struggling settlers. Darling's soldiers scored a passing success in their battle with them when, in the late afternoon of 1 September 1830, a detachment of troopers and police surrounded Jack Donahue and his gang in the Bringelly scrub near Campbell Town. Called upon to surrender, Donahue refused and, according to the official report, urged the police to 'come on, using the most insulting and indecent epithets'.

He fought to the end when a ball fired by Trooper John Muggleston took him in the head. And when the news rippled through Sydney's drawing rooms and grog shops, Venetian glasses and pewter tankards were raised to toast trooper and bushranger respectively. A tradesman began fashioning a line of clay pipes with the bowl a model of Donahue's head replete with bullet hole; and the surveyor-general Thomas Mitchell slipped into the morgue when the body arrived and made an evocative pencil sketch of his naked form. He even appended to it a quotation from Lord Byron:

No matter; I have bared my brow.
Fair in Death's face – before – and now.

This would not have endeared him to Darling. The governor was already at loggerheads with his surveyor-general.

By the end of 1830 Mitchell had made many changes to the roads from Sydney to Parramatta and Liverpool; he had also plotted a new road to the south through the area Hume had pioneered as far as Goulburn; and he had built the troublesome thoroughfare over the Blue Mountains to Bathurst. But Darling was not happy with this burst of activity, declaring Mitchell was 'getting ahead of himself' and that major alterations might need to be made. In fact, the line of road chosen by the surveyor and the bushman would endure, and travellers still follow in their footsteps today. And not surprisingly, Mitchell resented the implied criticism. Against Darling's orders he built a new road down One

Tree Hill (later Mount Victoria), the furthest peak of the Blue Mountains. The governor retaliated by attempting to remove the Department of Roads and Bridges from Mitchell's authority.

The increasingly tetchy surveyor was outraged. Having chosen Sturt over his own greater qualifications for exploration, Darling was now in effect removing the most substantial element of his role as the colony's road builder. It was intolerable. He claimed – with some justice – that his authority came directly from the crown rather than the governor, and he wrote to his patron Murray to press his case. Darling also penned a scathing letter to the secretary of state for the colonies claiming that unless Mitchell were punished there would be 'an immediate end to all subordination and to the Government [of New South Wales] itself'.

However, by then Murray had retired from the Colonial Office and in November 1830 the Whigs triumphed over the Tories. Darling was now on borrowed time; and the population of the colony counted the days until it finally ran out.

They did so without benefit of most civilised diversions such as the establishment of a public theatre, which he 'ruthlessly and implacably' opposed. He passed a law effectively banning all performance of drama without his specific approval. And he declined all requests. However, he did permit occasional musical concerts. Military bands were his preferred option. But young native-born Australians were still capable of asserting their rebellious spirit. In tribute to Jack Donahue, bush balladists composed songs to 'The Wild Colonial Boy', which the authorities tried desperately (and unsuccessfully) to ban.

CHAPTER SIXTEEN

Further Adventures of the Surveyor-General

Sturt is posted to Norfolk Island, Thomas Mitchell takes up the search for an inland sea, and a famous bushranger is born.

In March 1831, the secretary of state in the new Whig government, Viscount Goderich, notified Darling his time was up. As word spread the colony rejoiced, and when he and his family finally departed in the *Hooghly* in October they booed him through the Heads then breathed a collective sigh of relief.

Back in England in 1832, Darling faced a parliamentary select committee but they exonerated him from the colonists' charges, and the monarchy gave 'a dramatic display of official favour' when the king personally knighted him the following day.[1] No further military or political assignments followed for the still relatively young and active 59-year-old, and he died in Brighton on 2 April 1858 aged 85.

Hamilton Hume had been one of the few deserving beneficiaries of Darling's erratic and repressive rule. And he was fortunate in his reluctant decision to decline the terrible rigours of Sturt's second quest for the elusive inland sea, even though it cost the family's memoriam in Australia's greatest river.

An exhausted Sturt was rewarded by the governor with a posting to head the military garrison at Norfolk Island, and thereby provided a fascinating insight into the parallel worlds so strictly divided by the British class system. For while the South Pacific island only ten days sail from Sydney was the nadir of wretchedness for the convicts, it was regarded as a haven of rest and 'bounteous living' for the officers who ruled them. There were imported wines, fresh meat daily from the flocks of sheep and cattle, a free allowance of milk and butter, turkeys, geese, guinea fowls and even home-cured bacon. As one officer wrote, 'With all these advantages we lived most comfortably and almost for nothing.'[2]

However, soon after he arrived Sturt was confronted by a mutiny. As a chain gang returned from their work in the quarry they turned on their overseer, smashed him to the ground with pick-handles and left him for dead. They knocked off their irons, took his keys and returned to the jail, where they released other prisoners from their cells and prepared to rush the garrison. Unfortunately for the rebels, the overseer recovered sufficiently to stagger to the military fort and raise the alarm. Sturt acted quickly. He locked all exits from the jail and called out the guard.

Trapped inside, the prisoners spent the night planning their tactics, but in the morning Sturt was ready for almost anything and outmanoeuvred them at every turn. However, one bright spark called through his high window that he was prepared to name the ringleaders if Sturt would attend him. The explorer hurried to the prison wall beneath the cell and waited for the message. Instead he received the contents of a half barrel of urine and slops.[3]

The prisoner had misjudged his man. When they finally surrendered, all were placed in heavy irons and locked in tiny cells. Urged on by Morisset, Sturt had all 70 within the walls flogged on the courtyard triangle. But far from appeasing his anger, the experience played on Sturt's mind. His time on the island took on a nightmarish quality, and despite the offer of a residency in New Zealand, he was forced to take an extended leave in England.

His eyesight had been failing since the day he'd been forced to turn away from the sun's glare on the mountain summit during his expedition with Hume. On board ship to England, it broke down completely, leaving him totally blind. Though medical treatment would be moderately successful, he would never fully recover his health. Nevertheless, as we shall see, the vision splendid of that great inland sea would continue to haunt him. And in time he would answer its siren call from the red heart of his adopted land.

Hamilton Hume kept up a correspondence with him, but for the moment he was preoccupied with his property and his extended family. His younger brother John Kennedy Hume – now known as 'Happy Jack' – had married Elizabeth O'Neill in 1825 against the wishes of his parents because of her Catholic faith. However, since the records reveal their first child, Eliza, had been born the year before, it would seem that John was doing the honourable thing. Elizabeth was also known by the surname of 'Prendergast', so it may well be that she had become Catholic by an earlier marriage, and though she and John had most of their nine children baptised by Father Thierry, they repeatedly declared themselves 'Protestant' in New South Wales censuses.

However, this was of little moment to Hamilton, and when John took up a 60-acre grant at Appin in 1828 they were able to work their properties together. While Hamilton and his wife were childless, and would remain so throughout their marriage, John and Elizabeth had three little girls, and a boy on the way. John had been promised 120 acres at Gunning in the Yass district, so the brothers shared the pleasant prospect of remaining neighbours indefinitely.

Their sister Isabella – known universally as 'Belle' – who had married George Barber at only 17, was now relatively well off. Eventually they built one of the most beautiful Georgian homes in the colony on their 800-acre 'Glenrock' at Marulan. They had no fewer than 13 children, though one nine-year-old son died when he fell from a horse. George later bought valuable tracts of land in the Yass district as well. His step-father, the mercurial Charles Throsby, who had played such an important role in Hamilton Hume's early expeditions, had committed suicide in 1828.

Hume was also an assiduous correspondent with other fellow explorers, of whom Thomas Mitchell was among the most prolific. When Darling left the colony, Mitchell approached the acting governor, Colonel Patrick Lindesay, with a plan to explore the area between the Gwydir and Castlereagh rivers following reports of a large stream flowing west. Once again, the prospect of an inland sea beckoned. And this was his opportunity to trump his upstart rival, young Charles Sturt.

Lindesay was another Scot, the son of an army officer, educated at the University of Edinburgh with a particular interest in natural history. He had a relatively undistinguished military career, but it was through his influence that during Sturt's journey down the Murray the explorer shot and collected many bird skins. Lindesay sent them to the Edinburgh Museum where they formed a valuable part of the avian collection, the highlight of which was the Australian mound-building scrub turkey.

Lindesay willingly authorised Mitchell's request and once again Hume declined an opportunity to be part of the expedition, pleading continued ill-health 'within the family'. But while he might well have been concerned by Elizabeth's condition, he would have been perfectly aware that Mitchell was engaged in an exercise of one-upmanship against Sturt. Moreover, he would be covering much of the same country that Hume had already traversed with his good friend and travelling companion.

Then there was the Aboriginal question. While under Hume's influence Mitchell had ordered his surveyors to discover and employ Aboriginal names of geographical features and districts, his personal dealings with the native landsmen left much to be desired. Indeed, it was an attitude that would eventually bring the British-born surveyor down.

On this occasion, the party included 15 convicts, one of Mitchell's assistant surveyors, George White and his friend, the rigidly conservative Colonel Kenneth Snodgrass, a member of the Executive Council. They set out in November 1831 – starting at Boree station west of Bathurst – and travelled through settled country towards Tamworth. A second assistant surveyor, Heneage Finch, caught them up and was ordered to follow with additional supplies.

As they travelled further to the north-west, Mitchell procured the services of a half-assimilated Aboriginal guide he dubbed

'Mr Brown'. At his suggestion the party turned west to the Namoi River and followed it as far as Narrabri. However, when they encountered an old Aboriginal woman and Mr Brown spoke with her at length, he suddenly decamped and was not seen again.

Mitchell soon found himself desperately in need of water, and they began to hear taunting echoes of 'whitefella, whitefella' coming from the bush. It was an unnerving experience, and ended only when they broke out of the bushland on to the plains where for five days they trudged on under a merciless sun. Mitchell wrote, 'the very crows sat on the trees with their mouths open'. At last they reached a big lagoon, and for the next 12 hours it seemed he had found part of that elusive channel to the 'great lake'. However, the next day when he made his calculations he realised it was the river that Allan Cunningham had crossed twice, calling it the Peel at first and the Gwydir further upstream.

Heavy rain then began to fall, and in their confusion Mitchell and Finch failed to rendezvous until Mitchell finally came upon the assistant's camp. He was confronted by a shocking sight. Finch and his servant had been away from the camp at the time, and the two men left to guard the supplies had been killed by Aborigines who had then plundered the stores. Finch had just returned, and with Mitchell he and his men buried the bodies and salvaged what remained of the provisions.

Until then they had only rarely spotted the Aboriginal landsmen who followed them, but now they seemed to be all around. Without a negotiator of Hume's authority, Mitchell was aware of his vulnerability, but at the same time he wanted 'revenge' on 'these murderous savages . . . the plunderers of

Mr Finch's party'. As he wrote in his field book, 'It appeared necessary for the maintenance of our character amongst the natives of this part of New Holland, as well as for the security of subsequent travellers in this quarter, that we should not retire without endeavouring to avenge the murder of these men.'

But when they encountered an Aboriginal community, he and Colonel Snodgrass were thrown into disarray when the elders made a clear gesture of goodwill. They called some women over from beneath a nearby tree 'with unmistakeable invitations to visit these females who obediently dropped their cloaks and paraded themselves enticingly before us'. But comely and compliant as they were, wrote Mitchell, 'our party was much more disposed to fight than make love'. And when a 'sable nymph' was offered directly to Finch, the leader lost all composure and 'ordered the bullock driver to proceed'.[4]

When the whispering taunts from the bush were repeated, he decided to withdraw. He returned to Sydney in February 1832, disappointed that the mighty river to the inland sea had eluded him, but undeterred in his belief that further explorations would unveil the panacea.

At his first opportunity, Mitchell reported to the newly arrived governor, Major-General Richard Bourke, a very different character from his unlamented predecessor. Born in Dublin on 4 May 1777, he was from an Irish family who for generations had been popular landowners in Limerick and Tipperary. He was related to the distinguished and influential political philosopher of the Whig party, Edmund Burke. And at Richard's Westminster School, Edmund and his son – also Richard – kept a friendly eye on his progress and his finances.

Richard Bourke was a lively student, dubbed 'Merry Dick Bourke', and appeared in the school's stage productions and in its boxing ring before matriculating to Oxford at 16. He went down from Oriel College after four terms but returned to the university's Exeter College as a 'gentleman commoner' in 1796, graduating B.A. two years later. According to his biographer, 'He had a lively mind, an eagerness to learn, and his later career showed him to be energetic and industrious. He probably gained a good deal from his years there, and hugely enjoyed himself.'[5]

On graduation, he joined the Grenadier Guards and rose fairly smartly through the military ranks, seeing service in the Netherlands, South America and in the Peninsular Wars, where he was wounded on both sides of his jaw. While the disfigurement was minor, he was reticent thereafter to give public speeches. He was promoted to colonel in 1814 and after the war went on half pay. Along the way he had married Elizabeth Bourke, the daughter of the receiver-general of land tax for Middlesex, and they lived on his Limerick estate with their five children.

In 1825, he returned to service as major-general on the staff at Malta and when a political storm broke in Westminster over the conduct of the Cape Colony's governor, Lord Charles Somerset, Bourke was chosen by the then Tory government to step in as acting governor. He took up the post in March the following year. Six months later he was confirmed as governor by Viscount Goderich and tasked with reorganising the colonial government.

Under his rule the native population was accorded certain rights, improving conditions for the Hottentots and other free black Africans, though slavery remained an intrinsic element of British government policy. By 1828 his task was complete, and though offered the governorship of the Bahamas he declined as he felt the climate would be harmful to his wife's health. However, two years later when the Whigs took office, he accepted the vice-regal plum in rambunctious New South Wales.

He was rapturously received. His reputation in Ireland and at the Cape had preceded him, and bands played, fireworks exploded, bonfires were lit and the streets of Sydney illuminated to welcome him and his family. Bourke revelled in a new mood of colonial optimism. It was, nevertheless, universally regarded as a 'peculiar' colony. Having begun as a prison, it was now undergoing a painful transformation as emancipists increasingly demanded a renewal of their civil rights, and free emigration encouraged a wave of settlers from the vigorous lower classes of English society. Bourke's superiors in the Colonial Office warned him that 'recourse must be had to compromise and anomalies'.[6]

He set to with a will. He proposed trial by jury and the substitution of civil for military juries in criminal cases. He sought to reform the Legislative Council, which under Darling had been dominated by the 'exclusives'. And he reduced the power of magistrates over the convicts when charges were brought by their masters. But just as Darling had enraged the underclasses with his draconian regime, now Bourke raised the ire of the 'Bunyip Aristocracy' led by the Macarthurs, Blaxland, Campbell and their ilk.

The governor was unmoved by the opposition, but his morale suffered a terrible blow when, less than six months into his tenure, his beloved wife succumbed to the rheumatic carditis that had prevented their taking up the Bahamian post. She had been seriously ill on the voyage to New South Wales, and according to his biographer:

> Although suffering greatly from sea sickness himself, Bourke had saved her from many hours of terror. He often sat up half the night, holding a candle in his hand, and reading aloud to her to distract her thoughts. She arrived in Sydney in a state of 'debility' from which she never fully recovered.

She moved to the Parramatta residence and for a time revived, but it was only a brief reprieve. Bourke himself wrote to a friend, 'Surely there never left this world a purer spirit, nor ever lived in it a gentler or more affectionate creature. Thank God I was present to receive her parting breath, to close her eyes and leave her to her Maker.'[7]

Bourke resumed his duties deeply saddened but with an outward cheerfulness. He compensated by throwing himself into his work and in doing so endangered his own health. The wound to his jaw flared painfully and his eyesight suffered. His daughter Anne acted as his hostess and she retained the role after marrying Edward Deas Thomson, his clerk of the councils. They lived mostly at the Parramatta establishment, but by then as the metropolitan settlement had expanded it was more centrally positioned than in Brisbane's day. He welcomed the return of his surveyor-general despite the absence of any major discoveries. Indeed, Mitchell himself would have been hard pressed to justify the journey by its results.

However, Bourke's main concern was the state of the Survey Department in the face of an influx of settlers and landholders seeking security of title. Edward Stanley, the under-secretary for the colonies, had written to the governor demanding action, and he relayed Whitehall's concerns. Mitchell's response was prickly at best, and it would take him almost two years to deliver a map of the colony divided into 19 counties with a description of their boundaries. Moreover, he added a sharply worded memorandum declaring the need for a general survey before effective local surveys could be made.

Bourke did his best to placate both sides but without notable success. On 10 October 1834, he sent another more elaborate (and thoroughly provocative) defence by Mitchell, which was accepted as 'satisfactory' by Stanley's successor, Lord Glenelg, but with the pious hope that Mitchell would show no more 'insubordination'.

Bourke's concern for the convicts and emancipists was evident from the beginning of his incumbency. It was put to public test in a case against James Mudie, the owner of a very big property on the Hunter, who was notorious for his treatment of his Irish convict labour. In 1833, a group of six men rebelled and attacked his partner John Larnach during their escape. They were captured and Larnach survived with little more than a bruising. Nevertheless, the six were charged with attempted murder and the case quickly became a cause célèbre. Other landholders claimed that unless they were properly 'disciplined' their own convict labour force – which often outnumbered them 20 to one – might be tempted to rebel; and in the isolation of the bush they feared for their lives.

At trial the following year, the accused prisoners were defended by an avowed supporter of the governor, Roger Thierry, who was not only an Irish Catholic but a nephew of the leading Catholic clergyman, Father Joseph Thierry. Mudie asserted that Bourke himself had personally retained the defence lawyer. But if so, it was not money well spent – all six were found guilty; five were hanged and the sixth sent to suffer the tortures of the damned on Norfolk Island, for life.

Bourke commissioned the solicitor-general to report on the conditions of the convicts on Mudie's property and, while the findings were unfavourable, he chose not to act within his power to withdraw them from their servitude. Nevertheless, thereafter any signs of rebellion from convicts was routinely attributed to the governor's 'leniency'. He would remain in conflict with many of the colony's wealthy and conservative figures throughout his tenure.

Though unremarked at the time, 1834 also saw the arrival from Ross-shire, Scotland of a family whose second son, Francis, would later come to embody the bitter segregation of the underclasses of the colonial community from the wealthy and well connected. Charles Christie and his attractive and vivacious de facto wife Jane (nee Whittle), reached Sydney on the *James*. Both had previously been married – Jane to Charles's late brother, which by the laws of the day prevented their solemnising their relationship. Jane's children included Robina, sons Charlie and the five-year-old Francis, and daughters Archina, four, and Charlotte, only 12 months.

Also aboard was Henry Monro, the young bachelor scion of a wealthy and distinguished Scottish academic family but with a taste for the drink and a wild, ungovernable temper. Monro's departure from Scotland had not been exactly voluntary. His father was Alexander Monro, a professor at the University of Edinburgh, just as his father and grandfather had been before him. Henry had attacked Alexander in Craiglockhart House, the family seat. Professor Monro was not seriously injured but the son, then about 23, sailed for New South Wales soon afterwards. By the time the *James* berthed, Monro had engaged

Charles Christie, whose family had been in the South American shipping trade before falling on hard times, as his overseer.

He acquired a grazing property at Boro near Goulburn, which at the time was notorious for the fearsome triangle in the main street. Often on Sundays when the local families went to church they were treated to the public lashing of convict offenders. The young Monro had about a dozen convicts assigned to him, and under Christie's supervision they built the yards, sheds and rough homesteads on the property. He quickly adapted to the new regime; indeed he is said to have regarded his overseer as 'too soft' on the men under his command.

It was during this time that Monro and Jane Christie developed a secretive romantic liaison that resulted in the birth of a daughter, Maria Agnes, in 1836. While her birth certificate credits Christie as the father, Monro was in no doubt the child was his.

Young Francis, homeschooled by his mother, was soon inseparable from the stock horses Monro bought and bred on the property, and an eager listener to the men with their stories told around the camp fires at mustering. Among the other young people of the district, he also mixed with the Taylors and the Foggs, children of emancipist parents, especially Billy Fogg, his older contemporary. Billy would play a significant role in Francis Christie's later career as 'General' Frank Gardiner, Prince of the Tobymen, the most notorious and influential of Australia's bushranging paladins.

CHAPTER SEVENTEEN

The Inland Sea Beckons Again

Mitchell continues his explorations, the doctrine of terra nullius *is made law, and Bourke and Mitchell are at odds.*

In 1834, Hume began to concentrate most of his efforts on his Yass property. It was excellent grazing country ideally suited to merino breeding, and the quality of the wool would in time be among the very best produced in Australia. A small village had begun in 1830 where the rough road crossed the Yass River. That year, his neighbour, Henry O'Brien, built a small homestead on a bend in the river, which he named Cooma Cottage.

In March the following year, Mitchell left the surveying hackwork to his assistants and again set forth in quest of aquatic glory. Once again, Hume remained an interested – if increasingly sceptical – observer. Despite Mitchell's failings, Hamilton liked the man and respected his ability as a navigator. And as will be seen, the respect and affection was mutual. But Hume's continuing colloquy with the Aboriginal people provided him with not the slightest hint of a freshwater sea in the vast interior. However, he was aware that he was the odd man out; that for the general population – as for the European-bred explorers – the wish was father of the thought, and so he largely kept his opinions within the family.

Mitchell, like Sturt, was not to be swayed by doubters, at least at this stage. And he was headed once again to the area where Hume and Sturt had terminated their expedition on the banks of the Darling. Mitchell's plan, as presented to Governor Bourke, was to explore the Darling from the point where they had left it in 1828 down to its junction with the Murray. It was a wide enough brief to permit the explorer to follow the signs – perhaps even a mighty stream flowing into the Darling from the west – to the inland sea.

Once again he was well equipped with livestock and convicts. And though Colonel Snodgrass was unable to join him, having been appointed lieutenant-governor of Van Diemen's Land, his companionable replacement, Richard Cunningham, possessed an excellent pedigree. His elder brother Allan had made notable journeys in New South Wales as well as his discovery of Cunningham's Gap over the Great Divide. Moreover, the brothers were both botanists of some standing, Richard having curated Allan's remarkable Australian collection sent to the Royal Botanical Gardens at Kew. Indeed, that was where Allan was at present; while Richard had taken up the post of New South Wales botanist two years previously.

Since his arrival he had distributed vine cuttings and plants in many parts of the colony, including New Zealand, where he went bush in search of pine spars for the navy. He was accosted by Maoris but they had good memories of his brother whom he resembled, and he came to no harm. Allan said later his brother was careless of any danger posed because of his 'religious discipline and firm belief in the existence of a merciful, protecting providence'.[1] He had only just returned when offered the place in Mitchell's expedition. He accepted willingly.

The party travelled by easy stages to Boree station, which was then owned by Robert Barton, a former East India Company official with very little understanding of Australian conditions. In later years, the business would fail and his family would be forced to sell, a not uncommon fate for the British newcomers in an alien land. Mitchell's party then headed north-west to the Bogan River, which they reached in April. The journey had been uneventful until then, though they were conscious of Aboriginal people monitoring their progress through their homelands.

During a religious rest day on Good Friday 17 April, Cunningham left the riverside camp site and sallied into the bush on horseback in search of new plant species. He was soon lost, and in early evening he happened upon an Aboriginal group who took him in and fed him. Despite their nervousness of the whites, they allowed the botanist to remain with them that night, while back at camp Mitchell was preparing to organise a search party. Unknown to the Aboriginal people, the 42-year-old Englishman suffered from terrible nightmares, during which he often cried out and walked in his sleep. When one of these occurred in the dead of night, the terrified Aborigines clubbed him to death, then killed his horse.

Mitchell's search party discovered the dead horse and remnants of Cunningham's belongings, but it would not be until six months later that a party led by Lieutenant Henry Zouch of the 4th Regiment from Bathurst discovered his remains. Canadian-born and a graduate of Sandhurst, Zouch would play an important role in the 1860s gold rush near Yass. On this occasion, when some Aboriginal people told him the circumstances surrounding Cunningham's death, he dubbed it 'murder' but was unable to identify the perpetrators.

Mitchell continued his journey along the Bogan until it reached the Darling, then followed the larger stream south to the Menindee area. Again the Aboriginal people followed and at times harassed the explorers as they traversed the country they had nurtured unmolested for 40,000 years. The newcomers responded with gunfire that, according to the official report, 'killed and wounded several Aboriginals'. A frustrated Mitchell decided to abandon further travel and returned the way he had come.

The skirmish was typical of the early contacts between British explorers and the Aboriginal people. Historian Henry Reynolds says, 'Aborigines reacted in complex ways to the European invasion. Often the first glimpse of a white man produced outright terror at the arrival of these "ashen spirits of the dead".' At other times there was spontaneous violence to drive out the intruders, particularly when they realised they were humans riding alien beasts and driving fearsome creatures with whips and screams.

> In many cases they watched warily and curiously from hiding places to see how the newcomers behaved; and if they perceived no immediate threat they often extended the same courtesies they would show other tribes travelling through their territory. But when the intruders remained, and appropriated the land, they were faced with an existential threat. One can only speculate on the animated debates that must have ensued in the elders' councils on the best tactics to adopt.[2]

The colonists in Westminster were far more decisive. While they gave lip service to the notion that the 'natives' be treated 'humanely', they now paid little practical heed to the outrages perpetrated in their name. The majority of the English and Scottish settlers resented their presence and when challenged responded with rifle fire. Some individuals among the immigrants and Australian-born understood the consequences of the land-grab taking place, even as they participated in it. But their empathy was quickly compromised by the expectation of a bounteous future on the land.

In 1835, Hamilton Hume's childhood friend John Batman negotiated a treaty with the local Aboriginal people to acquire land in the Port Phillip area. This would precipitate a response from the British government that would give carte blanche to the total acquisition, without the slightest compensation, of the entire Aboriginal homeland.

After the fiasco at Western Port in 1826, nothing further had been done about settlement at Port Phillip for eight years, although the squatters began to follow Hume's tracks, and then the rivers, south of Yass and Wagga Wagga. Historian James Bonwick says:

> It is the connection of Hume and Batman, fellow townsmen, fellow natives of New South Wales, friends as well as neighbours, that really brought about the colonisation of Port Phillip. Batman acknowledged the indebtedness. Even others . . . opposed to Batman, traced their interest in Port Phillip to that exploration in 1824.[3]

It was a letter from Hume in the *Sydney Morning Herald* in 1833 that sparked Batman's interest in crossing Bass Strait from Van Diemen's Land where he had taken up grazing land around Ben Lomond. Hume included a section of the journal he had kept during the expedition with Hovell. His description of the area surrounding Port Phillip could hardly have been more encouraging.

In the final 100 kilometres of their journey, he says,

> We were passing over downs beautiful beyond description; the soil good, it being a black and brown loam, well covered with a thick sward of grass and herbage, and in many places the large sow-thistle was growing luxuriantly.
>
> In several parts of the downs are small woods or forests containing about 500 or perhaps 1,000 acres; these clusters are generally distant from each other from 5 to 10 and 15 miles, and being so disposed throughout the downs, had a picturesque appearance, and presented to the eye a scene beyond my powers of description.
>
> The downs were well watered by small rivulets, all of which run in a southerly direction and abound in fish and water fowl of many kinds . . . We came to a stream of fresh water, near which we fell in with some natives who at first gave us some reason to suppose they were hostile; we afterwards got on friendly terms with them.

Hume clearly enjoyed their company. 'The natives remained with us the greater part of the day,' he says, 'and we very soon learned that these ancient Australians were very admirable adepts in the art of thieving!'

> At this stream a white cockatoo 'of a new kind. Having a top knot of several colours, and a very singular note, was met with, and several other new birds. During the time the natives stayed with us I learned the names of several places in sight

> – the harbour they called Geelong, the downs Iramoo, and a remarkable high hill a few miles to the North-East they informed me was called Wilanmarnartar.
>
> I am now of [the] opinion that as soon as [the area] is known to the British Government we shall, in a few years, see it one of the most flourishing parts of this Colony as it possesses the chief advantages for an extensive agricultural settlement. There is adjoining a fine harbour, which is near the centre of our fisheries; at the lowest calculation one million acres nearly clear of timber and fit for any purpose of agriculture or grazing; and easy access to a good and unlimited interior.

Soon afterwards, Batman took ship to Sydney where he acquired a rare copy of Hume's original sketch map of his journey with Hovell to Port Phillip. Whether he actually received it from the hands of his childhood friend is unknown, but Hume later wrote that, 'I am well aware that my old friend after publication of my letter in the Sydney Morning Herald in 1833 was for a length of time very desirous to cross Bass Straits and visit the fine country I had described to him.'[4] In any case, thereafter he was bent on relocating his operations to what would become the Victorian capital.

Batman's actions and attitudes towards the Tasmanian Aborigines were ugly at best. With two of his own 'Sydney blacks' he had attacked a family group on his property in 1829. The following year he took part in the notorious 'Black Line' – the human chain across the island, driving the Aboriginal people from their lands into a 'manageable' area. His neighbour, the colonial artist John Glover, said, 'Batman was a rogue, thief, cheat and liar, a murderer of blacks and the vilest man I have ever known.'[5]

On the mainland, however, he treated the Port Phillip people with respect, and in the Dutigulla Deed, he undertook to lease their land on an annual basis for 40 blankets, 30 axes, 100 knives, 50 scissors, 30 mirrors, 200 handkerchiefs, 100 pounds of flour and six shirts. Whether the Aboriginal signatories were aware of the implications of the contract is highly doubtful, but it certainly raised serious questions for the British Colonial Office, and indeed Batman's rival settlers. It recognised prior ownership of the country, and that was anathema to Westminster. It fell to Governor Bourke – paradoxically one of the more enlightened of the colonial officials – to deliver the British government's proclamation that would carry the force of law until the Mabo decision of the Australian High Court in 1992.

The decree was issued by the Colonial Office and sent to the governor with Dispatch 99 on 10 October 1835. It stated that 'all people found occupying land without the authority of the government will be considered illegal trespassers'. It implemented the doctrine of *terra nullius* asserting that the land belonged to *no one* prior to the British crown taking possession of it. Aboriginal people therefore could not sell or assign the land, nor could an individual person acquire it, other than by distribution by the crown.[6]

Batman wrote in his diary on Monday 8 June: 'The boat went up the [Yarra] river that I have spoken of, which comes from the east, and I am glad to state, about six miles up found all good water and very deep. This would be a good place for a village'. According to a contemporary account, 'The site [had] already been noted for its virtues by numerous Britons including [his companion] John Helder Wedge and Batman's Parramatta friend Hamilton Hume.'[7]

While his 'treaty' was now invalid, he settled in the colonial camp established on the Yarra River in November that year. In 1836, he built a house at the western end of Collins Street, known as Batman's Hill. However, by then he had become victim of the devastating disease imported by the invaders that was now ravaging the Aboriginal people: syphilis. His was an advanced case, and early in the new year he seemed 'at the point of death'. He rallied but eventually became so physically helpless that he needed a 'rush-work perambulator' not unlike 'Claude's wheel-barrow' from the Hume and Hovel expedition, to get about.

His wife, the former convict Elizabeth 'Eliza' Callaghan, began a relationship with his storeman, William Willoughby, but in February 1839 she went back to England alone. Batman revised his will leaving her only £5 and tried to remove her legal right to his assets. Their seven daughters and one son, John Charles, moved to another house, and he engaged a widow from Van Diemen's Land to care for the girls.

At Batman's Hill, his Sydney natives became his only attendants until he died on 6 May 1839, deeply in debt. His home was requisitioned for government offices. The children were separated and sent to live with friends and relatives until Eliza returned later that year. In 1845, John Charles drowned in the Yarra while on a fishing trip, and soon afterwards Eliza disappeared, leaving Willoughby and her daughters in Melbourne. There is evidence to suggest that she was murdered in Geelong in 1852.

Batman was not the first immigrant to settle in Victoria. The Henty brothers Edward and Stephen arrived at the Portland Bay area in May 1834. The two young Englishmen had travelled with their father Thomas, a successful sheep breeder in his homeland, to Western Australia in 1832. After two dry seasons, they moved to Van Diemen's Land seeking freehold, but finding all had been snapped up, the boys headed over to Portland Bay in their ship the *Thistle* carrying bullocks, cows and pigs, along with baskets of tobacco, flour and salted meat. A month later their brother Francis joined them.

They were acting illegally. The Colonial Office had already refused Thomas's application for settlement rights, but the sons believed – with some justice – that, at least for the whites, possession was nine points of the law and they would eventually be granted the land. Either way, they were impatient with the trappings of officialdom, particularly Edward, who, according to his biographer, was, 'capable and energetic as a youth, but excitable and later socially ambitious and somewhat vain'. The 'backbone' of the settlement was undoubtedly his younger brother Stephen.[8] They established a small farm just back from the bay and also began a whaling venture.

Back in Sydney Mitchell was preparing for his third and most important journey of exploration.

By now relations between the surveyor and the governor had soured. Early in 1836, Bourke wrote to Lord Glenelg, 'The Surveyor General is a difficult man to manage, and I fear I am rather *en mauvaise odeur* with him at present.' The laconic tone concealed the depth of his displeasure.[9] His instructions to the explorer were to return to the Menindee then travel down the Darling to the sea; or if it flowed into the Murray or some other mighty stream, then he could follow that too. But he should return to Sydney via the settled areas around Yass. This meant his homeward trek would be along the course pioneered by

Hamilton Hume on his return from the 1824 journey. His map had now been published, along with Hovell's journal, edited and expanded by the idiosyncratic Dr Bland.

Hume was ready for a second journey, and wrote to Mitchell suggesting it. However, Mitchell seems by now to have become jealous of his position and unwilling to share the glory of discovery with someone as well regarded as Hume. The Australian's celebrity status had continued to grow, particularly among his compatriots and the beneficiaries of his explorations. Mitchell responded, 'I had the pleasure of receiving your obliging letter and . . . although I did not apprehend any difficulty in proposing [your suggestion] to the governor . . . I find that his orders from home are peremptory, that the survey department only is to be employed.'

It was a firm but polite brush-off, but a fortuitous one, as will be seen. However, Hume was not prepared to accept it without a further note to the governor himself seeking to lead a party of landseekers from Yass to Port Phillip. In response, Bourke's private secretary, George Kenyon Holden, pointed out that the government had yet to authorise the colonising of the port and suggested 'it would be better to await the results of Major Mitchell's tracing of the Darling and Murray to their opening before proceeding'. Hume bided his time.

Bourke also instructed Mitchell to use 'every possible means to conciliate the goodwill of the Aboriginal inhabitants' and 'show the utmost forbearance in the event of any hostility, resorting to firearms or force of any kind' only if his party's safety was in actual jeopardy. Bourke was well aware that on his earlier trips he – and particularly some of his men – had been aggressive to the Aborigines. There was a well-founded story that one of them – Joseph Jones – promised a woman a water kettle in return for sex, but when she claimed payment he knocked her down, seized her baby and dashed its brains out against a tree. As she tried to escape she was shot dead and several others were fired on by Jones and his mates. Bourke insisted the warning be included in the explorer's brief.[10]

In March, Mitchell again set out from Boree station with the surveyor Granville Stapylton and an impressive entourage of 23 heavily armed men, including several veterans of his earlier journeys. They were equipped with 12 horses, 52 working bullocks, five drays, two carts, two collapsible whaleboats and provisions for several months, including a flock of sheep to be eaten along the way. He had also engaged an Aboriginal guide, a Wiradjuri man they named 'John Piper'. They travelled south to the Lachlan and followed it down Hume's track to the Murrumbidgee and from there to the Murray (known to the Aboriginal people as the Milewa).

After leaving eight men at a base camp under Stapylton, he pressed on towards the Darling with the 15 others and 'John Piper'. Two days later, according to Mitchell's field book, they reached 'a fine Lake full sixteen miles in circumference' but 'swarming with Natives' who Mitchell recognised as 'our old adversaries from the Darling at a distance of nearly 200 miles from their usual haunts, and come across (as I was afterwards told) to fight us!'

This was not only unexpected, it revived memories of his earlier experiences with 'these murderous savages'. He wrote in his official report:

> Under such circumstances it appeared to me desirable to draw them after us first, to a greater distance from the depot camp

> and then to turn and attack them with as much effect as we could . . . [After] two days journey the numbers in our rear amounted to about one hundred and eighty.
>
> On the morning of the 27th of May they were following us closely . . . with tumultuous shouting, and our own safety and further progress evidently depended on our attacking them forthwith. But it was difficult to come at such enemies hovering in our rear with the lynx-eyed vigilance of savages. I succeeded however, by sending back a party of volunteers through a scrub to take them in flank, while I halted the rest of the party suddenly beyond a hill to which the savages were likely to follow our track.
>
> Attacked simultaneously by both parties, the whole betook themselves to the River – my men pursuing and shooting as many as they could. Numbers were shot in swimming across the Murray, and some even after they reached the opposite shore, as they ascended the bank. Amongst those shot in the water was the Chief (recognised by a particular kind of cloak he wore, which floated after he went down). Thus in a very short time the usual silence of the desert prevailed on the banks of the Murray, and we pursued our journey unmolested.

Having satisfied himself that the Darling did indeed meet with the greater stream, Mitchell crossed the Murray on 13 June and named Swan Hill seven days later. Travelling south-west, he climbed Pyramid Hill and was so impressed with the lush landscape that he christened it 'Australia Felix'. In early July, the party crossed the Loddon River and continued south-west to the Grampians and later to the mouth of a crystal clear stream he named – with an eye to his superiors – the Glenelg River.

It was now August, so he turned east towards Portland and reached the bay where to his astonishment – and that of the illegal settlers – he discovered a farm manned by the Henty brothers, Edward and Francis. At the time Stephen was captaining one of several whaling boats on the bay. The explorers and the pioneers greeted each other effusively and Mitchell was able to tell them of the excellent farmland he had crossed. He encouraged them to move their sheep north to the Wannon River, and they happily accepted his advice. By 1839 they were running 30,000 sheep and 500 cattle on the rich pastureland that for so long had provided the Aboriginal people with a bounteous living.

After a few days with the Hentys, Mitchell turned the expedition for home, and on 17 September he again split the party taking 14 men with him and leaving the rest in Stapylton's charge. He climbed Mount Macedon, from which he had a view of Port Phillip. Then, following Hume's track, he reached the Murrumbidgee on 24 October. From there it was an increasingly well travelled path to the closer settlement and Sydney itself, which he reached in early November. Stapylton and his men arrived soon afterwards.

By then Bourke had received his report of the mass slaughter on the Murray and he reported to Glenelg 'a very unfortunate conflict with the Aboriginal Natives in which I fear a considerable number of these unhappy Savages were slaughtered'. Accordingly, he had decided to hold an official inquiry. In December 1836, Mitchell faced a Legislative Council comprised of Bourke, Colonel Snodgrass, Alexander Macleay and the unhappy Thomas Scott's successor Archdeacon William Broughton.

Mitchell declined to testify himself but conducted a 'spirited cross-examination of his men, chiefly to elicit details of the dangers they faced and the fact that – not surprisingly – after the encounter they experienced no further "molestation"'.[11] In his defence, he said:

> . . . the collision took place, and although not exactly as I intended, I was satisfied with the result, as my men were not Soldiers. I still look back on that eventful day with entire satisfaction, and in a sense gratitude to God for such a deliverance from impending danger – in a cause in which I considered myself a humble instrument in His hands for the common benefit of the civilised and savage portions of our race.

The council was unimpressed by the Almighty's instrument. They found that 'while [Mitchell's] actions might have been "palliated" by the difficulties and dangers he faced, they could in no respect be justified'. Nevertheless, they concluded that, 'The council does not think it necessary to recommend that any other proceeding be now taken on the part of the Government than the communication of this minute to the Surveyor General.'

On the surface, it appeared no more than a tap on the wrist. However, when Bourke reversed an earlier decision and published a full account of the proceeding, Mitchell was publicly shamed for his conceit in claiming to be God's messenger in the outrage. Wentworth's *Australian* concluded that he had 'made an unprovoked attack on a harmless and well disposed tribe'. Mitchell, the paper said, 'is and always was dreadfully frightened of the blacks', as was proved 'by his having shot them just in the same indiscriminate manner on each of his previous expeditions'. His second-in-command, Granville Stapylton, later became a hopeless alcoholic. On 31 May 1840, while on a survey of the

Logan River in Queensland, he was speared by Aborigines and partly eaten.[12]

Mitchell had come a long way since his early association with Hamilton Hume. In the face of the uproar he applied for leave and departed for England in March 1837. He would remain there for four years – publish his best-selling *Three Expeditions into the Interior of Eastern Australia* and collect a knighthood – before returning to his post.

By then the immensely popular Richard Bourke had ended his service to the colony and was returning to Ireland. Even before his departure, a fund was rapidly filled by public subscription to erect a statue to commemorate his governorship. On the day he left, so many attended his levee at Government House that it took an hour for them all to file past and make their farewell bows. On the foreshores and the harbour, the 'shirtless and shoeless friends of the Governor' thronged to applaud him. According to *The Australian*, 'The ruffians followed him by land and water too. Those who had hats waved them triumphantly in the air; those who had not contented themselves with shouts that rent the sky.' As his ship rode down the harbour followed by a crowd of small boats, Bourke stood bareheaded on deck waving in response to the cheers. Never before (or since) has a New South Wales governor been so acclaimed.

His successor, Sir George Gipps, would prove a very different kettle of English fish. In 1837, a new monarch ascended the throne in the person of Queen Victoria, and the age of British imperial triumphalism reached new heights.

CHAPTER EIGHTEEN

The Death of John Kennedy Hume

Governor Gipps is installed, Aborigines are massacred by the settlers, and Hume's brother John is attacked by bushrangers.

By the time Brevet-Major Gipps arrived with his wife Elizabeth and their young son Reginald in February 1838, the colony's future as a convict slave economy was under threat. And neither by training nor experience was he fitted to manage the social and economic tumult in prospect.

Gipps was a son of the manse whose professional experience was confined to the military. He was educated at the King's School, where a classmate was William Broughton – now the New South Wales Anglican archdeacon – followed by the Royal Military Academy at Woolwich. He joined the Royal Engineers as a second lieutenant in 1809, and served in the Peninsular campaigns and in Wellington's army from 1814 to 1817. He was sent to the West Indies on administrative duties after the war. There he took a slave mistress and fathered a child whom he abandoned. But he impressed his superiors with his capacity for hard work and clarity of expression in his reports. Transferred to Canada, he helped to write the Gosford report on the grievances of the French Canadians and revealed himself as a Whig of cautiously liberal bent.

His wife was the daughter of Major-General George Ramsay, and at 47 he had become 'peppery, straightforward and frank when raising questions but asked none himself'. According to his biographer, he was regular in his devotions in the Anglican Church, though he admitted that the sermons of his erstwhile school chum Bishop Broughton 'were too much for him, and he occupied his thoughts with his official despatches'.[1] Throughout his tenure he would suffer from headaches, sick spells, malaria and finally a heart condition. Moreover, the colony was entering a severe drought that would devastate the agricultural economy over the next three years.

In Britain the Anti-Slavery Society led by William Wilberforce had secured an Act of parliament in 1833 abolishing slavery throughout the Empire, and the movement had naturally spilled over to the allied practice of transportation. In 1837, the urbane 26-year-old Member for East Cornwall, Sir William Molesworth, a radical politician who proudly sported a duelling scar (and who co-founded the Reform Club in Pall Mall following the passing of the Great Reform Bill of 1832) headed a committee of parliamentarians to consider the issue in its entirety.

He began it opposed in principle to the practice, and ended it appalled by the 'horrid details of the penal settlements' where:

> every kind and gentle feeling of human nature is constantly outraged by the perpetual spectacle of punishment and misery – by the frequent infliction of the lash – by the gangs of

> slaves in irons . . . till the heart of the immigrant is gradually deadened to the suffering of others and he becomes at last as cruel as the other gaolers in these vast prisons.

The parallels with black slavery were obvious, and not surprisingly his committee recommended that it should cease 'as soon as practicable'.

In the colony itself there were spirited contending views. The wealthy squatters and landowners were heavily dependent on the convicts assigned to them. But as the British penal code became less harsh, only the more hardened and dangerous English felons were being punished by transportation. So a deepening gulf had developed between these newly arrived lawbreakers and the rest of the population. On the other hand, the Irish politicals were increasingly well educated and were often the victims of police actions against their protests at the high price of British grain.

There was a sudden influx of convicts from Canada, many of whom were skilled tradesmen who on release congregated in the Parramatta suburb of Canada Bay. The Canadian connection is one of the lesser known aspects of early Australian history. It would lead to the arrival in 1852 of one of the more enduring characters of Australia's 'golden age' of bushranging, 10-year-old Johnny Gilbert.

At the same time there were growing waves of free settlers from Britain, and they feared that the 'hated stain' of convictism would blight their own reputations by association with the penal outpost. The newspapers and the churches pressed for an end to transportation on grounds that the convicts were not only competition to honest, free labourers, but also the source of vice and crime in the colony. Wentworth's *Australian* became particularly vociferous – if somewhat schizophrenic – after his law and business partner Robert Wardell was shot dead by an escaped convict, John Jenkins. Wentworth was torn between outrage at the loss of his friend and his desire for continued free labour on his big grazing properties.

One of Gipps's first tasks when he took over the vice-regal reins from the interim acting governor, the ubiquitous Colonel Snodgrass, was to prohibit the assignment of convicts for domestic service in towns. Thereafter they could only be allocated to relatively remote areas. This pleased neither side of the argument, and throughout his tenure Gipps would struggle to maintain a midway course between them.

Another of his early concerns was the rapid expansion of settlement north and south as the landseekers followed in the paths of the explorers, particularly Mitchell's well-marked track in Hume's footsteps to and from the Murray, then beyond it to 'Australia Felix'. This led to Gipps familiarising himself with Hume's various journeys and in 1837 he noted and approved his leadership of a party of family, friends and settlers to the lush valleys of the Murray basin. By then Hamilton had fully relocated his headquarters from Appin to Yass where that year he was a steward at the picnic races and a committee member of the Yass Hunt. As well, his brother John had moved to his 6,400-acre property, 'Collingwood', at Gunning, and his Eliza produced three more daughters who would survive the precarious childhood of the day.

The Hume brothers' youngest sibling, Francis Rawdon, remained at Appin where at 27 in 1830 he married 16-year-old Emma Mitchell. Together they would produce no fewer than 14 children, 12 of whom would reach adulthood. Rawdon, as he was known, had been granted 80 acres there in the 1820s and with subsequent purchases, this would be combined with his parents' 'Hume Mount Farm' and 'Beulah' to become 'the Rockwood Estate'.

Following Hume's tracks, a Goulburn squatter, William Faithfull, son of a private in the Rum Corps, sent a team of managers and convicts south with sheep and cattle to occupy land beyond the Ovens River. While his brother George took his sheep to the Broken River, William made for Oxley's Plains, discovered by Hume in 1824. The men with the sheep were caught in a violent affray with Aboriginal warriors resulting in fatalities on both sides. The trigger was the usual one: the men had trafficked with the Aboriginal women, and the articles promised for their favours were not forthcoming. The warriors then attacked the white men in their encampment and several were speared.

Also in the vanguard of settlers to the south was Henry Monro, who sold his 'Boro' property and moved his operation overland down 'Mitchell's line'. With Monro in the lead, the Christie family, together with assistant overseer Ferrier Liston and the dozen assigned convicts as stockmen and shepherds, set out in February 1838. Monro had built up his herds of cattle and sheep and they determined the party's progress throughout the journey. The squatter was armed with a shotgun and wore a shooting coat, straw hat and trousers strapped with leather and moleskin. He kept a short clay pipe between clenched teeth and was constantly on the alert for Aboriginal resistance. The natives appeared from time to time as moving shadows in the bush and when Monro spotted them he fired the shotgun above their heads to warn them off.[2]

It was a blazing hot summer and conditions were rough. When they finally forded the Coliban River and reached the Campaspe Plains four months after setting out, Monro took up a 50,000-acre run and named it 'Monro's Plains'.

They camped near Wild Duck Creek below Mount Alexander while the men built accommodation for Monro, the Christies and themselves. The shepherds took the flocks to grazing areas where the builders erected their huts. Nine-year-old Francis Christie and his sisters continued their studies, and their mother's instructions were supplemented by one of the convicts, Tom Clarke, who had been a teaching assistant in England and gave them lessons in arithmetic. They also had access to Monro's limited but eclectic library.

In July 1839 there was a big Aboriginal corroboree at Mount Alexander, a site of spiritual significance to the people of the area, and the gathering appropriated some of Monro's sheep for the occasion. It was not unusual for the shepherds to exchange a sheep for an Aboriginal woman to spend a night in their huts. The latest 'theft' would be noticed in the count, so they reported it to Monro, who was outraged.

Settlers had taken up neighbouring blocks and on an earlier occasion men from Bowman's and Yaldwyn's stations to the south had chased them away after similar thefts. The Aboriginal people had retreated to the flats behind the mountain and to 'teach them a lesson' the stockmen descended on them with massive rifle fire. They scored 'a great victory' in which an unknown number of Aborigines were killed. The whites thereafter dubbed the area 'Waterloo Plains'.

When Monro happened upon a hunting party of a dozen warriors, he charged his horse among them, firing his pistols.

The Aborigines responded with spears that brought down his mount and struck him in the back. Charles Christie spurred his horse into the melee and rescued the squatter who was seriously injured. As his wound healed over the following months, he headed raiding parties on their camps by the Coliban.

Clearly the 1815 Battle of Waterloo had become an iconic call to arms for the settlers north and south, for in the north-west plains another massacre took place at the same time in an area dubbed 'Waterloo Creek'. It followed the standard pattern of relatively minor Aboriginal resistance triggering a vicious, disproportionate response. In this case, the Aborigines appropriated a few cattle and sheep for food; shepherds interacted with the women; cattle stockmen shot and raped them and the Aborigines responded with spears. Five stockmen were killed in separate incidents and the government authorised a detachment of troopers under the commandant of the New South Wales Mounted Police, Major James Nunn, to the Gwydir valley to track down the Aboriginal 'murderers'.

On 26 January 1838 – the Jubilee of Arthur Phillip's arrival at Sydney Cove – Nunn and his heavily armed men surrounded a big tribal group and opened fire. Estimates vary, but at least 50 men, women and children were killed at camp or as they attempted to flee across the river. An inquiry into the incident would be held the following year but there would be no convictions and the matter was dropped.

Meantime, in the same area about 50 Aboriginal people of the Wirrayaraay tribe had moved to Myall Creek station, owned by an absentee landlord, Henry Dangar, at the invitation of a stockman. They had previously interacted with whites; most had English nicknames and the children could speak 'a degree of

English'.[3] In April 1838, John Fleming, a free settler with violently racist views, gathered a group of 11 convicts – ten English and one of African extraction – who had been assigned to squatters in the district. Together they set out on a killing spree.

When the young Aboriginal men were away hunting or working stock, Fleming and his gang overwhelmed the 28 women, children and elderly men at their camp, tied them together by the neck with a long rope and led them 800 metres away to a gully where they used swords to behead them. One woman was spared and repeatedly gang raped. The massacre was witnessed by an Aboriginal man, 'Davy', a stockman on the station. George Anderson, another convict on the property, refused to join the bloodbath and was able to save two of the Wirrayaraay boys. When the men of the tribe came back, Anderson told them to clear out in case the gang returned, but he was too late; the killers intercepted most of them and slaughtered them as well.

The station manager William Hobbs arrived back at the property several days later and discovered the headless bodies. Shocked, he passed the terrible news to a neighbouring squatter, Frederick Foot, who rode to Sydney to report it to Governor Gipps. But by the time the police arrived to investigate, the bodies had been cremated and only fragments of teeth and bone remained. Nevertheless, after taking evidence from Anderson and 'Davy', they arrested the culprits.

The owner, Henry Dangar, who was notorious for his treatment of Aboriginal people, then came on the scene, ordered Anderson and Hobbs to remain silent and organised The Black Association to contribute funds to the defence of the marauders. Hobbs refused to be silenced and Dangar dismissed him. Anderson stood firm but the instigator, Fleming, 'disappeared' (probably to the Hawkesbury), and the case against the convicts was confined to the murder of one man, an elderly Aborigine known as 'Daddy'. Aside from the convict Anderson's testimony, the case rested on circumstantial evidence and they were found not guilty to the general jubilation of the squatters. An article in the *Sydney Morning Herald* caught their mood: 'The whole gang of black animals are not worth the money the colonists will have to pay for printing the silly court documents on which we have already wasted too much time.'[4]

However, the convicts were remanded and seven faced a second trial for the murder of an Aboriginal boy. This time they were found guilty. On 18 December 1838, they were hanged. The other four men were remanded until 'Davy' could be found to give evidence against them. But according to a missionary, Henry Dangar had arranged for him to he killed.[5]

Gipps declared himself powerless in the face of 'the venturesome settlers whose philosophy is that the only good Aborigine is a dead one'. He wrote to Glenelg that he was confronted by, 'the extreme difficulty of devising any measure that shall effectively check the outrages, which I regret to say are now of frequent occurrence beyond the boundaries of location.'[6]

At the same time he was confronted by an upsurge of bushranging activity as escaped convicts formed themselves into gangs of young men totally alienated from the privileged classes who controlled the wealth and power within the colony. Two of the more notable were Archibald 'Scotchie' Thomson and Thomas Whitton who 'bolted' from 'Wangella', the Lachlan River property of the late Dr William Redfern, in the early months of 1838. A former convict who had been rehabilitated during the regime of Governor Macquarie, Redfern had died in 1834 and the management of his estate suffered. The convict overseer, Michael Peake, not only applied the lash; he was a regular informer to the manager.

In December, Scotchie and Whitton, together with another former convict, Tom Butts, returned to the property in search of their tormentor. Word spread quickly that they were seeking revenge and by now they were well armed and mounted. In a later statement, Whitton said, 'About sunset on the evening of that day Scotchie and myself, accompanied by Butts, went to the [dormitory] hut in which Peake then was. We remained outside while Butts went in and searched for Peake [and] discovered him under [his] bed.' Other inhabitants of the hut ran out. 'At this time Scotchie and myself were watching at the hut door when Scotchie . . . drew out his pistol and shot Peake.'[7] Butts was not happy, as he had been told they merely wanted to 'beat' the man. Whitton says, 'Butts expressed himself much annoyed,' so they parted 'as it was dangerous for him to be seen with us and he would be sure to be identified if taken in our company.'

On 22 January 1839, the government offered a reward of £20 and a conditional pardon for their capture. A further £25 was offered by Redfern's estate. However, the immutable social divide meant that they would be harboured and protected by convicts on outstations and emancipists with whom they shared a hatred of the privileged and the troopers who did their bidding. The *Australasian Chronicle*, a Parramatta periodical editorialised, 'There is no manner of doubt that the bushrangers are assisted by assigned servants and perhaps by others who are not servants . . . and these watch police movements for [them].'

Scotchie and Whitton withdrew to Bryan Gang station, where they learned that there was a great muster in progress at Rankin's station near Bong Bong to send flocks of sheep across the Murrumbidgee and into the 'new country' towards Port Phillip. Supplies for the great trek were on the way to the station from Sydney. The bushrangers headed out at first light, intercepted the drays and bailed them up. They then roamed the area from the Lachlan to Yass and Goulburn. And on 1 January 1840, with another escaped convict, Bernard Reynolds, they bailed up the house of magistrate Dr Benjamin Clayton, five kilometres north of Gunning. They paid a return visit a fortnight later prompting the doctor to seek shelter for his wife and children at 'Collingwood' with John and Eliza Hume.

On the 19th, the bushrangers turned once again to vengeance and sought out Francis Oakes, a landholder near Crookwell. They found him supervising a wheat harvest with 14 convicts and opened fire. One labourer, John Hawkins, was shot in the crossfire and killed. The squatter escaped to a neighbouring station and the bushrangers contented themselves with burning his homestead to the ground.

The next day they rode into Gunning and headed for the Grosvenor's Inn. However, they had been spotted on a back trail by the driver of the mail coach, Richard Robinson; he had reached the inn a few minutes before them and raised the alarm. As the bushrangers rode in, Robinson and James Grosvenor armed themselves and faced them. Whitton raised his gun and fired. Robinson returned the shot. Gunfire continued on both sides for the next hour when Grosvenor's musket exploded. Scotchie saw his opportunity and galloped towards the inn. Grosvenor grabbed a fowling piece, knocked him from his horse and ran inside. By sunset they had beaten off the attack and the bushrangers withdrew to 'Red John' Cooper's pub and store about 400 metres away.

The sound of gunfire had carried the four kilometres to 'Collingwood', where John Kennedy Hume and his family were entertaining Dr Clayton and his family as well as the youngest Hume brother, Rawdon. The two Humes, Dr Clayton and seven of John's convict labourers armed themselves and made for Gunning. John and his convict overseer William Hazel headed the party and went straight for Cooper's store. Hazel said later:

> As we entered Cooper's house, two women there [told] us to escape instantly as the bushrangers were on the premises. As we went out one of the bushrangers must have observed my master, as he came towards him and ordered him to lay down his arms. Mr Hume refused to do so – then the bushranger fired at him.[8]

Hume was struck and fell to the floor. According to *The Chronicle*, 'The robber, perceiving that the poor gentleman was not dead, fired a second and a third shot, all of which passed through different parts of his body.'

The bushrangers left the scene. *The Chronicle* said:

> Mr Hume's men were either very great cowards or were badly armed; it is perhaps owing to one or both of these causes that the whole of the bushrangers made their escape. The account of his death having reached his residence, a cart was despatched for the body, still warm and reeking with blood. Here was a sight for his disconsolate family – a wife and eight children, the greater number of the latter being little females, all of whom now deprived of a father and a protector.[9]

CHAPTER NINETEEN

The Bushrangers Meet Their End

Rawdon Hume helps track John Hume's killers, Alexander Maconochie briefly turns Norfolk Island around, and Sturt goes looking for the inland sea one last time.

Hamilton Hume was devastated by the news of his brother John's murder. He had been particularly close to John from their earliest years in the Hawkesbury and then as they explored their new surroundings at Appin with Dual and his mates. At 43, with his father a fixture at his Appin homestead, Hamilton was effectively the leader of an extended family with extensive land holdings and an enviable reputation throughout the colony. It was a fearsome blow. It reached him just as Magistrate Clayton was organising a posse headed by Goulburn Sergeant Freer and Rawdon Hume to track the bushrangers down.

By the time Hamilton arrived at 'Collingwood', they had left on the bushrangers' trail and there was little he could do but give comfort to Eliza and her brood and take charge of the arrangements for the funeral. Later he would take over the management of the property and the loss would haunt him for the rest of his days. It was scant comfort that his brother's killers would very soon meet their own violent ends.

Still on their mission of vengeance, Scotchie, Whitton, Reynolds and a fourth gang member, Jack Russell, rode to the homestead of Oliver Fry, the overseer on Dr George Gibson's station 'Narrawa'. Whitton called out, 'We've come to fry you in your own fat!' The overseer responded with a volley of shots, one of which hit Scotchie. Badly injured, he called on Whitton to 'finish the job'. His mate duly put a pistol to his head and pulled the trigger. Then he and Reynolds threw his body into the nearby Fish River.

By now Freer, Rawdon Hume and their party, which included Thomas Magennis, were bearing down on them. About 100 kilometres north-west of Goulburn, according to *The Chronicle*:

> The three bushrangers had alighted and just partaken of some tea when their pursuers got sight of them. The bushrangers each took a tree. The police party, knowing their men and knowing also that each bushranger had a double-barrelled gun, likewise got in shelter of trees. The police fired, as did the bushrangers – the former [then] charged them and in this they were well seconded by Mr Magennis.
>
> The police called on the bushrangers a second time to lay down their arms. When [they] did as they were ordered one of them [Russell], who was wounded by the police, and who lay on the ground from the effect of this wound, deliberately took out his own pocket-pistol, placed its mouth to his head and instantly put an end to his existence.[1]

Whitton and Reynolds – with Russell's body strapped to his horse – set out on the long journey to Goulburn. On the way, unnoticed by the police, Russell's body slipped off the horse. Reynolds had obviously retained his morbid sense of humour. He reckoned his mate could escape 'alive or dead'. The two remaining bushrangers were lodged in the Goulburn lock-up. 'Now that they are caught,' *The Chronicle* editorialised, 'it is most earnestly hoped that they will be kept safe.'[2]

It was not to be. When they were taken to Darlinghurst Gaol in Sydney, tried and sentenced to death, Reynolds cheated the hangman by contriving his own gallows with a torn blanket and his 'night tub'. Thomas Whitton, whose initial crime in England that began his tragic colonial chronicle is lost to history, met his fate with quiet resignation. Transported to Goulburn under heavy guard and with material for his gallows in a following dray, he faced a crowd of spectators encouraged to attend by the authorities. His open grave awaited behind the place of execution.

According to *The Monitor*: 'The prisoner, after swallowing a little coffee which was handed up to him in a tin dish, addressed a few words to the spectators, stating that whatever their masters might say or do to them, to abstain from using firearms for, he added "it was that which brought me here".' The hangman, Alexander Green, who had accompanied him from Sydney, then 'performed his duty. The unfortunate Whitton died after a few struggles . . . after hanging for about an hour he was lowered down and put in the coffin and then the grave. His aspect was little changed, his neck showed the mark of the violent ligature. He was twenty-six years of age.'[3]

While there was a sense of satisfaction among the landholders and the administration at the demise of the gang, they were but one of many still at large. And the assistance they'd received from the under-classes during their two years as free men gave Gipps and his police force serious concern, particularly when the punishment reserved for repeat offenders – exile to the terrors of Norfolk Island or Port Arthur – appeared to have very little effect.

Both of these penal colonies were drawn into focus when a message reached New South Wales later that year announcing the end of transportation to the colony. They were the two exceptions – hellholes that the British government believed would serve as deterrent to the Irish rebels, the English criminals and the colonial convicts who might otherwise be tempted to defy their masters or take to the bush. However, it was just at this time that one Alexander Maconochie would take Norfolk Island, Andrew Hume's introduction to life in the Antipodes, in exactly the opposite direction and with astonishing results.

A naval officer who had spent more than two years as a prisoner of war in France, he founded the Geographical Society of London, which soon attracted the royal patronage of William IV. It also introduced him to the dashing Captain John Franklin, a midshipman under Matthew Flinders in his circumnavigation of Australia. In 1837 Maconochie accepted the role of private secretary to Franklin when he was appointed lieutenant-governor of Van Diemen's Land on the understanding from Lord Glenelg that he would receive an independent appointment once he was established in the colony. Meantime, he had studied penology and come firmly to the view that the current policy was not only inhumane, it was utterly ineffective. His alternative was a system of 'marks' to be earned by the prisoners for good behaviour and self-responsibility within a team. It was a revolutionary concept in such a time and place. But it struck a chord with the Whig government and when he proposed to Gipps that he be given command of Norfolk Island to put his ideas into practice, the governor was torn.

Glenelg knew immediately that the 'exclusives' in the colony would be outraged yet he seemed at least prepared to give it a trial. Gipps reluctantly concurred and Maconochie's methods immediately bore fruit. But not in Westminster, and particularly not the following year when the Tories returned to power with Lord John Russell as their secretary of state and the colonies. From that moment, Maconochie's experiment in humanity was doomed.

Nevertheless, the vicissitudes of distance and communication would delay the inevitable for a full three years. And in 1843 Gipps appeared on the island unannounced. 'I visited every part of it,' he wrote, 'minutely inspected every establishment and separately questioned or examined every person holding some position of authority.' To his surprise, the system was working handsomely. But the vice-regal imprimatur notwithstanding, Maconochie was recalled and departed the island in March the following year.

Under his four-year regime, 920 old hands had been discharged and three years later less than 5 per cent had reoffended. More than 600 new hands earned their ticket-of-leave and departed, mostly for Van Diemen's Land as labourers and settlers. However, Norfolk Island then entered its most terrible phase with the appointment of a sadistic imbecile, Major Joseph Childs.

Back on the mainland, Gipps struggled with a multitude of contentious issues and a sense of utter aloneness but for the correspondence he shared with Charles La Trobe, who had been appointed superintendent of the Port Phillip district in 1839. The son of a Huguenot, La Trobe had been born in London in 1801, had led an adventurous life in the United States and been commissioned by the British government to inquire into the education of recently emancipated West Indian slaves.

He met with Gipps before taking up his new appointment, and the two men would exchange many hundreds of letters during their tenures. Gipps constantly referred to the opposition he experienced from all sides, not least in his own Legislative Council. By November 1843, he was writing testily that, 'There are about five or six men in the council who are personally my enemies for no better reason that I am aware of than because they were not received as dinner guests at Government House.' In fact, their enmity went considerably deeper and in the case of W. C. Wentworth it involved Gipps's refusal to sell him most of New Zealand's South Island for a song – 20 million acres at the rate of one thousand acres for a farthing.[4] Wentworth never forgave him, and never missed an opportunity to speak (and write) against him.

La Trobe had his own problems, and shared them with his superior. In 1840, the 3,000 inhabitants of Melbourne and settlers from further afield formed a Separation Association seeking a measure of self-government, and agitated strongly against receiving convicts or ticket-of-leave felons. The *Imperial Act of 1842* gave them only six seats in Gipps's Legislative Council and the time and distance involved meant their representatives were often unable or unwilling to attend.

La Trobe was also deeply concerned about the frontier war with the Aboriginal people. The whole of the Port Phillip district was aflame. On the Ovens, chaos reigned. George Faithfull, his cousin William Bowman and Colonel White retreated to New South Wales from the 'black avengers'. Dr George Mackay alone briefly stuck it out before rounding up his stock and making for the comparative safety of the Murray, claiming that 'It would have been certain death to remain.'[5]

Some 82 'pioneers of civilisation' signed a letter to Gipps demanding government protection. 'If adequate protection be not afforded . . . the settlers will undoubtedly take Measures to protect themselves,' they threatened

> as it is not to be supposed they will remain quietly looking on whilst their property is being destroyed and their servants murdered; and your Memorialists need hardly observe that such a mode of proceeding would inevitably be attended with consequences of the most painful nature.[6]

Among the signatories was the name Hamilton Hume.

The 'Aboriginal problem' in the country he had opened up south of the Murray was very different from that which pertained in Hume's home district of Yass, where the combination of closer settlement and imported diseases had decimated the Ngunnawal and Wiradjuri people. In 1839 Hume had expanded his Yass holdings with the purchase of Henry O'Brien's property, which included his Cooma Cottage. The following year he began a major building program and turned the cottage into a big rambling homestead.

Meanwhile, in Sydney when Gipps's six-year term expired in 1844 the governor applied for and received a two-year extension.

The drought had broken, and the colony was once again on a firm financial footing. However, the continuing influx of free settlers meant that the population of New South Wales had doubled since his arrival and now stood at almost 200,000. Among them was a growing number of children whose educational needs had been practically ignored from the beginning of settlement. Of the estimated 25,676 youngsters aged between four and 14, 7,642 went to public schools, 4,865 to private schools and the rest had no formal schooling at all.

The colonial government made grants to the schools on a half-and-half program, matching the funds raised privately by the school communities. Ironically, Gipps's attempts to reform the system were blocked by his old school friend Bishop Broughton. When his Anglicans combined with the dissenters to defeat him, Gipps abandoned his reform.

His support for further exploration of the interior was fitful and spasmodic. On his watch, the Polish aristocrat Paul Strzelecki made a geological survey of Eastern Victoria, named Gippsland in his honour, and in 1839 discovered gold there. Gipps feared the effects of the discovery on the colony and persuaded the Pole to keep it secret. Later the same year he led a party that included two Aboriginal guides that climbed Australia's highest peak and he named it Kosciuszko after a Polish hero. For the next two years he based himself in Launceston, and with the backing of Lieutenant-Governor Franklin explored most parts of the island before departing for Britain.

Charles Sturt had returned to Australia in mid-1835 and begun farming land granted to him in the area now occupied by the national capital. In 1838, he and a team of drovers took cattle overland to Adelaide, where he settled in 1839. He was appointed surveyor-general of the convict-free settlement, and a member of that colony's Legislative Council. But the siren call of the great inland sea still beckoned, and in 1844 he headed for the centre of the continent with a well-equipped expedition of 15 men, 200 sheep, six drays and the inevitable boat upon which to ride the waves.

They travelled along the Murray and Darling rivers before passing the buried riches of Broken Hill, but were then stranded for months by the extreme summer heat. When the rains finally came, they pressed on to the Stony Desert and across it to the even more desolate Simpson's Desert. Sturt dragged himself onward until his health broke down completely. The surgeon on the trip, John Harris Browne, then took over the leadership and helped him home.

He took leave in London and returned in 1849 to be appointed South Australia's colonial secretary. He threw himself into his many tasks but his explorations had undermined his constitution, and in 1853 he and his family sailed for England for the last time. He died suddenly on 16 June 1869.

His lifelong rival for pelagic honours, Thomas Mitchell, also set out for the interior in 1845 seeking, he said, 'a practical route to the Gulf of Carpentaria'. The previous year he had been elected to the Legislative Council for a Port Phillip seat in support of separation from New South Wales. But Gipps disapproved of his surveyor-general as a political activist and he duly resigned before heading north-west from his habitual starting point at Boree station.

By June 1846, he had established a depot on the Maranoa and for nearly four months explored the area that would become a rich Queensland grazing district. He was really searching for a great stream flowing north-west but instead found himself under threat from the Aboriginal people of the channel country. However, on his return this did not prevent him from suggesting that he had discovered the river that might possibly lead to the inland sea.

He again took an extended London leave, and in his absence the Survey Department languished. On his return, he resumed his fractious relationship with his superiors in New South Wales and the Colonial Office, even fighting a duel in 1851 with a critic, Stuart Donaldson, who would later become the state's first premier. Each fired three pistol shots – one went through Donaldson's hat, another within an inch of Mitchell's throat.

Finally, a royal commission was called to inquire into his departmental administration. But before it reported, Mitchell caught a chill while surveying the difficult line of road from Nelligen to Braidwood, developed pneumonia and died in his Sydney home on 5 October 1855.

By then Governor Gipps had long departed New South Wales with the hatred of the colonial press ringing in his ears. In 1846, as he set sail for London, the *Sydney Morning Herald*, somewhat unkindly, stated its firm conviction, 'from the matured observation of eight years . . . that Sir George Gipps has been the worst Governor New South Wales ever had.'

It was an overstatement, but not by much. He was a sick man when his ship passed through the heads towards a reunion with his son Reginald, whom he had sent back to England for schooling at Eton three years previously. Their time together was cut short; in February 1847 Gipps suffered a fatal heart attack. Reginald would himself be knighted and attain the rank of general in the British Army. He never returned to Australia.

CHAPTER TWENTY

Gold!

The rush for gold creates chaos in the colonies, Frank Christie begins his bushranging career, and Hamilton Hume begins to be concerned at Hovell's boasts.

Hume would be deeply affected by the wildly changing fortunes of the forthcoming gold rush, as would his fellow graziers in the Yass district. Gipps's decision to keep Strzelecki's gold discovery a secret only delayed the inevitable. In fact, discoveries had been popping up all over the colony since the 1820s but were treated with either derision or disbelief. In 1841 and 1842 the enterprising cleric Rev. William Branwhite Clarke did some prospecting between ecclesiastical duties and found gold traces in both the Bathurst and Goulburn districts. He told his parishioners of his good fortune but when he showed his prize to the governor, Gipps responded, 'Put it away, Mr Clarke, or we shall all have our throats cut.'[1]

The governor was acting on orders from the mandarins of Whitehall who said they feared a gold rush would turn the colony into chaos – the steady flow of wool for the industrial spinning mills would grind to a halt; officials would walk off their jobs; and the convicts might even defy the lash and bolt. And though Australian officialdom would escape the murderous fate Gipps envisaged, the Colonial Office was right on most other counts.

Gipps and his successor, the pampered aristocrat Sir Charles Augustus Fitzroy, would hold the line until 1848, when news of the California discoveries brought an immediate exodus across the Pacific. This prompted a reversal of government policy, and even a £10,000 reward for the discovery of a commercial field in Australia.

The winner was Edward Hargreaves, a scoundrel born in southern England in 1816, who went to sea at 14, and after knocking about the world arrived in Sydney in 1832. He worked on a property at Bathurst and four years later married Elizabeth Mackay, the daughter of a colonial merchant. He used her dowry to build a hotel and store at Gosford before taking off in March 1849 for the Californian goldfields.

His pickings were few, and when he returned in response to the reward, he enlisted a pair of young prospectors and made for the Bathurst area, where rumours of riches had circulated ever since the Rev. Clarke's discoveries. It was not long before they found traces, which Hargreaves inflated to become 'rich fields' in an overblown report to the *Sydney Morning Herald* in early May 1851. He named the area Ophir after the legendary source of King Solomon's gold, and within a fortnight, more than 300 diggers had descended on the district. The rush was on.

By the end of the year it had spread to other areas north and south of Sydney, and Hargreaves collected his reward from Fitzroy's government. However, the really big early finds would take place in the Port Phillip district, which in July 1851 achieved separation from New South Wales to become the colony of Victoria. Its inauguration could hardly have been more spectacular and auspicious for only days later news reached Melbourne of discoveries near Ballarat that triggered one of the biggest gold rushes the world had seen.

The infant colony was utterly unprepared. Melbourne was a hot, dusty place where bullock teams trundled down the pitted streets some 100 metres across; where Batman's Hill had yet to be renamed Spencer Street; and where the scattered population either collected their own water from the Yarra or bought it from the horse-drawn peddlers' drays. A ferry crossed the river at Elizabeth Street and when the Princes Bridge was opened later that year La Trobe declared a public holiday.

When the first big nugget was found at Ballarat, the townsmen departed en masse. A young English immigrant, John Chandler, who had arrived the year before and worked as a carter with his father, was on the town's outskirts with his bullock team. 'As we looked back the way we had come,' he says,

> there was one continued procession of vehicles of every description, for miles in single file, from a wheelbarrow to a ten-bullock team . . . very few men were left in Melbourne, and it was said that there was only one man left in Geelong, and the women were going to put him in a glass case.[2]

The squatters' shepherds and stockmen either departed for the goldfields as prospectors or, like Chandler, traded with the diggers. As tens of thousands of eager prospectors arrived from Europe and America, he says, 'Everything was very unsafe, for there were desperate characters about. In fact, you were not safe anywhere.'

On the Loddon riverlands, where Henry Monro had established his 'Monro's Plains' with the Christie family, the previous decade had wrought major changes. The love triangle between Jane, her de facto Charles Christie and Henry Monro had resolved itself in 1841 when she accepted Monro's proposal and they were married in Melbourne. A broken-hearted Christie left the property. He would later become a shearers' cook on New South Wales sheep stations.

The changed circumstances elevated 12-year-old Frank Christie and his siblings into the squatter class with 'social prospects'. Henry's brother David arrived for a visit on his way to New Zealand where he too would take up extensive farmland and eventually become Speaker of the House of Representatives. He was appalled at his brother's decision to marry beneath himself. 'I have never been able to find out why he married her,' he wrote in a revealing letter to his wife Charlotte.

> She must have been acting as his wife for some years and she is more than ten years older than him. I presume it must have been some consideration connected with his child, or some idea of doing justice to the woman that led him to take the step. However, it is a marriage to be very soon dissolved by the hand of death: the poor woman is lying in the next room to the one in which I am writing on her death bed. She suffers very great pain, and with much resignation, which it is impossible to have any feelings towards her but those of sorrow and compassion.

Nevertheless, Frank and his sisters retained some of their pastoral connections under Monro's patronage. These were loosened when in 1843 he sold 'Monro's Plains' and took up the

90,000-acre 'Crawford River' pastoral run at Hotspur, north of Portland Bay, after the previous owner had fallen to Aboriginal spears. They became more tenuous in 1846 when Monro married Catherine 'Kate' Power, the daughter of landed parents. And when, the following year, Kate gave birth to Alexander, the first of their ten children, they parted.

Frank was soon in trouble with the law. He and several mates stole a string of horses, and when captured he was sentenced to five years hard labour on the roads. He was held at the newly built Pentridge Gaol, where he led the first successful escape. He grabbed a pistol from the constable in charge, and while his companions scattered to the goldfields, Frank headed back to the Goulburn-Yass district of New South Wales. He was described as 'a sturdy, dark complexioned youth, not more than 20 years old'.[3]

By now Hume had turned his Yass property into a pastoral showplace. He had also 'adopted' one of his brother Rawdon's sons, 'Little Hamilton', who lived with him and Eliza at their Cooma Cottage homestead, and they ran his several holdings together. The young man had a flair for sheep breeding and fine wool growing and gradually built up his own flocks as well.

Hume's mother Elizabeth had died on 14 August 1847, aged 86 and in the knowledge that her eldest son had become a living legend, with dignitaries and newcomers calling by his property to pay their respects. His father Andrew would take his leave two years later, aged 88, at daughter Isabella's 'Glenrock' homestead. Her husband, George Barber, had been killed when swept away by floodwaters while riding home from Goulburn in 1844. Hamilton had offered a reward for the discovery of the body but to no avail.

Hamilton's wife – 'my poor Bess' – endured many fearful bouts of asthma and was constantly under the care of Dr John O'Brien, the local medico. However, she always recovered strongly and his affection for her is manifest in his letters to friends and relations. His own health in his fifties was robust, but he was becoming increasingly irritated by reports from friends and fellow travellers in the colony that his naval companion on the great journey to Port Phillip was boasting in public appearances about the part he played in the expedition. He was also concerned that Bland's bowdlerised and ornamented version of Hovell's journal was becoming the accepted wisdom. But for the moment he kept his peace. His properties required a great deal of his attention, particularly as convict labour was no longer readily available.

Transportation had been reintroduced in 1847 due to the overcrowding of British jails, and a public demand for it as a deterrent, but most convicts were sent to Van Diemen's Land and Victoria. They were designated 'exiles', and were permitted to work for pay while under sentence. However, once gold was discovered, free transportation was a positive boon to the felons, and the last convict ship to be sent from England to the Eastern colonies was the *St Vincent* in 1853.

By then the Victorian population was streaking upwards from 76,000 in 1851 towards half a million less than ten years later. The prospectors were attracted by the richest shallow alluvial goldfield in the world and the biggest nuggets ever unearthed. In Melbourne, John Chandler's business was booming. He ran his bullock team back and forth to the goldfields almost without a break. 'There was now a very large number arriving on the diggings and the government made a charge of 30 shillings per month for a licence to dig,' he says.

> This was very hard, as there were hundreds now on the diggings who could not get the colour, in fact not more than one in five was successful. The government was very harsh. They sent out four to six constables in a company with muskets and bayonets fixed. They were mostly old hands, or in other words, convicts from Van Diemen's Land.

If the diggers were unable to pay the charge immediately, they were either fined 40 shillings or taken to a lock-up for seven days.

They responded by banding together, so that whenever a squad of constables was spotted, the word 'Joe' (for Charles Joseph La Trobe) was quickly spread from one end of the diggings to the other. 'All the unlicensed men would vanish down their holes like so many rabbits,' Chandler says. 'The constables knew there were men down below but they dare not go down for accidents would be sure to happen.'[4]

This combination of disreputable lawmen and brutally oppressive regulations escalated in the early 1850s until wholesale anarchy threatened. 'Everyone had to go armed as there was so much sticking up and horse stealing,' Chandler says. 'Many a poor fellow was put out of the way during those times, and never heard of anymore. What few police we had were not to be trusted. It was every man for himself.'

In New South Wales, the rush concentrated in the area around Bathurst and Orange where the prospectors were well rewarded. In 1852 they extracted no less than 850,000 ounces (24 tonnes) and Mitchell's road across the Blue Mountains became choked with men from all walks of life. In Bathurst the local newspaper, the *Free Press* proclaimed, 'Complete mental madness appears to have seized almost every member of the community. There has been a universal rush to the diggings.' Prices of food and equipment rose alarmingly and fortunes were made by the men supplying meat and drink to the diggers.

In the south-west around the site of Sofala, alluvial gold was discovered in the Turon River and in late 1851 the government appointed Henry Zouch, the police officer who had found the body of Mitchell's botanical companion Richard Cunningham, as assistant commissioner of lands of the Lower Turon. He would hold the post until 1853 when he returned to Goulburn as superintendent of the mounted police in the southern districts, including the Gundagai and Braidwood gold escorts.

Meantime in Sydney, Fitzroy was wrestling with a turbulent Executive Council and a new secretary of state for the colonies, Earl Grey, who was certainly not the governor's cup of tea. The two men were constantly at loggerheads. When Grey made unpopular proposals, Fitzroy gave them full publicity while refusing to support them, thus allowing 'the storm to break over Grey's head'.[5] New Zealand had become a separate colony in 1841, and under Grey's watch gained representative government in 1852. New South Wales remained under London's control, but the Legislative Council gradually increased its powers and the same year developed a draft constitution.

The governor had lost his wife (and his aide-de-camp) in a carriage accident within the grounds of the Parramatta residence. Fitzroy was driving but escaped with minor leg injuries. When he recovered, his amorous antics with the ladies of the colony – both single and attached – set the colonial tongues wagging. He fathered at least one son out of wedlock – named by his teenage mother Augustus Charles Fitzroy. The child was later adopted by ex-convict John Fitzsimons and his family.

In 1851, Fitzroy wrote privately to Grey asking if his tenure might be extended beyond the agreed six years, since he had just received new commissions as governor of New South Wales, Van Diemen's Land, South Australia and Victoria as well as governor-general of all the Australian possessions, including Western Australia. Grey was not persuaded. The matter was left unattended when the colonial secretary fell from power in 1852.

CHAPTER TWENTY-ONE

The Colonies in Tumult

Governor Fitzroy's ineffectual reign continues, Sir Charles Hotham stirs up trouble on the goldfields, and Hume goes into print to contradict Hovell's accounts.

By 1853 the various strands of the colonial experience were coalescing to produce an extraordinary national transformation. Australia's role as a penal colony had virtually ended; only Western Australia would continue to receive a trickle of the British discards. By now the Aboriginal people were debilitated by forcible occupation of their lands as well as smallpox and other imported diseases; they would continue their sporadic resistance, particularly in Queensland, their most densely populated area, but their defeat was almost complete.

The settlers' demands for separation and self-government were spreading throughout the continent, and when Queensland achieved it in 1859, only distant Western Australia remained a statutory British dependency. The catalyst that drew the strands together to produce the metamorphosis was the gold rush. Its feverish repercussions rippled through all elements of colonial society.

Until then, the British notions of class had been sacrosanct. Wealth and privilege were reserved by birth to the ruling class, and the laws of the colony were designed to perpetuate the status quo. The police and the courts were their condign instruments to ensure its preservation. But in a single stroke, gold gave the lie to this 'natural order' of society. The nostrums the colonials had received in childhood about 'knowing their place' in the social structure no longer held sway. Suddenly the immutable truths of the past could be dashed to pieces by a well-placed miner's pick. And as the diggers were joined on the goldfields by American and Italian republicans with their rebellious democratic ideas, a radical new spirit swept through the colony.

John Chandler on his dray heading with a full load of supplies to the Bendigo diggings (with the contraband demijohns of hard liquor concealed at the centre) says, 'Work is plentiful and wages are high, and the [Port Phillip] bay is full of ships, for the sailors have run away as soon as they dropped anchor. Everybody has the gold fever . . . Jack is as good as his master!'

In New South Wales, Fitzroy was either unaware or unmoved by the turbulence that surrounded him. Encouraged by the departure of his bête noire Earl Grey, he wrote to his ministerial successor, the Duke of Newcastle, seeking a promotion to India. The duke declined but consoled him with a knighthood. Suitably mollified, Fitzroy resumed his role as the lofty conciliator in his tumultuous fiefdom. When Henry Zouch's Turon goldfields threatened rebellion, he suggested reducing the miners' licence fee. The Victorians protested and, according to his biographer, 'Fitzroy was unable to give a lead to either colony.'[1]

He brought the same air of lordly vacillation to the development of rail lines in the adjoining colonies, with the result that they chose differing gauges, an economic fiasco that would take more than a century to rectify. Fitzroy had become so inept that in the Legislative Council, John Dunmore Lang would brand him 'inefficient, extravagant, dilatory, oppressive, deleterious and morally bankrupt'. And he found a seconder in a rising young poet, journalist and politician who would soon play a major role in the transformation of the colony, Henry Parkes.

While Fitzroy was pursuing his laissez-faire administration in NSW, his newly appointed Victorian lieutenant-governor Sir Charles Hotham took a very different approach. The son of an English clergyman, he had joined the navy as a boy of 12 and risen to the rank of commodore stationed on Africa's west coast. He exhibited a talent for foreign languages, and in 1852 headed a commercial mission to Paraguay, but was caught in a political crossfire at Westminster. Newcastle resolved the issue by appointing him to distant Victoria, where he brought all the managerial subtlety of a naval officer whose whole adult life had been governed by unquestioning obedience to the chain of command.

John Chandler says, 'He thought he could do the same with a colony as he could on board a man-of-war.' In 1854 he decided to raise miners' licences from £1/10/- to £3 per month. 'This, with the arbitrary manner in which the licence was collected,' Chandler says, 'made the diggers desperate and they prepared to resist the imposition. They held meetings but no notice was taken of their complaints. They therefore armed and began to drill.'[2]

It was at this time, as the spirit of dissent from the old social strictures took hold, that Hamilton Hume chose to strike back against the mendacity of his fellow traveller on that great expedition of 1824–25. Hume and the other members of the party had never forgiven Hovell for his faint-heartedness in the face of every obstacle, and on 16 December 1853 at a public entertainment in Geelong, he had once again claimed the lion's share of credit for the journey.

As usual, he had ensured that his performance would be well noticed. Before he left his Goulburn seat he spread word of the engagement. It reached Hume in a chance meeting on the road with George Watson, his partner in a Yass flour mill, and from Watson's account Hume gave the occasion short shrift.

When he reached Geelong, Hovell led the local dignitaries to Bird Rock to the west of Point Wilson in Corio Bay. This, he claimed, was the actual spot the journey terminated. And that evening he attended the Woolpack Inn, where the mayor of Geelong made a fulsome toast in his honour. Hovell then responded in a written speech that has been preserved by the Geelong Historical Society. It is typical of the man in its flowery ornamentation, as he painted an imaginative picture of his and Hume's triumphant arrival at their destination:

> About this time 29 years back, my brother traveller Mr Hamilton Hume and myself were talking over what had passed during the journey, the present prospects, and the future . . . Thirst had kept us awake and we listened to the sound of thousands of water fowl which were then sporting on the waters of the bay then before us.
>
> In the morning while nine-tenths of mankind slept, we were on our feet watching for the light to show us the beauties which were then breaking in upon our view. When it did come, what was our delight to find with what success our outward journey had terminated! The eleven weeks of toil and

uncertainty was compensated by the result; and we considered ourselves the two most fortunate travellers on record.

We whereupon simultaneously embraced each other and, with extended arms, returned thanks to God for the shield of protection that He had thrown over us . . . Here we remained one day, the shortness of provisions and the mustering of the natives warned us that a longer delay would not be prudent, but the day we spent here was one of the happiest in our lives, for we had done that which a public record had claimed to be impossible . . .

The next happy day (five weeks later) was when we arrived among our family, to the surprise and astonishment of many, for there were those who would have been glad that we returned unsuccessful. That party was an influential one and therefore operated against us in a pecuniary way with the Government . . .

I have been asked what object we had in view in undertaking such a journey. My answer has been because it had been given out that it could not be done; and from what I recollect, I believe it was that statement and for the glory of the undertaking which were the only objects we had in view . . .

The next happy day in connection with the journey is the present. That I should live to be amongst the children of the land of my adopting after so many years absence, is to me a pleasure of no ordinary kind; *and that these children should with one accord meet and acknowledge me as the discoverer of their fine country*[3] shows that they can appreciate the services of the venerable parent.

Gentlemen, when we first saw this land it was an unoccupied wilderness . . . this land that I and my brother traveller

> Hume were the first to tread . . . A tree with my name cut on it, bearing the date 17 November 1824, and standing at the crossing place of the Hume River, is yet alive . . .

He retired to rousing applause, and the speech was widely reported. *The Argus* of 19 December 1853 captured the tone, if not the precise wording, of the written speech, when it said that Hovell

> felt no small degree of pleasure and pride at being the man who discovered the country which he found twenty-nine years ago to be a wilderness but which was now a thriving seat of civilisation, an infant nation capable of producing food to feed half the world, wool to clothe half the world, and gold to buy half the world.

When he returned home, Hovell wrote immediately to Hume – perhaps seeking to forestall an angry response – describing his trip to Victoria and ending with an invitation to accompany him to Melbourne and later to the Ovens River, which was now productive farmland. However, by then Hume had read the newspaper reports and he responded, with obvious restraint: 'I have had several of the Melbourne and Geelong papers sent to me lately by some friends, which have informed me of what has been going on there. All I now care to say is that I have not felt much gratified with the share assigned to me . . .'

Hume had not been well rewarded for his part in the expedition. As previously mentioned, he had to sell an earlier small grant of land to pay his half-share for the men and equipment. It was only later – after he had discovered a new and vastly better route than the half-completed track pioneered by

Blaxland, Wentworth and Lawson over the Blue Mountains to the western plains, led Captain Charles Sturt on his most successful expedition to the Darling, and made his own forays into the region surrounding what would become the national capital in the Limestone Plains – that he had been able to establish his own prosperous holdings at Yass.

But it was his leadership of that epic journey of 1824 that gave him his greatest pride and satisfaction. And now, 30 years later, Hovell (who lately insisted on pronouncing it Ho-*vell*) had visited its terminal point and claimed that *he* was 'the man who discovered . . . a wilderness which [is] now a thriving seat of civilisation'.

As he went about his work with Little Hamilton on 'Humewood' and sat with Eliza in the long evenings before the fireplace at Cooma Cottage, the injustice of Hovell's pretensions rankled. Finally Hume had had enough. He decided to respond with a factual account of the journey based on his own record. With his habitual care and thoroughness, he began to compile *A Brief Statement of Facts in Connection with an Overland Expedition from Lake George to Port Phillip in 1824.*

He wrote to the other members of the expedition such as Tom Boyd, Henry Angel and James Fitzpatrick for their recollections. It would take him almost a year to write and edit. By the time it was ready for publication in early 1855 it had become a devastating document. The former convicts, now respectable members of the community, had responded with detailed recall. Their testimony was supported by letters from the influential Alexander Berry and two of his most celebrated fellow explorers, Charles Sturt and Thomas Mitchell. The Introduction, written by the Reverend William Ross of Goulburn – where Hovell then lived – concluded that:

> When New South Wales becomes the Great Britain of the Southern Hemisphere, the name of Hamilton Hume may be mentioned in history with the honour due to the native explorer who, almost unaided, opened the way to some of the finest tracts of country in the world.
>
> The name of his companion will not be forgotten, the credit due to him will be awarded . . . the colony owes its gratitude to Mr Hovell but the colony is bound to grant the laurel crown to Mr Hume.

The letters of the convicts were much less generous to Hovell. They recorded even more graphically than Hume himself the manner in which the naval captain quailed before the rivers that barred their progress. Time and again, Hovell wanted to turn back, sometimes even attempting to rouse the men to mutiny. According to James Fitzpatrick, 'I positively assert that the journey would never have been accomplished but for the indomitable perseverance of Mr Hume and that he was, in fact, the sole leader of the party.'

Moreover, throughout the enterprise Hovell's much vaunted expertise with his compass and other navigational instruments proved useless. Indeed, he insisted that he had led the expedition to Western Port rather than Port Phillip and the resulting confusion delayed the establishment of Melbourne for a decade.

For 30 years Hovell had apparently believed that the strictures of colonial society would forever protect him from the 'currency lad' and that the convicts would keep their silence. To have his behaviour broadcast around the drawing rooms at the instigation of his social inferiors would be almost unbearable.

Meanwhile, back in Victoria, the diggers were organising to hit back against Hotham's latest provocations. Almost 1,000 of them drilled in companies, but they lacked both discipline and expertise. And the tempting prospect of a big strike was a constant diversion from the demands of soldiering.

On 6 October 1854, a Scottish miner, James Scobie, was beaten to death at the Eureka hotel by the proprietor James Bentley. When, ten days later, Bentley was acquitted of murder by a corrupt magistrate, thousands of miners rioted and burned down the pub. Hotham's troopers arrested seven of their number and more than 4,000 gathered in protest. They formed the Ballarat Reform League and passed a resolution: 'It is the inalienable right of every citizen to have a voice in making the laws he is called on to obey, that taxation without representation is tyranny.' They even resolved 'to secede from the United Kingdom' if the situation didn't improve.

Hotham immediately established a royal commission on the miners' grievances, but appointed Robert William Rede, a former British government spy with a grudge against the miners, to conduct it. He took only two weeks to reach his conclusions. On 28 November, he recommended that the agitation be 'crushed', and deliberately provoked the rebels by ordering another licence hunt. He attempted to split the miners by attacking the Irish activists among them. Instead, he forced them all into open rebellion. 'They built a stockade on a hill called Eureka,' says John Chandler, 'and here they raised a flag called the Southern Cross.'

Elements from two regiments in Melbourne, including most of the 40th and one company of the 12th, set out for Ballarat with four field artillery pieces. As word spread, 200 Americans calling themselves the Independent Californian Rangers, under the leadership of James McGill, arrived from their diggings at about 4 pm on 2 December. The Americans were mounted and armed with revolvers and Mexican knives. But in a fateful decision, McGill decided to take most of the Rangers away from the stockade to intercept rumoured British reinforcements coming from Melbourne.

Rede's spies noted their departure and also that many of the miners went back to their own tents after the traditional Saturday night carousing. The diggers had assumed that the Queen's military forces would never be sent into battle on the Sabbath, so only a small contingent remained at the stockade overnight. They misjudged their opponents. At 3 am the government forces attacked. According to Chandler, who was in the area, 'The diggers fought well but discipline and numbers soon told, and they were routed with over 40 killed and twice that number wounded.'

By 8 a.m., Captain Charles Pasley, the second-in-command of the British forces, sickened by the carnage, saved a group of prisoners from being bayoneted and threatened to shoot any police or soldiers who continued with the slaughter. Victory on the field was complete. And though the Bendigo diggers also began to drill, the government's tactics had crushed the diggers' appetite for battle.

Chandler resumed his trading to the Ballarat fields. 'As we travelled down, we met many stragglers on the road,' he wrote, 'some of them had evidently been in the fight but they were very quiet and anxious to keep out of the way. The troopers were hunting men down like dogs. We got safe back to Melbourne and loaded again for Bendigo.'

The Eureka leaders were rounded up and taken to Melbourne for trial. 'They were tried for high treason,' he says, 'but no jury would convict them. About the court house there were gathered about 3,000 men, most secretly armed – this I know from what I heard and saw. They were determined to rush the court and release the prisoners if they had been brought in guilty.'

They were acquitted, and three months later the rebel leader Peter Lalor, who lost an arm in the fight, wrote:

> The unusual proportion of killed to the wounded is owing to the butchery of the military and troopers after the surrender. There are two things connected with the outbreak which I deeply regret. The first is, that we shouldn't have been forced to take up arms at all; and the second is, that when we were compelled to take the field in our own defence, we were unable (through want of arms, ammunition and a little organisation) to inflict on the real authors of the outbreak the punishment they so richly deserved.[4]

According to Chandler:

> Everybody was excited and incensed against the government for the diggers had been treated shamefully. The government found it best to draw in their horns for the whole colony was on the side of the diggers. One member in the Assembly speaking in defence of the diggers said the government 'was not fit to govern a colony of cats'.

Hotham was reprimanded by the new colonial secretary, Sir William Molesworth who had been so instrumental in ending transportation. In response, he lowered the cost of a licence to dig to ten shillings then five shillings a month as a concession to the diggers. Molesworth raised the Victorian post to a full governorship in February 1855. Alas, Hotham would have scant opportunity to savour his vice-regal status. He died in December from pneumonia after catching a chill while opening the Melbourne gasworks. He was 49.

Victoria remained in a state of barely controlled lawlessness and the gold fever had spilled over to the Chinese of their country's southern provinces. Their homeland was ablaze with the Taiping Rebellion as a fanatical pseudo-Christian sect rose up against the hated Manchu emperors. Their love of gambling was legendary, and emigration to 'New Gold Mountain' provided an attractive alternative to the chaos in Fujian and Guangdong. But on their arrival, European notions of racial superiority would find them under attack from a new and unexpected source.

They were not the first Chinese to reach the colony. Since the end of transportation, some of the big landholders – notably the Macarthur-dominated Australian Agricultural Company – had imported indentured labourers from Fujian to work as shepherds and irrigation experts. Between 1848 and 1853 more than 3,000 took up their posts in the New South Wales countryside. But their orderly arrival bore little resemblance to the sudden influx of their countrymen in Victoria and New South Wales. The consequences would alienate the newcomers from the colonial authorities and disfigure Australia's national politics and perceptions for more than a century.

Frank Christie added to his aliases at this time the surname of his convict maths tutor John Clarke. However, it failed to save him from arrest on 3 March 1854 at the Royal Hotel in

Yass. He and a mate, Henry Prior, the son of a well-known publican, were celebrating after selling 16 horses, which they had 'found before they were lost', at the local auction. They stood trial at the Goulburn courthouse and on 14 March both were sentenced by Judge Stephen to seven years hard labour.

Christie was sent to Cockatoo Island in Sydney Harbour, where the prisoners laboured in chains cutting the island's sandstone into blocks for transport by whaleboat and dray to the building sites of burgeoning Sydney Town. It was a devastating blow to his family, and soon after his arrival he attempted to escape. He and several others decided to risk the shark-infested waters between the island and Balmain. They slipped their bonds at night and made for the water's edge, but before they reached it they were caught, and Christie was punished with 50 lashes 'laid on hard'.

He worked on 'the rock' during the day, and at night he kept to himself, carving oddments from the bones of sheep and cattle slaughtered for the prison pot. Late in 1857 he was joined by another rebel, John Peisley, who at 23 was already serving part of a second five-year sentence. Peisley had been born in Bathurst and knew the area from Goulburn to Cowra and Wagga Wagga as well as Frank himself. While both held a deep-seated grievance against the colonial regime, Christie retained a curiously romantic view of the life he anticipated once they had served their sentences. Frank, it is said, sought out the prison poet, Owen Suffolk, whose latest quatrain embraced his rebel aspirations.

Place me in a forest glen, unfettered, wild and free,
With fifty tried and chosen men – a bandit chief to be.
'Tis there, when fighting with my foes amid my trusty band,
I'd freely leave this world of woes and die with sword in hand.[5]

CHAPTER TWENTY-TWO

The Feud between Hume and Hovell

Hamilton Hume's Brief Statement of Facts *is published, Governor Denison takes the helm, and Chinese prospectors are persecuted.*

Hamilton Hume's *Brief Statement of Facts* was published by a Sydney printer in February 1855. It gave a broad-brush account of the expedition but detailed Hovell's recalcitrance and backed it with damning detail from other members of the party. Hovell was appalled. He wrote immediately to Hume in barely controlled rage: 'There is one passage compels me to take immediate notice of,' he said. 'On page 17 and in [Henry] Angel's statement are these words: "Mr Hume got in a passion and I think called both Mr Hovell and Claude [Bossawa] cowards." In order that there may be no ambiguity on the subject, I now want, Sir, an immediate answer from you, whether you did or not apply the word coward to me.'

It was tantamount to an invitation to a duel. And Hume refused to back down. 'I am not a little surprised to find you are in possession of a pamphlet which I was not aware was in circulation,' he wrote. 'I have been informed that you were very solicitous to obtain one from my printers . . . In reply to your last paragraph referring to Angel's statement, in which he says he thinks I called both you and Claude cowards, he may be right.'

Hovell stewed, but failed to carry out his implied threat. By now he was a gentleman farmer on the rich pastures of Grabberdrack near Goulburn, and he gathered his fellow 'exclusives' to support him. He accused Hume of 'mendacious innuendoes' and of 'cooked sentences'.

Though he had kept a relatively succinct journal and a detailed, progressive sketch map of the journey, Hume had not previously written at any length about the expedition. Hovell's fulsome journal entries, written during the evenings of their journey, had been greatly enhanced by the fellow 'exclusive', Dr William Bland, a London surgeon who had killed a naval officer in a duel. He'd been found guilty of murder, transported to New South Wales, but quickly pardoned and welcomed into society. He would rise to become a leading figure in colonial politics. He supported Hovell's 'plain good sense', which, he said, had permitted 'the return of the party at all, and still more, its triumphant return without the loss of a single life'. While he could hardly call Hume's word into question, it is clear nevertheless that he discounted the former convicts' testimony.

Hovell now turned to Dr Bland for support. But while he might well have reassured his friend privately, Bland's public stance was strictly impartial. Hume's partnership with Charles Sturt in the subsequent expedition to the Darling ensured his credibility in the dispute. Indeed, Bland himself asserted that he had been 'invaluable as a teacher' to the military man. He explained that putting Hovell's name first in his account was 'purely coincidental and not unpardonable', since 'the merits of the two travellers appeared to be equal'.

By now the press had begun to revel in the 'human interest' elements of the expedition, which until then had been cloaked in Bland's banalities. Angel, Fitzpatrick and Boyd had emerged from the *Brief Statement* as vigorous characters whose courage and stamina had been vital to the journey's success. At the same time, Hovell and Bossawa were pictured as either faint-hearted or deliberately obstructionist.

The various judgements of the newspapers reflected the predispositions of their readership. The *Yass Courier,* for example, reported Hovell's visit to its town 'not in a manner to flatter his excessive vanity' and referred to his having 'accompanied Mr Hume on that journey'. It also recalled Hovell's trip to London 'out of which the former gentleman has made so much capital in Europe as well as in the colonies'. It noted with undisguised satisfaction that 'no knighthood' was awarded.[1]

The *Sydney Morning Herald* summed the issue up in a leader:

> Both Hovell and Hume were men of strong wills, self-assertive and obstinate to a high degree. Incontestably, Hume, the native, and an explorer who gave proof of his ability with the great Sturt and with Mitchell and Berry in exploring the South Coast, was a fine bushman; and Hovell the sea captain was not.

Hume's reputation was enhanced. Indeed, soon after the *Brief Statement*'s publication he was asked to stand as a candidate for the new Legislative Assembly, but declined the offer 'as he had had a bout of pneumonia white staying at Appin'.[2]

The election of the assembly took place under the vice-regal eye of Sir William Thomas Denison, who took up his new colonial post from the departing Fitzroy in January 1855. Since 1846 he had been governor of Van Diemen's Land, which remained largely a convict colony. He was no Alexander Maconochie. His rule there had followed his self-imposed dictum that, 'to everyman the full penalty which the law allots to his offence should be carried out.'

Denison had followed a well-trodden path of the minor aristocracy from Eton to the Royal Military Academy, graduating in 1826 as a lieutenant in the Royal Engineers. He had a modest literary bent and, following a Canadian posting, had won a silver medal for an essay on timbers. In 1838 he married Caroline, the daughter of Sir Phipps Hornby, who would become one of the Lords of the Admiralty.

Denison sent soldiers across Bass Strait to support Hotham's assault on the Eureka Stockade, and just prior to his appointment as governor-general he had recommended that Van Diemen's Land be renamed Tasmania. London approved and the name change took effect in 1856. However, his first year as the country's titular head was dominated by fears of a Russian attack as Britain went to war against that nation in the Crimea. He strengthened the batteries at Dawes Point and built a fort in Sydney Harbour that now bears his name: one of the few memorials to a largely undistinguished career.

In Victoria, Hotham was succeeded temporarily by Lieutenant-General Edward Macarthur, the eldest son of John the wool baron who had died insane 20 years previously. Edward had been a babe in arms when he arrived in Australia with his parents in 1790. He returned to England aged nine and spent most of his life in the British Army. In Melbourne he held the fort until the arrival of Sir Henry Barkly, a compatriot of Henry Monro in Scotland's Ross-shire.

Barkly had followed his father into a business career in the slave colonies of the West Indies and was elected to an English seat in the British House of Commons in 1845. Prior to his Victorian appointment, he was governor and commander-in-chief of Jamaica. He reached Melbourne with his family on Christmas Eve 1856, but like others before him, he suffered the personal tragedy of losing his wife – in childbirth – within a year of their arrival.

He was disappointed to discover that, with representative government having just been granted, his role in the governance of the colony was circumscribed; and as Victoria wrestled with the tumultuous social adjustments forced upon it by the gold rush he was forced to rely on a succession of politicians ranging from the inferior to the mediocre. Government was haphazard and ineffective. Those who suffered most were undoubtedly the Chinese prospectors who joined the rush in their thousands from 1854. Most were from Guangdong province, and had endured a three-month voyage under British captains, usually in shockingly overcrowded conditions, before reaching Melbourne; and only the smallest handful were women. The men were regarded 'a problem' since they kept to themselves and thereby gave the mistaken impression that they were more successful prospectors than the Europeans. More importantly, an inherent racism in the community aroused wild and illogical fears. Not least was the widely believed rumour that they were 'fanatically loyal to a despotic foreign emperor who could order them to rise up at any moment'.[3] In fact, many were rebels against the Manchu dynasty.

Rede's royal commission, which resumed after Eureka, did nothing to expose the anti-Chinese canards or calm the fears of the British miners or the Victorian community. In 1855, the Victorian parliament passed the *Immigration Restriction Act*, forcing the Chinese alone to pay a £10 head tax on arrival. It also restricted the number of Chinese travellers per tonnage of shipping. Both measures caused a slowdown in arrivals in Melbourne from 10,000 between 1853 and 1855 to only hundreds passing through the port subsequently.

Instead, they landed in Adelaide or the town of Robe in South Australia, which soon became the favourite sea terminus before a long overland trek to the Victorian goldfields. In the beginning, Chinese hopefuls would pay local guides, who often abandoned them in the bush. But as more followed, the Chinese organised their own route. They even dug wells and established overnight lay-bys beside the bush tracks. However, that was just the beginning of their travail. When they reached the Ballarat and Bendigo fields, they were scorned and derided by the Europeans. This descended into open violence in 1857 in the Buckland Valley between Mount Buffalo and Falls Creek.

On 4 July, more than 100 European miners – reportedly led by 'Americans inflamed by liquor' – torched 50 Chinese huts and bashed nine Chinese miners to death. Those who escaped the first assault were forced into the Buckland River where an unknown number drowned. Some of the Chinese had by now married white women and they too were bashed, one almost losing her finger when her wedding ring was ripped off. The police finally arrived and charged nine of the rioters with major offences. The jury dismissed all but the most trivial – 'unlawful assembly' – much to the delight of the crowded courtroom.

The government established a system of Chinese 'protectors' in Ballarat, Bendigo and Beechworth but these were as ineffective as the Aboriginal protectors previously appointed to oversee the welfare of the native people. They did little more than record second-hand versions of the white immigrants' abuses of their Asian neighbours. In the wake of the Buckland Valley attack, more than 3,000 Chinese miners gathered in a Bendigo park to denounce the discriminatory laws. They sent a petition to the government in Melbourne, but without result. The Chinese developed their own self-sustaining communities in most of the areas where a substantial strike was made. They often arrived from China in groups, with men selected for their special skills such as scribes, herbalists and even opium traffickers.

By 1857, William Gilbert, a distiller by trade, had been in Victoria with his family for five years. William had emigrated from England to Canada in 1830 but joined the Australian gold rush with his children from two marriages in 1852. Among them was the youngest son of his first marriage, ten-year-old John who, according to family history, left home two years later to find work as a stable boy in Kilmore.

As the gold seekers moved north into the Snowy Mountains, Johnny (as he was universally known) joined the crowd of men and women who serviced the prospectors with their food, transport and entertainment. At 17 he was already a dashing horseman, and it was during this time that he met up with another who sat easily in the saddle, Frank Christie, who by now had adopted the surname Gardiner after the man who gained national fame by droving the first mob of cattle down Hume's track from Sydney to Melbourne: John Gardiner. Legend has it that the meeting took place at a poker table in Kiandra in 1860.

By then, Frank Gardiner had been released from Cockatoo Island on a ticket-of-leave that required him to remain in the Carcoar district. Instead, he teamed up with his former cellmate, John Peisley, and embarked on a career of bushranging. They held up stores and mail coaches together, but Peisley had a fondness for liquor that made him a dangerous companion, and they soon parted company. Gardiner headed for the Kiandra diggings where he – perhaps in partnership with Gilbert – supplied the diggers' butcheries with cattle they acquired by fair means or foul.

Hamilton Hume remained an active member of the Yass community and a frequent correspondent to a wide circle of friends and relatives as well as the colonial press. He was not only a prominent pastoralist but a local magistrate, founder of the Mechanics Institute and a trustee of the Anglican Church. In 1858 he wrote to the *Sydney Morning Herald* encouraging the renewed search for the explorer Ludwig Leichhardt, who in 1848 had set out from the Condamine to cross the continent to the Swan River in Western Australia. Leichhardt's expedition consisted of five Europeans, including the leader, two Aboriginal guides, seven horses, 20 mules and 50 bullocks. They were last seen on 3 April 1848 departing the Darling Downs.

Four years later, the New South Wales government under Fitzroy sent out a search party but they found nothing but a single camp site with a tree marked 'L'. Now in 1858, Augustus Gregory was preparing to lead a second search, which would traverse the Warrego and Barcoo rivers of the channel country. Hume suggested Gregory should travel by ship to Port Essington on the north coast and work his way south. He set out a detailed plan and volunteered at least £50 to start a fund for it. The offer was declined and Gregory kept to his original overland course, but after finding two further trees marked 'L', he abandoned the search and made for Adelaide.

Governor-General Denison sounded the expected demise of the Aboriginal people in a letter to the colonial secretary (and popular novelist of the day) Bulwer Lytton. 'Due to the physical peculiarities of the race,' he said, 'their want of stamina to resist the slightest access of disease seems to render their gradual extinction almost a matter of necessity when coupled with the unproductiveness of the females.' Lytton responded in masterly non sequitur: 'I can only press upon the local government the consideration that is our duty, on Christian no less than on political grounds, not to relax our efforts in despair.'

The puzzling dispatch reached Denison while he was engrossed in the establishment of Queensland, where the Aborigines were fighting a rearguard action for survival. He resisted the temptation to 'despair' but, according to his biographer, 'he never seemed to detect their spiritual malaise'.[4]

Denison was concurrently governor of Norfolk Island and he decided that it should once again be abandoned. His recommendation was approved by Bulwer Lytton, who then took the fateful decision to transfer the descendants of the mutiny on the *Bounty* who had been living in incestuous propinquity on tiny Pitcairn Island to the much larger Norfolk. Denison's tangled negotiations with the islanders gave them the false impression that their new home had been deeded to them by the crown. In fact it remained within the New South Wales polity, but the confusion surrounding the various official statements of intent would encourage the Pitcairners to resist full integration into Australian governance until the second decade of the 21st century.

It was Denison's last act of any note, and he received his marching orders to his next posting – as governor of the presidency of Madras – in 1860. He left behind a New South Wales government in which 'Slippery Charlie' Cowper was colonial secretary and would become premier the following year. The third son of the Rev. William Cowper who brought him to the colony in 1809 aged nine, he was educated in the manse by his parent, and at only 19 was appointed clerk of the Clergy and School Lands Corporation. He later acquired several properties near Hume's original holdings in the Argyle and married Eliza Sutton before embarking on a career in politics.

He quickly rose through the ranks and became a prominent, if somewhat opportunistic, figure in the various ministries that rose and fell in the 1850s. However, the most powerful and disruptive voice in the Legislative Assembly would come from Henry Parkes, who made his first public speech at the City Theatre in January 1849. He demanded universal suffrage as 'the best guarantee of the people growing in enlightenment'. And the following year when John Dunmore Lang established the Australian League to work for a 'Great Federal Republic', Parkes wrote to him denouncing their conservative opponents as 'the dung-hill aristocracy of Botany Bay'.

Charles Cowper welcomed him into the fold, and his subsequent election to the Chamber of Commerce signified his acceptance into the inner councils. Two years later, he was elected to the first Legislative Assembly in the Sydney City constituency. He supported Cowper in the complex manoeuvres to establish a working government until he was forced to resign on the failure of his newspaper the *Empire*. But it was a brief interregnum, and he re-entered parliament in 1859. He was a man of conflicting passions, and almost impossible to control. So in 1860 Cowper offered him a tour of England as a commissioner of emigration at the tempting salary of £1,000 a year. He found it irresistible, and left his wife and six children on a rented farm in Sydney's west for the next 14 months.

These years were to be among the most momentous of any in New South Wales' colonial history. The effects would echo down the years for more than a century. And by coincidence Hamilton Hume would play a peripheral part in the tumult. In 1860, he was unanimously elected a Fellow of the Royal Geographical Society, and as he went about his pastoral duties with Little Hamilton he was utterly unprepared for the social hurricane about to strike his beloved Yass and district.

CHAPTER TWENTY-THREE

The Lambing Flat Riots

Gold is discovered at Lambing Flat, to the benefit of Hume, and European miners attack the Chinese.

On 4 June 1860, Denis Regan, the manager of James White's Burrangong station in the Lachlan Valley, was crossing a creek in the grassy, sheltered paddock they called the Lambing Flat – only a day's ride from Hume's Cooma Cottage – during a sheep muster. Riding beside him in the shallow stream was the station's American cook known as Alexander the Yankee, a veteran of the 1849 gold rush in California. As Alex looked down from his horse he glimpsed a 'golden flash' in the water. When they reached the other side, they climbed down and, using the tin lid of Regan's billycan, 'washed' two handfuls of dirt from the creek bed. It yielded six shillings worth of gold. Word quickly spread and the rush was on.

James White had followed Hume's track to the south-west of settlement in 1826 only two years after the expedition with Hovell. He had then veered further west and made friends with the local Aboriginal people. White was soon followed by

Hazleton and McGee, who squatted on the adjoining 'Marengo', and by 1860 he had built up a steady pastoral business running sheep, cattle and horses. He was totally unprepared for the onset of thousands of prospectors who would soon overwhelm his property. However, they would make him a very wealthy man.

The strike could hardly have come at a more opportune time for the 'freelance' prospectors. The Victorian fields had given up their surface treasure, and companies had been formed to sink the deep shafts needed to extract the precious metal. The Kiandra field was proving to be a 'flash in the pan' and some miners were already heading to New Zealand following reports of big strikes in the South Island. At Lambing Flat, the good finds were being made on and near the surface.

George Preshaw, a young employee of the Bank of New South Wales, was sent from Kiandra to the area to buy gold and establish a branch on the fields. The *Yass Courier* reported in August that about 1,500 had reached the diggings and the miners were earning between £3 and £5 a week. A correspondent wrote, 'It is such a splendid-looking auriferous country for miles around. There are a great number of diggers flocking here every day.' Most passed by Hamilton Hume's property and, like other graziers in the area, he too would benefit from the rush as the demand for beef and mutton escalated.

By October there were at least 6,000 diggers on the field. The *Courier* reported, 'The diggers continue to find new ground every day, and it is expected that the richest part of the neighbourhood has not yet been struck. Provisions are cheap and procurable in abundance.' The Yass paper was also the first to report the arrival of 'a great many Chinese', and commented, 'The labour being light, this place is likely to become a favourite with them.'

However, it very soon became clear that they would come under fire from the Europeans who consistently outnumbered them by at least eight to one. According to George Preshaw, the Europeans comprised 'many creeds and almost all nations, many of whom [were] reckless in the extreme and without character'. And on 13 November 1860, they staged their first 'riot' against the Chinese.

The *Courier* said:

> Some 500 Europeans attacked a party of Chinese and maltreated them to such an extent as to cause the death of at least one of their number. We are informed that the 'pigtails' of the unfortunate Celestials were cut off in so barbarous a manner as to detach the skin from the back of the head; and further that the brutality was carried to the length of cutting the ears off several.

And that was just the beginning. Despite the stationing of a gold commissioner and three mounted troopers on the field, the following month, according to an official report:

> a vigilante group, to the accompaniment of a musical [German] band took it upon themselves to burn down some disreputable grog shanties and pour away the liquor which was allegedly drugged. They also drove off 50 Chinese, scalped two men and cut the ears off others. Police reinforcements arrived but no evidence of assault was found.

Preshaw says the population was now 15,000, of which 2,000 were Chinese. 'These Mongolians were scattered about in small encampments of a few hundred in each of the various parts of the diggings,' he says.

> I am no apologist for the Chinese. I do not advocate their claims as equal to those of our own countrymen; but still they have certain rights which ought not to be trampled upon.
>
> The Europeans take up certain localities, work it for a short time, become dissatisfied, rush off to a new place, and the abandoned ground is forthwith occupied by the Chinese. Perhaps within a few weeks the same Europeans are disappointed and return to their old quarters to find they have really abandoned a good claim which is being assiduously worked by John Chinaman.
>
> The consequence of all this was an appeal to the gold commissioners with the usual list of complaints against the Chinese – that they spoil the water, are dirty and filthy in their habits [and] take up more ground than they are entitled to. The commissioners can do nothing so the diggers will; and at it they go to drive John off the field. Such are really the facts of the case. The water question had in truth as little to do with the riots as the writer of these lines; it was simply that the Europeans wanted, and would have, the ground occupied by the Chinese.[1]

The goldfields commissioners applied to the government for more police protection, and the response was an addition of troopers, foot police and detectives. Head of the police contingent was Captain Henry Zouch, the former lands commissioner at the Lower Turon who had been stationed at Yass. On the last Friday of January 1861, his men were suddenly called to arms when about 4,000 Europeans assembled for a concentrated attack on the Chinese.

According to the *Courier*: 'About two o'clock a large body came in from Stony Creek, headed by a brass band playing martial airs, with the Union Jack on either side floating over them. They came on horseback, on foot, and in vehicles, and the band occupied a "jaunting car" drawn by two-fine horses.'

Several boxes were placed together on a small hillock and the Union Jacks on either side of them forming a platform around which the dense assemblage collected. They debated 'whether Burrangong was a European or a Chinese territory'. The answer was not long in coming, and after a series of rabble-rousing speeches the German band struck up.

The commissioner, James Griffin, with Captain Zouch and seven troopers, all well armed, and with detectives Carnes and Scarlett, were occupying a position a short distance away. 'After threatening to burn the police barracks if they interfered,' Preshaw says, 'the crowd advanced on the biggest Chinese camp.' The Chinese retreated, but not before one of their number was knocked down and killed. Captain Zouch and his troopers intervened and the miners withdrew.

Zouch summoned police reinforcements from Yass and they arrived the following day, bringing their number to 30. Nonetheless the miners rallied again two days later and, ignoring police threats and pleas, again attacked the Chinese, this time killing an unknown number and mauling scores more.

The police arrested 11 of the rioters, and in the late afternoon 4,000 miners gathered at the rough timber courthouse and demanded their release. According to Preshaw, 'Not many minutes passed before the suspense was brought to an end by the mob firing several shots at the police, whereupon the foot police (sixteen in number under Inspector Sanderson) were ordered to fire.'

One man was killed and another injured. However, says Preshaw, 'Nothing daunted, the mob fired again and again. The mounted police (twenty-four in number led by Sub-Inspector McLerie) then charged; the effect was instantaneous, the mob making a most ignominious retreat.' The police took casualties, with four seriously wounded, while the rioters suffered shocking sabre cuts, one man losing his nose and much of his face. The dead miner – named Lupton – was taken to the Empire Hotel, where Zouch established a temporary headquarters and sought to discover the miners' plans. When he learned that 'some thousands of bullets had been moulded' to attack the courthouse and release their comrades from custody, he called a meeting with the commissioners, and it was decided to retreat to Yass, and there await reinforcements. 'They opened the prison doors,' Preshaw says, 'released the prisoners and beat a retreat, thus leaving the goldfield to the mercy of the mob.'

Premier Charles Cowper visited and lived up to his 'Slippery Charlie' nickname when he claimed to 'sympathise' with the Chinese, yet said he would restrict their entry but for a British treaty with the Chinese government that he was powerless to change. On 11 March, more than 150 troops with three 12-pounder field guns arrived, setting up fortifications at the corner of Campbell and Berthong streets. However, they soon became very friendly with the miners, and the Chinese were restricted to Blackguard Gully. Meanwhile, a Gold Fields Bill, intended to separate the warring factions, lapsed when parliament was prorogued and the troops departed.

Soon a rumour spread that 1,500 Chinese had landed in Sydney and were bound for Lambing Flat and this prompted a 'roll-up' on 30 June that resulted in the biggest onslaught of all. More than 3,000 Europeans armed with pick-handles, bludgeons, guns and whips assembled in a paddock beside their encampment. The German band was again called to service and the Europeans advanced on the Chinese waving British, Irish and American flags.

As they reached the Chinese camp they surged forward and all hell broke loose among the tents. The Chinese were vastly outnumbered and fell before the charge. An unknown number were bashed or shot to death, their bodies tossed down nearby mine shafts, and an estimated 250 were gravely injured. At least one European died and others were wounded in the fracas that lasted until the Chinese scattered and the entire camp was torched.

The police arrested several Europeans, and on 14 July about 1,000 miners laid siege to the jail in a rescue attempt. More shots were exchanged and at least one miner was killed outright. Once again the police departed for Yass and, as they left, the miners burned their quarters.

Captain Zouch contacted the authorities in Sydney and Premier Cowper persuaded Captain Henry Carr Glynn of the British warship HMS *Fawn* in Sydney Harbour to detach 75 marines to become part of a force headed for the goldfield.

They set out immediately with a police contingent and an artillery unit totalling 200 officers and men for the journey in a horse-drawn omnibus towards Lambing Flat. When they arrived at Yass, they disembarked and prepared for the march to the goldfields. Hamilton Hume gave them the run of his orchard, and after an overnight stay they arrived at Lambing Flat on 31 July.

They spread out through the fields, arrested a further five men and quelled the rioting. The prisoners were charged with affray and assault while the miners raised £400 as a defence fund. At their trial in Goulburn, all but one were acquitted. The miners celebrated; the servicemen returned to Sydney. Thereafter the Chinese were restricted to designated fields by government decree, and further assaults went unpunished, since it was now clear to all that no European jury would convict. Four months later, the New South Wales Legislative Assembly passed the *Chinese Immigration Restriction Act*.

When the dust settled, Cowper decided to draw a symbolic line under the lawless uprising by giving Lambing Flat a new name. And what better, he decided, than that of the new governor of New South Wales Sir John Young. It was so proclaimed in 1863. But the effects of the uprising, and the racist fires it kindled, would not be so easily extinguished. Queensland would introduce similar anti-Chinese restrictions in 1877 and Western Australia in 1886. The racist stain would spread through all the mainstream political parties, and in the wake of Federation in 1901 the White Australia Policy would be enshrined in the first Bill passed by the Commonwealth Government.

CHAPTER TWENTY-FOUR

The Golden Age of the Bushranger

The most famous bushranging robbery takes place, the gold rush fades, and Hume battles ill-health.

As the Australian continent surrendered its buried treasure, the colonies' political and economic forces produced a class of sturdy, law-abiding individuals like Hamilton Hume and other prosperous pastoralists and farmers in the scattered rural communities of New South Wales and Victoria. But the stratified society also created a sense of hopelessness and injustice among those denied the 'fair go' that was coming to define the peculiarly Australian outlook. So when the more alienated and belligerent among them took up arms against the symbols of authority – particularly the corrupt and ineffectual police force – the 'have nots' offered their support and assistance. The country was ripe for social rebellion in the so-called 'golden age' of the Australian bushranger.

On his arrival in Sydney in March 1861, Governor Young had been confronted by a raging constitutional crisis. Premier

Cowper was demanding that the Upper House – the Legislative Council – be democratically elected. But when Young gave his approval, council members resigned en masse and the Bill stalled in the legislature. The colonial secretary, the Duke of Newcastle, accused the governor of 'dangerous democratic tendencies'. Having risen through the parliamentary and colonial ranks, Young found himself buffeted on all sides.

In the countryside, the latent anarchy rumbling beneath the gold rush broke to the surface. As the gold strikes expanded east and west from Young, the squattocracy revelled in the economic boom while the inflated prices for goods and services meant the emancipists and small settlers struggled to survive. And when the police troopers quailed before the mob, the seeds of defiance and insurrection were suddenly blowing in the wind.

In Hume's Yass district, no one was better placed to gather and propagate the germs of dissent than Frank Gardiner. Now 31, he was slightly above medium height, solidly built, fine-featured, with a well-trimmed curly beard, a neat moustache and his dark hair at collar length. He had acquired a devil-may-care charisma that attracted younger men into his orbit and breathless glances from their sisters. He rode a beautiful black horse he called 'Darkie', and they were a formidable team as he rounded up cattle and sheep for the butchering business he had established with his boyhood friend William Fogg to supply the Lambing Flat miners. And when demand exceeded legitimate supply, he 'duffed' them from the back paddocks of the graziers in the area from Forbes to Yass to Cowra that would soon become known as 'bushranger country'.

In May 1861, he was arrested as Frank Christie and charged with stealing cattle, but was granted bail and immediately absconded. He took refuge in the nearby Weddin Mountains (from the Wiradjuri word for 'waiting place'), a 19-kilometre volcanic range between Forbes and Grenfell. The thickly wooded peaks overlooked a community of small settlers – many of whom were the sons and daughters of emancipists – and at its centre Mount Wheogo rose beside the station of that name owned by the Walsh family.

It was there that Gardiner met and courted Catherine 'Kitty' Brown. She was one of three Walsh sisters and was then married to John Brown, the Wheogo station manager. However, their widowed mother was also charmed by Gardiner and she turned a blind eye to their extramarital activities.

Johnny Gilbert had been working as a stockman on Marengo station, but soon responded to Gardiner's call of the wild. He wore his hair at shoulder length and dressed 'flash' in thigh boots and blue Crimea shirts. Like Gardiner, he could read and write and, according to his biographer, 'was witty of speech, of happy disposition and a fine horseman'.[1] In 1861, he was in his nineteenth year.

In June, they began their bushranging careers in earnest, holding up coaches and travellers on the Cowra Road and, after the first race meeting at Lambing Flat, Gardiner made off with the winning horse. About this time they were joined on the highways by Ben Hall, who had been forced to sell his grazing property after being arrested on suspicion of an association with Gardiner. The charge was dropped after several weeks in the Forbes lock-up, but when he returned to his Sandy Creek station his wife had departed and his yarded stock had died of thirst. Thereafter he became a committed member of Gardiner's gang.

Hall's arresting officer was Sir Frederick Pottinger, whose father, Sir Henry, had been a high-ranking member of the British East India Company and the first governor of Hong Kong after the Opium War of 1842. He died in 1856, and Freddie lived with his mother in London, where he dissipated the family fortune in gambling and high living before departing for the colony in disgrace. He tried gold prospecting in Victoria but without success, and in 1858 joined the New South Wales constabulary as a mounted trooper under an assumed name. However, when the inspector-general John McLerie discovered his titled identity in 1860, he was immediately promoted to officer rank and given charge of the Southern District.

With his superior airs and rakish behaviour he quickly became a figure of fun for the bushrangers and the newspaper satirists of the day. And as Gardiner's fame-cum-notoriety grew, he wrote taunting letters to the newspapers as 'The Highwayman' or 'Prince of the Tobymen', asserting his gentlemanly conduct towards women and challenging Pottinger to capture him or to meet him in a duel. 'Silver I never took from a man yet,' he told the *Burrangaong Courier*. 'And as for a mean, low or petty action, I never committed it in my life.'[2]

This was a very different character from the surly ex-convicts bent on revenge like Scotchie and Whitton. An air of chivalry and wild humour surrounded him. Soon reports of his gang's activities poured in from all points of the compass. The newspapers blamed 'the General' for simultaneous hold-ups in distant locations. While he fell short of his 'fifty tried and chosen men in a forest glen', he became the inspiration for the rise of bushranging across southern New South Wales and northern Victoria. 'Gardinerism' swept through the backblocks.

Cowper and his successors were under pressure from the squatters to declare martial law. Time and again, small gangs held up their homesteads then retired to their mountain redoubts with the bounty, which they shared with a 'bush telegraph' that offered them sanctuary and information on police movements. They chose their targets carefully, particularly the squatters who threatened or scoffed at them or those with a poor reputation in dealings with their hired hands. But such was Hamilton Hume's reputation that he was never targeted.

In June 1862, Gardiner and his gang executed the most famous incident of bushranging history, the robbery of the Lachlan gold escort at Eugowra Rocks. They held up the coach from Forbes to Orange carrying £14,000 worth of gold and banknotes ($1.4 million in today's money). When the first shots rang out, the driver, Jack Fagan, and the four police guards leapt from the coach. One bullet had passed through Fagan's hat; another clipped the testicles of a trooper. The coach overturned but all were able to flee the scene on foot.

The gang headed to Gardiner's hideout on Mount Wheogo to divide the loot. Pottinger and his men set out that night, and by dawn had picked up their tracks. That day they followed them to the mountains and the gang scattered. The police followed in a posse that included Thomas Mitchell's son Richard and captured an exhausted packhorse carrying some of the gold that the bushrangers had released in the hope they could return to it later.

The Eugowra robbery catapulted Gardiner to national prominence, and the story of the police pursuit spread like wildfire over the colonies of Australia.[3] Pottinger and his men surrounded Kitty Brown's house at night, believing Gardiner to be inside. And when he left he rode straight into the police. Pottinger said, 'The man on the white horse was Gardiner. I called upon him to stand. I prepared to shoot him but the cap of my piece missed fire . . . and he bolted into the bush.'

Black trackers found in the morning that Gardiner had dismounted about 500 yards away and actually seated himself at the foot of a tree. The community at large was unforgiving. Pottinger's name would enter the vocabulary as 'Blind Freddie'.

In the wake of Gardiner's escape, poems and songs were written and sung around the country camp fires. To an eager readership it seemed as though 'the General' had disappeared like some mythical will o' the wisp. The authorities, by contrast, were unamused. And as the months passed they raised the reward on Gardiner's head to a remarkable £1,000.

Just as the lawless upheaval ran its course, so too did the gold rush, which roared north and west like a flash flood and then slowly subsided. In New South Wales a sense of collective anticipation was replacing the riotous extravagance of the early 1860s.

The population had soared, and when the gold fever passed most stayed and put down roots. Some of the wealth had been exported, but much had been invested in the founding of a vigorous young economy. A new, democratic aspiration had spread through the colonies, gathering followers in the provincial towns and fledgling cities. New roadworks snaked across the country and the routes of the red Cobb & Co coaches wove a filigree between the towns and villages.

Yass had been at the epicentre of the eruption and now it became an 'exemplar of the new' – a centre for flour milling, for cattle and horse sales, and for some of the finest merino wool in the country. Hamilton Hume's 1842 venture into milling was in full production under the guiding hand of Tom Barber, the son of his sister Isabella. And the tall rangy explorer had been elected a Fellow of the Royal Geographical Society and appointed a magistrate in the town. However, he was feeling the rigours of his early career battling the rough country he had done so much to open to his fellow settlers. There were even suggestions that 'he suffered such ill-health he was inclined to seek relief in the soothing powers of liquor'.[4] In 1865, he quarrelled needlessly with his nephew, Andrew 'Little Hamilton'. The subject was Andrew's in-law, Dick Furlong, a 'Romeo' and racing enthusiast whom Hume couldn't abide.

Andrew had been managing 'Humewood' as well as Hamilton's other properties, 'Eurolie', and 'Marshmont'. When they parted, the younger man selected three runs in the district and 'Mandamah' on Mirool Creek. It was a serious blow to Hume, but he helped to set the younger man up with the gift of 2,000 sheep and 250 head of cattle. He was also worried about his wife Eliza, who was staying at her family's property near Windsor in an effort to find relief from her asthma. 'I fear the worst for my dear, good wife,' he wrote to his sister-in-law Emma Rawdon Hume. 'I am all alone and low spirited.'

Nevertheless, he attended to his magisterial duties every day and, despite growing deafness, took a keen interest in the activities of St Clement's Anglican Church, of which he was a trustee, and other local community organisations. In between, he returned increasingly to his *Brief Statement of Facts*, developing a third edition in which he responded to Hovell's protests.

Hovell was equally engaged in the bitter dispute from his Goulburn property where he now lived with his second wife and doughty supporter, Sophia Wilkinson. A wealthy woman in her own right, she would endow the Sydney University with £6,000 to found the William Hilton Hovell lectureship in geology and physical geography.

CHAPTER TWENTY-FIVE

Hume's Final Years

Frank Gardiner is caught and tried,
Henry Parkes comes to prominence, and
Australia moves towards nationhood.

The mystery of Frank Gardiner's whereabouts continued to titillate colonial newspaper readers with reports of his sighting from wildly different locations. He had left the district with Kitty Brown in disguise, dressed as a boy. He might well have driven a buggy down Hume's now well-worn track to Melbourne where he was not so well known. The *Sydney Mail* strongly suggested they had travelled 'via Goulburn for Portland Bay' where he had relatives. But when they reached Queensland, Kitty resumed her female identity and they undoubtedly drove north with 'Darkie' in harness until they arrived at the small gold mining town of Apis, near the Peak Downs diggings about 160 kilometres inland from Rockhampton.

There, as Mr and Mrs Frank Christie, they operated a store and hostelry in association with a couple named Craig, who were unaware of their background. For two years they led a blameless life, during which Frank became the trusted guardian of prospectors' gold from the diggings.

Early in 1864, in response to a tip-off, Detective Sergeant Daniel McGlone and Constable Andrew Pye travelled to Apis, where they caught Gardiner unawares. The following day, the party set out for Rockhampton, with McGlone mounted on Gardiner's 'Darkie'. They then travelled in stages to Sydney, arriving in the harbour at midnight on the steamer *Telegraph*.

Gardiner's sudden presence was a sensation; and when he was remanded in Darlinghurst Gaol there was a rush to see him in his cell. He was first charged in May 1864, before Judge Sir Alfred Stephen, with wounding two policemen in an earlier fracas. According to *The Gazette*, 'Whilst the jury was considering its verdict the courtroom was in uproar as people surged forward to speak with Gardiner, including "professional gentlemen and men with respectable positions in society". Greater uproar yet when the jury returned a verdict of Not Guilty!'

The *Sydney Morning Herald* recorded, 'Notwithstanding the demands of his Honour for silence and the efforts of the police, the cheering, shouting, whistling, stamping of feet and clapping of hands continued for some seconds.' Sketches and plaster models of Gardiner's head and bust were offered for sale in a George Street shop and sold out immediately. But when two months later further charges of robbery under arms of several travellers succeeded, Judge Stephen made the sentences cumulative, a total of 32 years imprisonment.

Gardiner was returned to Darlinghurst to serve his sentence. In January 1865 he attempted to bribe a jailer to set him free, but another prisoner learned of it and informed the warden. Thereafter he became a model prisoner. Assigned to the coir-matting group, he wove a series of distinctive mats featuring 'Darkie' as a centrepiece. He also engaged in bookbinding, and bound a small prayer book with 'CATHERINE' stamped on its front cover. Inside, in copybook lettering, he inscribed, 'Presented to Catherine by her Affectionate Frank, 1865.'

They would never meet again. Kitty lived for a time with her sister Bridget and James Taylor. In December 1867, she went to the New Zealand goldfields with James's brother Richard. A few weeks later on 14 January, she shot herself. She lingered for almost two weeks, finally dying on 26 January 1868.

By the early months of 1867, all the major figures of the 'golden age' of bushranging were either dead or locked away in New South Wales prisons. Henry Manns had been gruesomely hanged for his part in the Eugowra Rocks robbery; Dan Morgan was gunned down on Peechelba station in Victoria; and the Braidwood desperados John and Tommy Clarke would end their young lives on the Darlinghurst scaffold.

Ben Hall, Johnny Gilbert and their gang had led the troopers a merry dance in 1864, but in November, Gilbert shot Sergeant Edmund Parry in a horseback duel defending the mail coach between Gundagai and Jugiong; and in January 1865 both were present when their confederate John Dunn shot Constable Sam Nelson dead before his family at Collector. In doing so they sacrificed the goodwill of their 'telegraph', and in May both were cut down by police parties within a week of each other. Thereafter, Darlinghurst Gaol housed more than a score of their rebellious confederates.

Sir Frederick Pottinger also met his end during this time. His cavalier behaviour and hapless reputation came to a head in January 1865 when, against police regulations, he rode his own horse in the Wowingragong races. He was dismissed from the force shortly afterwards, and with some support from friends and confederates in the Riverina he set out from Forbes in March to confront his accusers at Sydney headquarters. But at a stopover at Wasco's Inn he tarried too long, and when he tried to mount the moving coach his pistol discharged into his abdomen. He recovered sufficiently to reach Sydney and then to be moved to the Victoria Club, but complications ensued and he died on 9 April. He was buried at St Jude's Anglican Church, Randwick.

At 'Humewood' the ageing Hamilton Hume retained a lively interest in the wider world where in the New South Wales parliament, Henry Parkes had at last achieved ministerial office in the government of James Martin. In January 1866 they had conspired to bring Charles Cowper down with a no-confidence motion on the floor of the assembly. They then combined as premier and colonial secretary.

It was an unusual match, even for the rambunctious New South Wales parliament. Against Parkes's English background, Martin had been born in Ireland's County Cork in 1820. His father John was a castle steward who, after a chance meeting with Sir Thomas Brisbane, travelled to the colony with his wife and baby son the following year and worked as a groom for Brisbane at the governor's preferred residence in Parramatta. James showed great promise in his early school days and his parents invested all their savings in his further education at Sydney's premier school in Castlereagh Street, opened by Governor Brisbane in 1824. While still at school, he contributed articles to Wentworth's *Australian* and would retain a lifelong interest in journalism.

He combined this with legal studies, and at 20 became an articled clerk. He was eventually admitted to the bar, where he built a substantial practice. He rose to the editorship of *The Australian,* while in his barrister's robes he defended Frank Gardiner's gang members charged with the Eugowra Rocks robbery, and saved all but one from the gallows. By the time of Gardiner's trial he was attorney-general, and prosecuted both cases against him.

However, his political life was devoted to a deep concern for the native-born with whom he identified, having arrived in the colony as a babe in arms. And in this he sparked Hume's vigorous support. Hume's dispute with Hovell continued to echo down the years and Hume was even then preparing another printing of his *Brief Statement of Facts* to answer his former travelling companion's protests. Hume also favoured the kind of movement towards a more independent Australia that Parkes was coming to be identified with. But the parliamentarians, like the explorers, were engaged in a marriage of convenience, since they differed on the tariff and state aid for church schools as well as electoral and land reform. Soon they too would part in mutual recrimination.

In Victoria, the colonial administration was similarly unruly, but from late 1863 the Scottish landholder James McCulloch had held the reins as premier in a coalition government. He would do so until 1871 and would remain the most influential member of the Victorian parliament until 1878. His influence would extend far beyond his political activities, for it was on his outback New South Wales property with its stark 'broken hill', managed by his nephew Alexander, that the greatest silver, lead and zinc mine the world had known was discovered. In time it would lay the foundation for Australia's industrialisation by the Broken Hill company.

In Queensland, too, the miners led the way to prosperity, closely followed by grazing and agriculture. It was also the location of a reversion to the slave labour that had marked the earliest days of the colony. The American Civil War of 1861–64 had interrupted the flow of cotton to the British mills, and an English merchant mariner turned trader, Robert Towns, sought to fill the gap with a plantation on the Logan River.

Towns claimed that to make a success of the venture it was necessary to import indentured labour, and after beginning with Chinese coolies he turned his attention to the South Pacific. In 1863, with the support of Queensland's Governor George Bowen, Towns sent his ship the *Don Juan* to Melanesia where the captain recruited 67 islanders, and though the practice was highly controversial the plantation was a commercial success. However, when the Americans resumed their cotton production Queensland farmers turned to sugar, where slave labour had a long history in the West Indies.

For the next 30 years some 60,000 Islanders were captured or otherwise induced to work in degrading conditions in the Queensland industry. While the Australian press, led notably by G. E. Morrison writing in *The Age,* campaigned against it in the 1880s, it was the White Australia Policy and the desire to protect jobs for white Australians that finally ended the labour trade. In 1901 it formally ceased, and the Federal Government took steps to deport South Sea Islanders who had established homes in Queensland back to the islands.

Tasmania had enjoyed a self-governing bicameral parliament since 1856 and, though the gold rush largely passed it by, the state had strong independent trade links with the Empire, and was among the most prosperous of the colonial administrations. It raised a local defence force that not only fought at Eureka but would send its own contingent to the Boer War where Tasmanian soldiers won the first two Victoria Crosses awarded to Australians. The *Sydney Morning Herald* recorded on 16 May 1902 that 'an old Yassie', Corporal Dick Furlong, the son of the 'Romeo' at the centre of Hume's break with 'Little Hamilton', had been killed in action in South Africa. 'Furlong was regarded as a thorough loyalist and a staunch friend of democracy,' it said.

Events in South Australia and Western Australia barely impinged on the daily life of Hamilton Hume, though the periodicals and journals of the Royal Geographical Society kept him up to date with developments. South Australia had always been a special case, since Sir William Molesworth, the Duke of Wellington, and other British luminaries of the Reform Club had persuaded their parliament to pass the *Colonisation Act of 1834*, which outlined its boundaries and made it the only state to be entirely convict free. It also promised self-government when the population reached 50,000 and guaranteed the rights of Aboriginal people to the lands 'they now occupy or enjoy'.

Two years later the first fleet of nine ships containing settlers and officials reached Kangaroo Island – and then Glenelg – while their surveyor Colonel William Light selected a site on the River Torrens for the first settlement to be known as Adelaide after the wife of William IV.

But despite the good intentions, the Aboriginal people were devastated by the smallpox brought in by the settlers, and after they killed the 25 passengers and crew of the wrecked brigantine *Maria*, bound from Adelaide to Hobart in 1840, their land rights went the way of their compatriots. Squatters were permitted to appropriate Aboriginal country without protest from the authorities. The colony did not become self-governing until 1856, by which time it contained more than 100,000 people, but the following year they elected a bicameral parliament and subsequently led the way in female suffrage.

Hume had followed with interest and concern the activities of his old friend Charles Sturt, whose health had been seriously impaired by his final expedition through South Australia in search of the elusive inland sea in 1844. He had welcomed Sturt's award of the Royal Geographical Society's gold medal; still more his decision to settle back in Adelaide as the colony's colonial secretary in 1849. They continued their correspondence, but since Sturt had departed Australia four years later he had heard little until news of his death reached 'Humewood' in 1869.

By then, Hamilton had followed the reports of John McDouall Stuart's 1862 expedition to the north coast of Australia and despaired at the mad folly of the Burke and Wills tragedy in the waterless wastes of the Red Centre. Another eccentric explorer, Edward John Eyre, who Hume had known in his early journeys to the Monaro via Yass, had pioneered a route across the Nullarbor Plain in 1840 to St George's Sound on Western Australia's south-west coastline. It was a tenuous link to the Swan River settlement, which valued – and often seemed to prefer – its independence from the other colonies. They received their final convict ship, *Hougoumont*, in January 1868.

The young John Forrest, son of Scottish servants who had arrived in 1842 and become farmers in the new colony, had joined the Surveyor-General's Department. In 1869, he was engaged in his first major journey of exploration searching for the elusive Ludwig Leichhardt. He would continue his rise through the colony's ranks to become its first premier.

The notion of some kind of continental entity began to find a place in community discourse, and slowly the building blocks of nationhood were being assembled. In 1867, Henry Parkes announced: 'These colonies should be united by some federal bond of federation,' and in the early 1870s, briefly out of parliament in the wake of yet another bankruptcy, he became convinced that a federation of the colonies was not only desirable but might also be possible. When he returned in 1871 as the Member for Mudgee, he helped bring down the latest Martin ministry. Within a year, he had at last become premier, in his own right in a government that would last for nearly three years.

A month after his first Cabinet was sworn in, the new governor, Sir Hercules Robinson, arrived and gave notice of his intention to play a major role in the issues of the day. 'The masses,' he declared, 'instead of resenting the outspoken sentiments of a governor on great questions, welcome them.' Parkes's response is not recorded but it would not be an easy relationship. Its most public bone of contention would surround Frank Gardiner, who by 1872 had spent eight years in Darlinghurst Gaol. Throughout his incarceration, his sisters Archina and Charlotte and his elder half-sister Robina had provided whatever support they could. And when Robinson declared his desire to be involved in the affairs of the day they immediately redoubled their efforts to secure his release with a direct vice-regal approach.

They had chosen their mark well. Sir Hercules was Irish on both sides of his family, and after Sandhurst had joined the Royal Irish Fusiliers as a second lieutenant in 1843. The enforced sale of the family estates compelled him to resign three years later and, after marrying into the minor aristocracy in 1846, he supervised relief works for victims of the Irish famine. This secured him preferment in the British colonial administration, and he served in the West Indies, Hong Kong and Ceylon before taking up his current post. He had enjoyed executive power as well as privilege in his earlier postings, and was loathe to abandon either among the unruly antipodeans of New South Wales.

The Monro connection was helpful to Gardiner's sisters. Though the Scottish grazier had sold his Australian interests and returned to England in 1860, they now lived in the home of a respected businessman, Henry Griffith, in Sydney. Monro's brother David had entered politics in New Zealand and in 1861 had become Speaker of the country's House of Representatives, a post he held until 1870. His daughter Maria, born to Frank's mother Jane, had married Dr John Grier in Portland where they were highly respected.

Archina and Charlotte's petition to the governor was signed by 500 Sydneysiders pleading for Frank's release. They said he had repented his deeds and reformed, had led an honest life in Queensland, and had not only behaved well in jail but had invented a new technique of selvedge of the matting processed in the prison. His health had suffered so badly that he was constantly under the care of a doctor, and that now 'the crime of bushranging has been happily and effectually suppressed', his continued detention was no longer a deterrent to others.

The former colonial secretary, William Foster, supported the petition and the principal jailer, J. C. Read, wrote that 'his conduct is very good, and [he] sets a good example to others in every way'. The sheriff, Harold McLean, added his support suggesting that Gardiner's sentence be reduced to ten years, and pointed out that he was only one of a number of bushrangers serving very long sentences. Only the trial judge, Sir Alfred Stephen, remained adamantly opposed. Indeed, he claimed that if only Gardiner had served his full sentence on Cockatoo Island the whole saga of Australian bushranging would not have taken place. 'He would have had no opportunity of commencing cattle stealing or of robbing the Gold Escort afterwards.'

Three weeks later, Sir Hercules decided that 'if his conduct continues in the meantime should be good, I should feel disposed to grant him a pardon, after serving ten years of his sentence, conditional upon his leaving the country'.

By 1871 Hamilton Hume, according to the *Yass Tribune,* a successor to the *Courier,* was 'on the scene of his peaceful triumphs' at 'Humewood', 'having fallen into the yellow leaf with all those things that accompany old age, as honour, love, obedience, troops of friends . . .' Later that year, a public meeting was called to name the new bridge at Yass after him. The motion was carried on the voices, though Hamilton was not well enough to attend its opening 'due to the accumulation of troubles arising from the privations he endured on his journeys'. Nor was his wife Elizabeth, who was again debilitated by her asthma.

On 30 June that year, *The Tribune* again blasted 'Mr Hovell', stripping him of his naval title and stating that he was 'nothing more than the skipper of a coastal barge' and that he was 'once again earwigging newspaper editors to keep himself prominently before the public'.

In 1872 Hamilton wrote to his old friend Alexander Berry, then 91, to say he had lumbago and had recently been stung by a scorpion, which caused painful swelling. He was 'well off', but would like to be back on the Shoalhaven where once, so many years ago, they had fought their way through the thick bush on bright mornings with the smell of eucalyptus in their nostrils as they climbed the steep hills and crossed the shaded gullies and the swift-flowing mountain streams together.[1]

It was the last letter he wrote which has survived. It was fitting that it should have been to the friend who put him forward to Governor Brisbane as the man to lead the most momentous of the early journeys of European exploration in the vast Australian continent.

Hamilton Hume died at Cooma Cottage on 'Humewood' station on 19 April 1873, aged 75. His wife and his nephew 'Little Hamilton' were by his side. Despite her lifetime of illness, Eliza would outlive him by 13 years.

AFTERWORD

A Fitting Tribute to Hamilton Hume

For his last few months of life Hamilton Hume had supervised the construction of his tombstone and his final resting place in the Yass cemetery, as well as the drafting of his extensive will, but his principal concern was with the preservation of his name and the regard in which history would hold him. Though he knew very well that his extended family held him in high esteem, the fact that he and Eliza had remained childless added a special poignancy to his disquiet.

He had been the pathfinder to much of the most valuable country in Australia: the Southern Highlands, the Illawarra and South Coast districts; the Goulburn, Breadalbane and Yass plains; the Murrumbidgee, Tumut, Murray, Mitta Mitta, Kiewa, Ovens and Goulburn river valleys; and the rich downs north and west of Melbourne. But perhaps the greatest service he rendered Australia was his understanding of the mood and quality of his homeland as only a native-born could. To this he added a visionary appreciation of its potential and a unique respect for the Aboriginal people.

According to Robert Webster, 'Those who followed his tracks generally did so in peace, and in the sure knowledge that they could succeed in their venture if they respected his guidelines and his example.' He could not know that by chance or design they would devastate his 'friends of the forest' and all but destroy their culture.

His anxiety for recognition was reflected in the epitaph he wrote for the tombstone: 'For the sake of those who bear my name, I should wish it to be held in remembrance as that of one who, with small opportunities but limited resources, did what he could for his native land.' It is striking that he chose to emphasise the place of his birth in his farewell to the living. But it is not surprising, for he had lived in the shade of British hubris and condescension to the Australian-born. And his fear, as we have seen, was well merited. He had named the country's greatest river the Hume after his father Andrew, but they had taken that from him and replaced it with the name of an obscure and quickly forgotten Scottish politician.

His 'native land' was then just beginning the process of defining itself as a separate entity from the British progenitor that had compromised it at birth with inherent notions of race and class. It would be an endlessly difficult endeavour. It was as though its escape from the colonial chrysalis was being impeded by these unrelenting snags within. And no one was more conscious of the struggle ahead than the new premier, Henry Parkes.

In the early months of 1874, Parkes confronted the dilemma posed by the governor's decision to release Frank Gardiner, the symbol of the conflict between the classes. Once word leaked out that he would be pardoned, petitions flooded in from squatters demanding that Parkes stand firm. His daughter Menie wrote to him, 'I can hardly understand it,' she said. 'Before Gardiner was taken I used to be shocked by hearing him spoken of in only a half-condemnatory manner, as a rather fine fellow etc . . . They seem to be more afraid of the lion when his claws are plucked out than ever they were when he was raging in the woods.'[1]

But confront it he did. In a grand speech to the Legislative Assembly, Parkes announced that the time had come to put the whole bushranging era behind the colony and, in addition to Gardiner, would release all 23 prisoners held on various bushranging charges. When his motion was put to the house, the numbers were evenly split and it passed only on the casting vote of the speaker.

On 20 July 1874, Gardiner, accompanied by his weeping sisters and a small crowd, was taken to the Sydney docks, where he boarded the SS *Dandenong* for the journey to Newcastle. After two days, he embarked upon the *Charlotte Andrews* and travelled to Hong Kong and then San Francisco. There his 'friend' and captor, the former police inspector Daniel McGlone, having liquidated his hotel business in Sydney, had established himself in a hostelry only a few months before. Frank bought his own Twilight Saloon no more than half a kilometre from his Australian compatriot. And there begins – and ends – the yet unfathomed mystery of Gardiner's final years in the United States.

But while the chances are that they will remain so, there is yet another passing sidelight to his role in the national story. Gardiner's step-brother Charles Carmichael Monro, born on Henry Monro's returning journey to London in 1860, rose through the British military ranks to become a general and, later still, a baronet. His most decisive success on the battlefield came about in December 1915. That was when he organised and commanded the stunningly successful withdrawal of the Australian soldiers from Gallipoli.

Back in Sydney, Parkes survived the outrage over Gardiner's release and would occupy the post of premier no fewer than five times. His 1867 declaration for federation would become his guiding star. He reiterated his ambition in speeches at the 1880–81 inter-colonial conference. On 24 October 1889, he engaged the nation with an address to a town hall meeting in Tenterfield. He called for 'a great national government for all Australians' to be brought into being by 'a convention of leading men from all the colonies, delegates appointed by the authority of parliament, who would fully represent the opinions of different Parliaments of the colonies'.

He brought all the passion of a lifetime to the cause, and in 1890 he instigated the inter-colonial conference in Melbourne, which ended in broad agreement on the way forward on issues such as tariffs, trade and defence. The following year he presided over the first federal convention, held in Sydney. It produced a draft constitution that would be tempered and refined over the next ten years of discussion and negotiation between the colonies.

Ill-health forced him to retire from proceedings in 1895 but, after one failed attempt when Western Australia voted against it, a Bill was presented to the British Imperial Parliament with an address requesting Queen Victoria to enact it into law. Finally the *Commonwealth of Australia Constitution Act* was passed by Westminster in 1900 and the Commonwealth of Australia officially established on 1 January 1901.

Henry Parkes had died on 27 April 1896, so did not live to see his dream become a reality. In this he shared the fate of

Hamilton Hume, whose name would adorn the largest and most fitting memorial imaginable. Though it had begun in piecemeal fashion in the early days of settlement, when he died the great thoroughfare that would be known as the Hume Highway was in its infancy.

In 1830, his travelling companion Thomas Mitchell had marked a line of road south from Sydney through Campbell Town to just east of the present town of Alpine in the Southern Highlands. He envisaged this as the beginning of three great roads of the colony, the others being to the north and west. The southern line then went along almost flat country immediately north of an existing rough track towards Goulburn.

Two years later Mitchell was walking along Macquarie Street in Sydney when he happened upon a worker cutting stone for the low wall in front of the Legislative Assembly. Struck by his expertise, Mitchell engaged him in conversation. His name was David Lennox, a 44-year-old Scotsman who had taken passage to Sydney in the wake of his wife's untimely death. In his bereavement he had sailed in the *Florentia* arriving only weeks before the chance meeting. He was a master mason who had worked on major bridges in Britain.

Mitchell hot-footed it to Governor Bourke, and by October Lennox was appointed to the roads department, and within a year he was the colony's superintendent of bridges. He then built a series of stone bridges, some of which are still standing, his masterpiece undoubtedly the classic Lansdowne Bridge over Prospect Creek. The design was based on an arch near Gloucester in England, and he built it with 20 hand-picked convicts who had worked with him on earlier projects in the Blue Mountains and over the Medway Rivulet. It was opened by Governor

Bourke with great ceremony on 26 January 1836. It still carries traffic on the Hume Highway.

By 1847 the main southern road passed through Goulburn and Yass. Lennox designed and built the bridge over the Yass River in 1854 and the Humes no doubt entertained the superintendent at Cooma Cottage. A track then continued to Jugiong and Gundagai, the site of the horseback duel between Sergeant Parry and Johnny Gilbert. And along its length, hotels and coaching inns proliferated as it gradually made its way along Hume's homeward-bound track to Albury on the Victorian border.

The road from Melbourne began much later but the gold rush provided the incentive – and the funding – to begin construction towards the Great Dividing Range. Some of the country rising to Kilmore was heavily timbered; other parts cleared for grazing as it levelled out near Seymour to cross flat, mostly cleared farmland country from Euroa, Benalla, Glenrowan and Wangaratta to Wodonga across the Murray from Albury.

The expansion of the rail system during the 1860s and '70s lessened the need for the road to be improved, and its development slowed. But in the early 1900s, as the motor car era began, there was increasing activity, though in the beginning most travel was by bus, taking over from the stage coaches of the nineteenth century. Horses remained common, as did travelling stock as drovers plied their trade down the long paddock.

As cars became more common the highway was the setting for amateur speed trials running until the mid-1930s when the police stepped in. By then the record for the Sydney–Melbourne run had dropped progressively to eight hours and 56 minutes. In 1928, the New South Wales *Government Gazette* proclaimed the road the 'Hume or Great Southern Highway', but since to Melburnians travelling Highway 31 was a *northern* journey, Australians on both sides of the Murray would inevitably opt for Hume.

During the Great Depression, the Hume Highway provided the location for some major unemployment relief projects that kept men in work and made mighty improvements for travellers. By the start of World War II it was sealed its full length and it became a major artery – together with the railway – for matériel heading to Australia's northern defences. In the early 1950s, this association with our wartime effort was commemorated in the northern section when the New South Wales premier, 'Joe' Cahill, launched the Remembrance Driveway scheme as a living memorial to all those who served; and the following year the Queen and the Duke of Edinburgh simultaneously planted trees at each end of it at Canberra's Australian War Memorial and Macquarie Place in Sydney. Since the mid-1990s, the rest areas have been dedicated to Victoria Cross recipients from World War II and the Vietnam conflict.

In 1974 it had become a truly national project when the Federal Government took over full responsibility for its funding and embarked on a massive effort to create a dual carriageway over its entire length. This was finally achieved in 2013. And in 2015 a volunteer force of enthusiasts, supported by the National Trust, came together over its length to turn the Old Hume Highway 31 into a tourist attraction in its own right – some 200 years after the 18-year-old explorer embarked with his brother John and his Aboriginal mate Dual on those first vigorous forays into the virgin bushland.

The old man of the bush, the great Australian pathfinder, can now rest easy. His remembrance is assured.

Bibliography

Andrews, Arthur, *Settlers of the Upper Murray*, Oxford University Press, 1920.

Barrallier, Francis Louis, *Expedition into the Interior of New South Wales*, Marsh Walsh, Melbourne, 1802.

Bayley, William A., *Early Exploration of Southern Highlands of New South Wales*, Halstead, Sydney, 1965.

Bennet, George, *Wanderings in New South Wales,* Bently, London, 1834.

Berry, Alexander, papers in the Mitchell Library, State Library of New South Wales, Sydney.

Bigge, John Thomas, *Report of the Commission of Enquiry into the State of the Colony of New South Wales*, London, 1822.

Bland, William, *Journey of Discovery to Port Phillip, Now New South Wales,* [etc.], A Hill, Sydney, 1831.

Bonwick, James, *John Batman, the founder of Victoria*, Samuel Mullen, Melbourne, 1867.

Boyes, Rosemary, *Overland to Port Phillip*, Interprint, Melbourne, 1972.

Collins, David, *An Account of the English Colony in New South Wales*, London, 1798.

Cox, William, *A narrative of proceedings of William Cox, Esq. in the years 1814 and 1815*, F. W. White, Sydney, 1888.

Gammage, Bill, *The Biggest Estate on Earth: How Aborigines Made Australia*, Allen & Unwin, Sydney, 2011.

Glover, M. K., *Map of Sturt's 1828 Journey*, Mitchell Library, State Library of New South Wales, Sydney.

Harvard, Olive, 'Mrs Felton Matthew's Journal', read before the Society, *Journal of the Royal Australian Historical Society*, 29, Part II, 1943.

Harvard, Ward L., 'Hamilton Hume and the Road to Bathurst', *Journal of the Royal Australian Historical Society*, 21, No. 2, 1935.

Hovell, William Hilton, 'Journal Kept on the Journey from Lake George to Port Phillip, 1824–1825', *Journal of the Royal Australian Historical Society*, 7, No. 6, 1921.

——*Reply to Hume's Brief Statement of Facts*, Thomas Daniel, Sydney, 1855.

Hume, Hamilton, *Brief Statement of Facts in Connection with an Overland Expedition from Lake George to Port Phillip in 1824–1825*, J. J. Brown, Yass, 1855.

——*Journal of Journey Made from Lake Bathurst to Pigeon House*, Mitchell Library, State Library of New South Wales, Sydney.

Hume, Stuart, *Beyond the Borders: An Anecdotal History of the Hume and Related Pioneering Families in Australia from 1790*, Jennifer Hume Macdougall and Prudence Grieve, Canberra, 1991.

Kennedy, Donald Edward, *Sturt of the Murray*, Robert Hale, London, 1958.

MacAlister, Charles, *Old Pioneering Days in the Sunny South*, Chas MacAlister Book Publication Committee, Goulburn, 1907.

Macklin, Robert, *Fire In The Blood: The Epic Tale of Frank Gardiner and Australia's Other Bushrangers*, Allen & Unwin, Sydney, 2005.

Lachlan Macquarie, Governor of New South Wales, *Journals of His Tours in New South Wales and Van Diemans Land 1810–1822*, Trustees of the Public Library of New South Wales, Sydney, 1956.

Pinkstone, W. E., 'Early colonial days: the biography of a reliable old native John McGuire', *Hawkesbury Herald*, 1906.

Mitchell, Thomas, Journals, letters and papers in the Mitchell Library, State Library of New South Wales, Sydney.

Musgrave, Sarah, 'The Wayback', *West Wyalong Advocate*, 1926.

Robinson, George Augustus, *Journey into South Eastern Australia*, Australian Historical Monographs, No. 3, 1844.

Scott, Ernest, 'Hume and Hovell's Journey to Port Phillip', read before the Society, *Journal of the Royal Australian Historical Society*, 7, No. 6, 1921.

Sturt, Charles, *Two Expeditions to the Interior of Central Southern Australia*, Smith Elder & Co, London, 1833.

Throsby, Charles, Papers and reports in the Mitchell Library, State Library of New South Wales, Sydney.

Walsh, Robin, *In Her Own Words: The Writings of Elizabeth Macquarie*, Exisle, Wollombi, 2011.

Webster, Robert H., *First Fifty Years of Temora*, J. A. Bradley and Sons, Temora, 1950.

Webster, Robert H., *Bygoo and Beyond*, Halstead Press, Sydney, 1956.

Webster, Robert H., *Currency Lad*, Leisure Magazines, Sydney, 1982.

White, Charles, *History of Australian Bushranging*, Volumes 1 and 2, Lloyd O'Neil, Melbourne, 1979.

Williams, Stephan, *Lowry, Foley & Cummins: The Mudgee Mail Robbers*, Popinjay, Canberra, 1992.

Williams, Stephen, *The Last Days of Scotchie and Whitton*, Popinjay, Canberra, 1994.

Endnotes

INTRODUCTION

1 Harvard, Olive, 'Mrs Felton Matthew's journal', read before the Society, *Journal of the Royal Australian Historical Society*, 29, Part 2, 1943.

2 Webster, Robert H., *Currency Lad*, Leisure Magazines, 1982, p. 53.

CHAPTER ONE

1 Letter from Williams to his agents in London, *The Public Advertiser*, 6 August 1790.

2 ibid.

3 From the translation of the letter from Schaeffer to Nepean, in J. Cobley, *Sydney Cove 1789–1790*, Sydney, 1980, p. 244.

4 Schomberg, Isaac, *Naval Chronology*, Vol. 2, T. Egerton, London, 1815, p. 123.

5 *Spirit of the English* magazine, 1823.

6 *Dublin Chronicle*, 23 October 1790.

7 Hazzard, Margaret, *Punishment Short of Death: A History of the Penal Settlement at Norfolk Island*, Hyland House, Melbourne, 1984, pp. 37–38.

CHAPTER TWO

1 They included 12-year-old Mary Wade, among whose descendants would number an Australian prime minister, Kevin Rudd.

2 *The Bee*, 15 March 1792.

3 Gelke, A., great-grandson of Francis Rawdon Hume, quoted in Webster, p. 5.

4 Macklin, Robert, *Dark Paradise*, Hachette Australia, Sydney, 2013, p. 103.

5 Hunter to Colonial Office, 3 July 1796.

6 Webster, op. cit., p. 10.

7 White, Charles, *History of Australian Bushranging*, Lloyd O'Neil, Melbourne, 1970, Vol. 1, p. 2.

8 Gammage, Bill, *The Biggest Estate on Earth: How Aborigines Made Australia*, Allen & Unwin, Sydney, 2011.

9 Warren, Christopher, *'Smallpox at Sydney Cove – Who, When, Why?', Journal of Australian Studies*, Vol. 38, Issue 1, 2014.

10 Reynolds, Henry, *This Whispering In Our Hearts*, Allen & Unwin, Sydney, 1998, p. 1.

11 Evans, Raymond and Orsted-Jensen, Robert, 'Assessing Violent Mortality on the Queensland Frontier', Australian Historical Association, 33rd Annual Conference, University of Queensland, 7–11 July 2014.

CHAPTER THREE

1 Barnard, Marjorie, *Macquarie's World*, Melbourne University Press, 1946, pp. 32–53.

2 ibid.

3 ibid.

4 'Mrs Macquarie's Diary', Mitchell Library, State Library of New South Wales, Sydney.

CHAPTER FOUR

1 Williams, Shayne and Karskens, Grace, *Heritage NSW*, Heritage Council of NSW, Sydney, 2012.

2 Karskens, Grace, *The Colony: A History of Early Sydney*, Allen & Unwin, Sydney, 2009, pp. 506–14.

3 Wallis to Macquarie, April 1816.

4 Webster, op. cit., p. 19.

5 Dunlop, E. W., 'John Joseph Oxley', *Australian Dictionary of Biography*, Vol. 2, Melbourne University Press, 1967.

CHAPTER FIVE

1 McGuanne, J. P., 'Centenary of Campbelltown – Appin's Pride,' *Lone Hand*, 1920.

2 Broomfield, Frederick J., *Lone Hand*, 1 May 1913.

3 McGuanne, loc. cit.

4 Gammage, op. cit., p. xix.

5 Webster, op. cit., p. 33.

6 In fact it would be eight years before the formalities were completed.

7 Walsh, Robin (Ed.), *In Her Own Words: The Writings of Elizabeth Macquarie*, Exisle, Wollombi, 2011, pp. 31–32.

CHAPTER SIX

1 Hume, Hamilton, 'A Journal kept by Mr Hamilton Hume in a tour through the interior for Lake Bathurst to the sea coast, 1821', Alexander Berry papers, Mitchell Library, State Library of New South Wales, Sydney.

CHAPTER SEVEN

1 Teale, Ruth, *Thomas Brisbane*, Oxford University Press, 1971, p. 3.
2 ibid., p. 4.
3 ibid., p. 12.
4 Macklin, op. cit., p. 125.
5 The town of Coolangatta on the Queensland/New South Wales border is named after Berry's vessel, the *Coolangatta*, which was wrecked off Point Danger, Queensland, in August 1846.

CHAPTER EIGHT

1 Hume's quotations throughout the journey – and those of the convicts – are taken from his *Brief Statement of Facts*, first published in 1855 together with letters from the men.

CHAPTER TEN

1 Webster, op. cit., p. 79.
2 ibid.

CHAPTER ELEVEN

1 Hume, Hamilton, *A Brief Statement of Facts of Facts in Connection with an Overland Expedition from Lake George to Port Phillip in 1824–1825*, J. J. Brown, Yass, 1855.
2 Berry is unlikely to have asked him to bring his journal unless he knew Hume did keep one, however rough in form and content. But if so it has been lost to history.
3 Author's emphasis.
4 Teale, op. cit., p. 22.

CHAPTER TWELVE

1 Shaw, A. G. L., *Ralph Darling*, Oxford University Press, 1971, p. 1.
2 Webster, op. cit., p. 92.
3 ibid., p. 95.
4 Clarke, Marcus, *Old Tales of a Young Country*, 'Sir Ralph Darling's Iron Collar', Melbourne, 1871.

CHAPTER THIRTEEN

1 Shaw, op. cit., p. 18.
2 Webster, op. cit., p. 104.
3 Sturt, Charles, *Two Expeditions into the Interior of Southern Australia*, Smith Elder, London, 1833, p. 19.
4 ibid., p. 39.
5 ibid., p. 40.

CHAPTER FOURTEEN

1 Sturt, op. cit., p. 40.

2 ibid., p. 43.
3 ibid., p. 71.
4 ibid., p. 83.

CHAPTER FIFTEEN

1 Sturt, op. cit., p. 143.
2 ibid.
3 Robinson, George Augustus, Journal, January 1830.
4 Milliss, Roger, *Waterloo Creek: the Australia Day Massacre of 1838, George Gipps and the British Conquest of New South Wales,* McPhee Gribble, Melbourne, 1992, pp. 68–69.

CHAPTER SIXTEEN

1 'Sir Ralph Darling', *Australian Dictionary of Biography*, Vol. 1, Melbourne University Press, 1966.
2 Macklin, op. cit., p. 165.
3 ibid., p. 138.
4 Milliss, op. cit., p. 90
5 King, Hazel, *Richard Bourke*, Oxford University Press, 1971, p. 9.
6 ibid., p. 140.
7 ibid., p. 166.

CHAPTER SEVENTEEN

1 Parsons, Vivienne, 'Richard Cunningham', *Australian Dictionary of Biography*, Vol. 1, op. cit.
2 Milliss, op. cit., pp. 99–100.
3 Bonwick, James, *John Batman the Founder of Victoria*, Samuel Mullen, Melbourne, 1867, p. 19.
4 Scott, Ernest, 'Hume and Hovell's Journey to Port Phillip', read before the Society, *Journal of the Royal Australian Historical Society*, 7, No. 6, 1921.
5 *Who's Who*, National Museum of Australia, retrieved 9 September 2014.
6 The document was retained by the Colonial Office and is in the UK National Archives. The copy sent to Governor Bourke is lost.
7 Boyce, James, *The Founding of Melbourne and the Conquest of Australia*, Black Inc., Melbourne, 2008, p. 74
8 Bassett, Marnie, 'Edward Henty', *Australian Dictionary of Biography*, Vol. 1, op. cit., pp. 531–34.
9 Milliss, op. cit., p. 128.
10 ibid., p. 128.
11 ibid., p. 133.
12 Webster, op. cit., p. 112.

CHAPTER EIGHTEEN

1 McCulloch, Samuel Clyde, 'Sir George Gipps', *Australian Dictionary of Biography*, Vol. 1, op. cit., p. 1.

2 Macklin, Robert, *Fire in the Blood,* Allen & Unwin, Sydney, 2006, pp. 95–210.
3 Australian Heritage Database, Relations between Aborigines and Colonists.
4 McCulloch, op. cit., p. 2.
5 Australian Heritage Database, op. cit.
6 McCulloch, loc. cit.
7 Williams, Stephan, *The Last Days of Scotchie and Whitton*, Popinjay, Canberra, 1994, pp. 2–3.
8 ibid., p. 14.
9 'Awful and outrageous conduct of bushrangers', *Australasian Chronicle*, 28 January 1840.

CHAPTER NINETEEN

1 'Capture of Whitton and death of Scotchie', *Australasian Chronicle*, 31 January 1840.
2 ibid.
3 *Sydney Monitor*, 25 March 1840.
4 £2,300.
5 Milliss, op. cit., p. 261.
6 ibid., p. 265.

CHAPTER TWENTY

1 Macintyre, Stuart, *A Concise History of Australia*, Cambridge University Press, 1999, p. 86.
2 Chandler, John, *Forty Years in the Wilderness*, Loch Haven Books, Main Ridge, 1990, p. 40.
3 MacAlister, Charles, *Old Pioneering Days in the Sunny South*, Chas MacAlister Book Publication Committee, Goulburn, 1907, p. 263.
4 Chandler, op. cit., p. 49.
5 Ward, John M., 'Sir Charles Augustus Fitroy', *Australian Dictionary of Biography*, Vol. 1, 1966.

CHAPTER TWENTY-ONE

1 Ward, John M., op. cit.
2 Chandler, op. cit., p. 80.
3 Author's emphasis.
4 Lalor, Peter, (1855). *Peter Lalor's Narrative: Eureka on Trial,* Public Record Office Victoria, 2003, retrieved 21 February 2007.
5 Suffolk, Owen, 'For Frank Gardiner'.

CHAPTER TWENTY-TWO

1 *Yass Courier* files.
2 Webster, op. cit., p. 121.

3 Kok, Hu Jin, 'The Followers of Hun Xiu Quan in Australia', paper presented to the Eighth Biennial Conference of the Chinese Studies Association of Australia, 10–12 July 2003, Bendigo.
4 Currey, C. H., 'Sir William Thomas Denison', *Australian Dictionary of Biography*, Vol. 4, Melbourne University Press, 1972.

CHAPTER TWENTY-THREE

1 Preshaw, George, *Banking under Difficulties*, Dunlop, Edwards and Co., Melbourne, 1888, pp. 13–14.

CHAPTER TWENTY-FOUR

1 Penzig, Edgar, *Happy Jack*, Tranter Enterprises, Katoomba, 1990, p. xv.
2 23 April 1861.
3 Williams, Stephen, *Seven Poems About Frank Gardiner*, Popinjay Publications, 1992, pp. 20–23.
4 Webster, op. cit., p. 121.

CHAPTER TWENTY-FIVE

1 Webster, op. cit., p. 123.

AFTERWORD

1 Williams, op. cit., p. 46.

Acknowledgements

An earlier Hume biography – *Currency Lad* by R. H. 'Bob' Webster – could not find a commercial publisher and was privately printed by his family in 1982. As it happens, Bob Webster, who died in 1994, was my father-in-law and in the years after I married his daughter Wendy we became close friends.

His research occurred before the internet provided authors with a nimble assistant named Google. So Bob's quest involved endless hours in the Mitchell Library – and to a lesser extent Canberra's NLA – to build a picture of the man and his career of exploration. His book, as edited by his daughter Lindy Webster Cayzer, was a work of genuine scholarship and, while it reflected the attitudes of an earlier age, it is almost impossible to overstate the assistance it provided to me in the development of this current work.

I offer once again my thanks to my dear friend and long-time collaborator, Peter Thompson, who read the manuscript and provided excellent suggestions for its improvement. Thanks also to my agent Margaret Kennedy and to my regular and valued publisher Matthew Kelly.

I am particularly indebted to Robyn Condliffe, a descendant of Frank Gardiner's sister Archina, for her assistance in telling the true story of the 'Prince of the Tobymen'. Thanks also to Dr Rick Williams of the National Trust's Cooma Cottage for permission to use the Hume photographs; to Ken McInness for his material on Hume's sketch map and his later association with John Batman; Frank Burke, the convenor of the Old Hume Highway 31; the Historical Societies of Appin, Yass and others along the great thoroughfare; and of course it would not have been possible without Bob's finest creation, my wife Wendy.

Robert Macklin, Canberra

Index